英语经典散文
翻译与赏析

刘士聪 选译
谷启楠 审译

创于1897 商务印书馆 The Commercial Press

图书在版编目(CIP)数据

英语经典散文翻译与赏析/刘士聪选译.—北京:商务印书馆,2017(2023.6重印)
ISBN 978-7-100-14333-2

Ⅰ.①英… Ⅱ.①刘… Ⅲ.①散文—英语—翻译②散文—文学欣赏—世界 Ⅳ.①H315.9 ②I106.6

中国版本图书馆CIP数据核字(2017)第139323号

英语经典散文翻译与赏析
刘士聪 选译
谷启楠 审译

商 务 印 书 馆 出 版
(北京王府井大街36号 邮政编码100710)
商 务 印 书 馆 发 行
北京市白帆印务有限公司印刷
ISBN 978-7-100-14333-2

2017年8月第1版 开本880×1230 1/32
2023年6月北京第3次印刷 印张15⅝
定价:76.00元

前　言

《英语经典散文翻译与赏析》包括英语散文(主要是英国散文)60篇,皆选自英国作家亚瑟·奎勒-库奇爵士(Sir Arthur Quiller-Couch)编辑的《牛津英语散文读本》(*The Oxford Book of English Prose*,1925)。其中多数是2010年前后几年为《英语世界》杂志所作的译文,还有几篇曾收录于《英汉·汉英美文翻译与鉴赏》,且将其移至此凑个整数。

文章编排大体依据作者出生年月先后。关于体例,每一篇目各有四个部分,“作者简介”“原文”“译文”和“译后语”。如前所说,因文章曾分别用于不同书刊,“译后语”部分的写法略有区别,为保持原貌,并未对其做统一处理,特此说明。

在翻译过程中,得到美国朋友帕特·麦克德米德博士(Dr. Patt McDermid)和伊丽莎白·舒尔茨教授(Prof. Elizabeth Schultz)的悉心帮助,释疑了很多难点。在此,对他们表示衷心感谢。

用于《英语世界》的有些文章曾得到好心读者和专家的批评指正,所提意见中肯、中的,重审译文时颇受启发,对修改不当和误译之处多有帮助，趁译文结集出版之际，表示诚挚的谢意，并希望继续提出批评意见。

译　者

2015 年 8 月

目　录

Joseph Addison（约瑟夫·艾迪生） ······ 1

Westminster Abbey（威斯敏斯特教堂） ······ 2

Richard Steele（理查德·斯梯尔） ······ 9

My First Grief（初识悲哀） ······ 10

Alexander Pope（亚历山大·蒲柏） ······ 17

A Tragic Pastoral（田园悲剧） ······ 18

Philip Dormer Stanhope（菲利普·多默·斯坦诺普） ······ 25

The Art of Pleasing（取悦于人的艺术） ······ 26

Samuel Johnson（塞缪尔·约翰逊） ······ 33

Congregational Music（聚会音乐） ······ 34

William Collins（威廉·柯林斯） ······ 38

David Hume（大卫·休谟） ······ 45

Foreign Trade（对外贸易） ······ 46

Gilbert White（吉尔伯特·怀特） ······ 53

The Bat（蝙蝠） ······ 54

Edmund Burke（埃德蒙·伯克） ······ 61

Cultivating Generous and Honest Feelings（培养慷慨正直的感情） ······ 62

William Cowper（威廉·考珀） …… 67
A Candidate for Parliament（议会候选人） …… 68
Country Music（乡村音乐） …… 74
William Hazlitt（威廉·黑兹利特） …… 81
On Going a Journey（谈旅游） …… 82
The Pleasures of Reading（读书的快乐） …… 90
Dorothy Wordsworth（多萝西·华兹华斯） …… 97
The Beggars（乞丐） …… 98
Robert Southey（罗伯特·骚塞） …… 103
Nelson's Departure from Portsmouth（纳尔逊驶离朴次茅斯） …… 104
Charles Lamb（查尔斯·兰姆） …… 109
The Old Margate Hoy（古老的马盖特客船） …… 110
Washington Irving（华盛顿·欧文） …… 115
Poets' Corner（诗人角） …… 116
The Stage Coach（公共马车） …… 122
Dulce Domum（回家真好） …… 134
Jane Taylor（简·泰勒） …… 143
A Young Lady's Education（一个年轻女士的教育） …… 144
Thomas De Quincey（托马斯·德昆西） …… 151
A London Waif（一个伦敦孤苦女孩） …… 152
Frederick Marryat（弗雷德里克·马里亚特） …… 159
Naval Politeness（海军的礼貌） …… 160
John Gibson Lockhart（约翰·吉布森·洛克哈特） …… 167
The Death of Sir Walter（瓦尔特爵士之死） …… 168

John Henry Newman（约翰·亨利·纽曼）…………………… 175
The Classics（古典文学）………………………………………… 176
Definition of a Gentleman（什么样的人是有修养的人）……… 182
James Frederick Ferrier（詹姆斯·弗雷德里克·费里尔）……… 189
The True End of Man（人生的真正目的）…………………… 190
Charles Dickens（查尔斯·狄更斯）………………………… 193
The Widow at the Grave（墓旁的寡妇）…………………… 194
Benjamin Jowett（本杰明·乔伊特）……………………………… 201
Socrates Under Sentence of Death Hears the Voice of the Laws of Athens（被判死刑的苏格拉底听见雅典法律的声音）……………………………… 202
Last Words on Plato（最后评说柏拉图）……………………… 206
James Anthony Froude（詹姆斯·安东尼·弗劳德）………… 213
The End of the Middle Age（中世纪的终结）………………… 214
Thomas Hughes（托马斯·休斯）………………………………… 221
Coaching to School（乘坐马车去上学）……………………… 222
Henry Walter Bates（亨利·沃尔特·贝茨）……………………… 231
A Naturalist's Day in the Tropics（一个博物学家在热带丛林里的一天）……………………………… 232
Lord George Sanger（乔治·桑格勋爵）……………………… 241
A Fair and a Fire（一场娱乐和一场大火）…………………… 242
Thomas Henry Huxley（托马斯·亨利·赫胥黎）………………… 249
A Game of Chess（一盘棋）……………………………………… 250
Walter Bagehot（沃尔特·巴奇霍特）………………………… 257
The Old Private Banker（从前的私人银行家）……………… 258

Henry Kingsley（亨利·金斯利） ······························ 265
The Children at a Wedding（婚礼上的孩子们） ············ 266
Leonard Courtney（伦纳德·考特尼） ·························· 277
Justice（正义） ·· 278
James Whistler（詹姆斯·惠斯勒） ···························· 285
Nature and Art（自然与艺术）··································· 286
Robert Falcon Scott（罗伯特·福尔肯·斯科特）··············· 295
The Death of Captain Oates（奥茨上校之死）················· 296
William Stanley Jevons（威廉·斯坦利·杰文斯） ·········· 305
True Science（真正的科学）····································· 306
William Henry Hudson（威廉·亨利·哈德逊）················ 313
Pilgrims at the Land's End（"陆地尽头"的朝圣者） ·········· 314
Birds and Death（鸟儿与死亡） ································ 326
Oliver Wendell Holmes（奥利弗·温德尔·霍姆斯） ········· 329
The Lost Sloop（失踪的战舰）·································· 330
Archibald Philip Primrose（阿奇博尔德·菲利普·
普里姆罗斯）·· 335
The Elder and the Younger Pitts（老少皮特）················· 336
Richard Jefferies（理查德·杰弗里斯）························· 343
The Wheat（麦子） ·· 344
Robert Louis Stevenson（罗伯特·路易斯·史蒂文森） ········ 353
Night among the Pines（松林之夜）···························· 354
George Gissing（乔治·吉辛） ·································· 361
Shakespeare's Island（莎士比亚之岛）························· 362
Arthur Clutton-Brock（亚瑟·克拉顿-布罗克）················ 369
The Cardinal Virtue of Prose（散文最重要的品质） ··········· 370

Charles Edward Montague（查尔斯·爱德华·蒙塔古） ………… 377
The Faculty of Delight（感知快乐的天赋）………………………… 378
Harold Fielding Hall（哈罗德·菲尔丁·霍尔） ……………………… 385
A Burmese on the English（一个缅甸人谈英国人） ………… 386
George Moore（乔治·穆尔） ………………………………………… 393
Esther's Son（埃斯特的儿子）…………………………………… 394
Olive Schreiner（奥利夫·施赖纳） ………………………………… 401
Waldo（沃尔多） ………………………………………………… 402
Goldsworthy Lowes Dickinson（戈兹沃西·洛斯·迪金森） …… 411
Literature in Cathay（文学在中国）…………………………… 412
George Santayana（乔治·桑塔亚纳） ……………………………… 415
The Weather in His Soul（英国人灵魂里的气象）……………… 416
Rudyard Kipling（拉迪亚德·吉卜林） ……………………………… 429
The Spring Running（春跑）…………………………………… 430
Edward Verral Lucas（爱德华·维拉尔·卢卡斯） ………………… 439
The Windmill（风车磨坊） ……………………………………… 440
Mark Rutherford（马克·拉瑟福德） ………………………………… 449
A Londoner's Holiday（一个伦敦人的假日） ………………… 450
Robert Bridges（罗伯特·布里吉斯） ……………………………… 459
A School Portrait（一幅肖像）………………………………… 460
Max Beerbohm（马克斯·比尔博姆） ………………………………… 469
The Morris Dancers（跳莫里斯舞的人们）……………………… 470
John Masefield（约翰·梅斯菲尔德） ……………………………… 479
The Clipper（快帆船） ………………………………………… 480

Joseph Addison

约瑟夫·艾迪生(1672—1719),英国散文家、诗人、剧作家和政治家。发表于1713年4月的剧作《加图,一个悲剧》(*Cato, a Tragedy*),描写古罗马政治家(小)加图(Marcus Porcius Cato Uticensis,95—46 B.C.)在他最后岁月里所经历的历史事件。据说他的思想和政治主张对美国开国元勋产生重要影响。艾迪生与他的朋友理查德·斯梯尔(Richard Steele)创办杂志《旁观者》(*The Spectator*),该杂志于1711年3月1日出版第一期。后文"Westminster Abbey"选自该杂志的第26期。艾迪生的散文以朴素、条理和准确著称,他将英语散文提到了一个新的高度。

Westminster Abbey

Joseph Addison

When I am in a serious humour, I very often walk by myself in Westminster Abbey, where the gloominess of the place, and the use to which it is applied, with the solemnity of the building, and the condition of the people who lie in it, are apt to fill the mind with a kind of melancholy, or rather thoughtfulness, that is not disagreeable ...

... for my own part, though I am always serious, I do not know what it is to be melancholy; and can therefore take a view of nature in her deep and solemn scenes, with the same pleasure as in her most gay and delightful ones. By this means I can improve myself with those objects, which others consider with terror. When I look upon the tombs of the great, every emotion of envy dies in me; when I read the epitaphs of the beautiful, every inordinate desire goes out; when I meet with the grief of parents upon a tombstone, my heart melts with compassion; when I see the tomb of the parents themselves, I consider the vanity of grieving for those whom we must quickly follow; when I see kings lying by those who deposed

威斯敏斯特教堂

约瑟夫·艾迪生

每逢我心情庄重之时，我常常一个人去威斯敏斯特教堂走走。这里阴沉沉的气氛和它令人肃然的功能，加之其建筑的庄严以及长眠于此的人们，都易于使人产生一种悲伤的情绪，或让人陷入沉思——但你并没有不快的感觉……

尽管我的心情总是庄重的，但就我个人而言，我不知道什么是悲哀；因此，在自然万物处于深沉和庄严的状态时，我能以愉悦的心情看待之，如同其处于最欢乐和最愉快的状态时一样。以这样的态度观看这些景象，可以完善自己，而别人却怀着恐惧心理看待这些。当我看那些伟大人物的墓冢时，所有嫉妒的情绪都熄灭了；当我读那些美好人物的碑文时，所有的奢望都消失了；当我在一个墓碑上看见父母表露的悲痛时，我的心被怜悯之情融化了；当我看见父母们自己的墓冢时，我想，我们很快将尾随其后而去，为他们而悲伤就不那么重要了；当我看见国王们躺在那些废黜他们的人们身旁

them, when I consider rival wits placed side by side, or the holy men that divided the world with their contests and disputes, I reflect with sorrow and astonishment on the little competitions, factions and debates of mankind. When I read the several dates of the tombs, of some that died yesterday, and some six hundred years ago, I consider that great day when we shall all of us be contemporaries, and make our appearance together.

时,当我想到那些比肩而卧的睿智的对手,或者那些因为竞争和纠纷而使世界分裂的圣人时,我怀着悲哀和惊奇思考人类的那些微不足道的争斗、派系纷争和争论。我察看几块墓碑上的生卒年月,有的墓主昨天刚去世,有的则死于大约六百年前。这让我思考,我向往一个伟大的日子,那时我们将会与这些人为伍,一起出现在此地。

译后语

关于几个句子的翻译：

（1）... and can therefore take a view of **nature** in her deep and solemn scenes, with the same pleasure as in **her** most gay and delightful ones.

译文将 nature 略作调整，如将其译作“大自然”很合适，物主代词 her 也跟着译作“她”，代词与所代之词在词性和数量上保持一致。这里译者将 nature 译作“自然万物”，是为了说得具体些，使其接近当时的场景。但代词 her 需作相应调整，应与“万物”保持一致。用汉语的“他们”或“它们”代“自然万物”似不妥，故用“之”和“其”代之。译文如下：

> ……因此，在自然万物处于深沉和庄严的状态时，我能以愉悦的心情看待之，如同其处于最欢乐和最愉快的状态时一样。

（2）... when I meet with the grief of **parents upon a tombstone**, my heart melts with compassion ...

译者对这句话的理解有变化。最初在《英语世界》上发表的译文是这样的：

> ……当我遇见抚摸墓碑而万分悲痛的父母时，我的心被怜悯融化了……

那时认为 parents upon a tombstone 是父母出现在墓旁，现在看来不是，因为没有定冠词 the 的 parents 是泛指。应是父母在碑文里表达的悲痛心情。故做如下修改：

……当我在一个墓碑上看见父母表露的悲痛时，我的心被怜悯之情融化了……

(3) ... when I see the tomb of the parents themselves, I consider the **vanity** of grieving for those whom we must quickly follow ...

这里的 vanity，应是“不重要”的意思。

Richard Steele

理查德·斯梯尔（1672—1729），爱尔兰散文家、剧作家、政治家。主要剧作有 *The Funeral*（1701）、*The Lying Lover*（1703）、*The Tender Husband*（1705）和 *The Conscious Lovers*（1722）。他以创办杂志而闻名，他于 1709 年创办杂志《闲谈者》（*The Tatler*），旨在揭露生活中的虚假，撕下狡诈、虚荣和做作的假面具，倡导朴素的服饰、话语和行为。他自己为杂志撰写大部分文章，约瑟夫·艾迪生撰写一部分，二人合作撰写一部分。他还与艾迪生合作创办了《旁观者》（*The Spectator*）杂志，很有影响。后文“My First Grief”选自他创办的 *The Tatler*（第 181 期）。原文编辑者所加的标题是“His First Grief”，译者将其改为“My First Grief”。

My First Grief

Richard Steele

The first sense of sorrow I ever knew was upon the death of my father, at which time I was not quite five years of age; but was rather amazed at what all the house meant, than possessed with a real understanding why nobody was willing to play with me. I remember I went into the room where his body lay, and my mother sat weeping alone by it. I had my battledore in my hand, and fell a beating the coffin, and calling Papa; for, I know not how, I had some slight idea that he was locked up there. My mother catched me in her arms, and, transported beyond all patience of the silent grief she was before in, she almost smothered me in her embraces; and told me in a flood of tears, Papa could not hear me, and would play with me no more, for they were going to put him under ground, where he could never come to us again. She was a very beautiful woman, of a noble spirit, and there was a dignity in her grief amidst all the wildness of her transport; which, methought, struck me with an instinct of sorrow, that, before I was sensible of what it was to grieve, seized my very soul, and has made pity the weakness of my heart

初识悲哀

理查德·斯梯尔

我初次懂得悲痛是在父亲去世的时候，那时我不到五岁；然而，与其说因为我明白了别人为什么不愿意跟我玩而苦恼，还不如说家里的状况让我感到惊诧。我记得走进停放他尸体的屋里时，母亲正一个人坐在他旁边哭泣。我手里拿着板羽球的球板，扑上去拍打棺材，一边喊着“爸爸，爸爸”，因为，不知怎的，我隐约有一种感觉，似乎他是被人锁在里面的。母亲一把将我抱住，因为情绪激动，先前默默忍受悲哀时的耐心不见了，她紧紧抱住我，憋得我几乎喘不上气来；她泪流满面，对我说，爸爸再也听不见我说话了，再也不能和我玩了，因为他们就要把他埋入地下，他再也不能回来看我们了。母亲非常漂亮，气质高贵，于悲痛欲绝中透露出尊严；我觉得，这尊严让我突然产生了悲哀的本能，在我意识到什么是悲哀之前这本能已经控制了我的心灵，从那以后，怜悯之心就变成我情感世界的弱点。

ever since. The mind in infancy is, methinks, like the body in embryo; and receives impressions so forcible, that they are as hard to be removed by reason, as any mark, with which a child is born, is to be taken away by any future application. Hence it is, that good nature in me is no merit; but having been so frequently overwhelmed with her tears before I knew the cause of any affliction, or could draw defences from my own judgment, I imbibed commiseration, remorse, and an unmanly gentleness of mind, which has since ensnared me into ten thousand calamities; and from whence I can reap no advantage, except it be, that, in such a humour as I am now in, I can the better indulge myself in the softness of humanity, and enjoy that sweet anxiety which arises from the memory of past afflictions.

我觉得，幼年时期的心理如同胚胎阶段的身体，那时所生成的印象非常牢固，很难用理智将其消除，如同初生婴儿身上的胎记，以后用什么药都除不掉。因此，我的好脾气不算优点。但是，在我还不懂是什么使人痛苦，或也无力经自己的判断而筑起防线时，我便常常被她的眼泪征服，之后才滋生了同情、懊悔，以及男性少有的柔情，此后这种柔情使我陷入千万次灾难之中。它并没有给我带来多少好处，只是，以我的性情（我现在依然如此），我能更好地沉湎于人性的温柔，并能更好地欣赏因回忆痛苦往事而产生的伤感和焦虑。

译后语

关于几个句子的翻译：

（1）I remember I went into the room where his **body** lay, and my mother sat weeping alone by it.

这个句子包含一个宾语从句，宾语从句包含一个状语从句，从句里的主句为“… my mother sat weeping alone by it”，是这个句子要表达的主要意思。译文应凸显这个主句：

> 我记得走进停放他尸体的屋里时，母亲正一个人坐在他旁边哭泣。

句中的“body”一词，还应译为“尸体”，尽管文中提到“I had some slight idea that he was locked up there.”，孩子还是知道父亲死了。

（2）She was a very beautiful woman, of a noble spirit, and there was a dignity in her grief amidst all the wildness of her transport; **which**, methought, struck me with an instinct of sorrow, **that**, before I was sensible of what it was to grieve, seized my very soul, and has made pity the weakness of my heart ever since.

这句话里有两个关系代词，which 和 that，弄清它们之所指，能帮助理清句子结构和意思。which 应指 a dignity，that 指 an instinct of sorrow，即母亲悲哀中透露出的尊严让“我”产生了悲哀的本能，而这本能控制了“我”的心灵，并使得怜悯之心成了“我”情感世界的弱点。

（3）… I **imbibed** commiseration, remorse, and an unmanly

gentleness of mind ...

to imbibe，英文词典解释为 to absorb sth，意为“吸收，接受”，因这里所谈的是情感，故将其译为“滋生”：

……之后才滋生了同情、懊悔和男性少有的温柔情愫……

Alexander Pope

亚历山大·蒲柏(1688—1744),英国诗人,被认为是奥古斯都时代(Augustan Age),即18世纪早期英国文学最伟大的诗人。因翻译荷马史诗《伊利亚特》(*Iliad*,1715—1720)和《奥德赛》(*Odyssey*,1725—1726)而闻名。主要著作有讽刺诗 *The Rape of the Lock* (1712)、长诗 *The Dunciad* (1728—1742),以及 *Epistle to Doctor Arbuthnot* (1734)、*Essay on Man* (1733—1734)。后文"A Tragic Pastoral"选自 *Letter to Lady Mary Wortley Montagu* (1 Sept.,1718)。

A Tragic Pastoral

Alexander Pope

I have a mind to fill the rest of this paper with an accident that happened just under my eyes, and has made a great impression upon me. I have just passed part of this summer at an old romantic seat of my Lord Harcourt's, which he lent me. It overlooks a common-field, where, under the shade of a haycock, sat two lovers, as constant as ever were found in romance, beneath a spreading beech. The name of the one (let it sound as it will) was John Hewet; of the other, Sarah Drew. John was a well set man about five and twenty, Sarah a brown woman of eighteen. John had for several months borne the labour of the day in the same field with Sarah; when she milked, it was his morning and evening charge to bring the cows to her pail. Their love was the talk, but not the scandal, of the whole neighbourhood; for all they aimed at was the blameless possession of each other in marriage. It was but this very morning that he had obtained her parents' consent, and it was but till the next week that they were to wait to be happy. Perhaps this very day, in the intervals of their work, they were talking of their

田园悲剧

亚历山大·蒲柏

我想在信纸空余的地方写一写我亲眼见到的一个意外事故，这个事故给我留下极深的印象。今年夏天，我在哈考特勋爵借给我的古老的乡村房舍里刚刚度过一段时间。这座房舍富有浪漫情调，俯瞰着一块公共用地，在那里一个草垛的阴影里坐着一对恋人，正如浪漫故事中常见的那样，他们是在一棵树冠很大的山毛榉的荫庇之下。一个名叫约翰·休伊特（任它怎么念吧），另一个叫萨拉·德鲁。约翰身体结实，25 岁左右；萨拉的皮肤晒得黝黑，18 岁。好几个月以来，约翰白天和萨拉在同一块地里干活；早晨和晚上萨拉挤牛奶时，约翰就把牛领到她的奶桶旁。他们的爱情成了附近人们茶余饭后的话题，但没有人说他们的闲话；因为他们追求的只是婚后的相互拥有，这无可非议。就在那天早晨，他征得了她父母的同意，他们只需等到下个星期就开始幸福生活了。或许就在那天，劳动间歇的时候，他们讨论婚礼那天

wedding clothes; and John was now matching several kinds of poppies and field-flowers to her complexion, to make her a present of knots for the day. While they were thus employed (it was on the last of July), a terrible storm of thunder and lightning arose, that drove the labourers to what shelter the trees or hedges afforded. Sarah, frightened and out of breath, sunk on a haycock, and John (who never separated from her) sat by her side, having raked two or three heaps together to secure her. Immediately there was heard so loud a crack as if heaven had burst asunder. The labourers, all solicitous for each other's safety, called to one another: those that were nearest our lovers, hearing no answer, stepped to the place where they lay: they first saw a little smoke, and after, this faithful pair; —John with one arm about his Sarah's neck, and the other held over her face, as if to screen her from the lightning. They were struck dead, and already grown stiff and cold in this tender posture. There was no mark or discolouring on their bodies, only that Sarah's eyebrow was a little singed, and a small spot between her breasts. They were buried the next day in one grave, in the parish of Stanton Harcourt in Oxfordshire; where my Lord Harcourt, at my request, has erected a monument over them.

穿戴的服饰，约翰正在试几种罂粟花和地里的野花，看哪一种与她的肤色相匹配，做一个象征喜结良缘的礼物，婚礼那天送给她。这时(那是7月的最后一天)，突然电闪雷鸣，风雨大作，正在干活的人们赶紧跑到树下和树篱底下避雨。萨拉很害怕，吓得喘不上气来，躺倒在草垛上，约翰(他一直没有离开她)把两三个草垛堆在一起保护她，就坐在她身旁。突然一声震耳欲聋的霹雳，似乎天空被炸成碎片。干活的人们惦记互相的安全，你喊我，我喊你：距离我们的恋人最近的人们没有听见应答，便来到他们躲避的地方；他们先看见一股烟，后来看见这对忠诚的恋人——约翰用一只胳膊搂着萨拉的脖子，另一只胳膊护着她的脸，似乎是替她挡住闪电。他们已经被雷击死了，身姿充满温情，但身体已经变得僵硬冰凉。他们身上没有雷击的痕迹，也没有变颜色，只是萨拉的眉毛烧焦了一点，胸间有一小块伤痕。第二天，人们在牛津郡斯坦顿-哈考特教区把他们合葬在一座坟墓里，哈考特勋爵应我的请求为他们立了一个纪念碑。

译后语

关于几个词语的理解和翻译：

（1）It overlooks a **common-field** ...

《牛津高阶英汉双解词典》有一个词条 common land，是这样解释的：land that belongs to or may be used by the local community，应该和 common-field 意思一样，即“公共用地”，人们可在那里种植庄稼、牧草或放牧牲畜。

（2）The name of the one（**let it sound as it will**）was John **Hewet**...

作者为什么要在括号里加上 let it sound as it will？笔者请教过美国人，说这是作者的诙谐，因为 Hewet 的发音很像 Hew it，用斧子砍东西（木头之类），暗示他并非来自贵族家庭。是否还有别的意思，待查考。

（3）Their love was the talk, but not the scandal, of the whole neighbourhood; for all they aimed at was the **blameless possession of each other** in marriage.

此句里的“... blameless possession of each other”，在英语里，这种“形容词＋名词”的搭配很自然，汉语如译成“无可非议的相互拥有”虽然意思清楚，但将 blameless 提出来单独处理更符合汉语习惯：“……因为他们追求的只是婚后的相互拥有，这无可非议。”这样译正好和前面的“没有人说他们的闲话”相照应。

（4）They were buried the next day in one grave, in the **parish** of Stanton Harcourt in Oxfordshire...

关于 parish,《牛津高阶英汉双解词典》有两个解释:一为 an area that has its own church and that a priest is responsible for,一为(in England) a small country area that has its own elected local government。文中没有明显的迹象指向后者,这里将其译为“教区”:

> 第二天,人们在牛津郡斯坦顿-哈考特教区把他们合葬在一座坟墓里……

Philip Dormer Stanhope

菲利普·多默·斯坦诺普(1694—1773),称号切斯特菲尔德伯爵四世(4th Earl of Chesterfield),英国政治家、外交家,以写给儿子和教子的书信闻名。他有两本书信集,*Letters to His Son* (1774)、*Letters to His Godson* (1890)。信中讲如何讲究礼貌,如何取悦于人,如何在社会上取得成就等。后文即选自 *Letters to His Son*。

人在成长过程中主要受三方面影响,家庭、学校和社会。其中,家庭教育对孩子性格的形成和品质的培养尤为重要,是为他们走进学校和走向社会之前做准备,而家长良好的文化修养和人文素质对孩子产生直接影响。在这方面,切斯特菲尔德伯爵值得效仿。

The Art of Pleasing

Philip Dormer Stanhope

Dear boy,

The art of pleasing is a very necessary one to possess; but a very difficult one to acquire. It can hardly be reduced to rules; and your own good sense and observation will teach you more of it than I can. Do as you would be done by, is the surest method that I know of pleasing. Observe carefully what pleases you in others, and probably the same things in you will please others. If you are pleased with the complaisance and attention of others to your humours, your tastes, or your weaknesses, depend upon it, the same complaisance and attention, on your part, to theirs, will equally please them. Take the tone of the company, that you are in, and do not pretend to give it; be serious, gay, or even trifling, as you find the present humour of the company: this is an attention due from every individual to the majority. Do not tell stories in company; there is nothing more tedious and disagreeable: if by chance you know a very short story, and exceedingly applicable to the present subject of conversation, tell it in as few words as possible; and even

取悦于人的艺术

菲利普·多默·斯坦诺普

亲爱的孩子：

掌握取悦于人的艺术很必要，但学会这种艺术很困难。很难将它归纳成几条规则；你自己好好体会好好观察，会学到很多，比我能教给你的多。就我所知，按照别人对待你的做法去做，是最稳妥的取悦于人的方法。仔细观察别人身上有什么东西让你感觉愉快，或许你身上同样的东西也会让别人感觉愉快。假如别人附和并注意你的幽默、你的口味或你的嗜好而使你感觉愉快，你就这么做，附和并注意别人的幽默、口味或嗜好也同样会使他们感觉愉快。要接受你所在场合的气氛，不要试图去制造气氛；要表现得认真、快活，甚至微不足道，要看当时大家的情绪而定：每个个人对多数人应该考虑这一点。和大家在一起时不要讲故事，没有比这更乏味更讨厌的了；假如你偶然知道一个很短的故事，而且与谈话内容特别契合，就尽可能用简短的话来讲，即使如此，也要婉转地说

then, throw out that you do not love to tell stories, but that the shortness of it tempted you. Of all things, banish the egotism out of your conversation, and never think of entertaining people with your own personal concerns, or private affairs; though they are interesting to you, they are tedious and impertinent to everybody else: besides that, one cannot keep one's own private affairs too secret. Whatever you think your own excellencies may be, do not affectedly display them in company; nor labour, as many people do, to give that turn to the conversation, which may supply you with an opportunity of exhibiting them. If they are real, they will infallibly be discovered, without your pointing them out yourself, and with much more advantage. Never maintain an argument with heat and clamour, though you think or know yourself to be in the right; but give your opinion modestly and coolly, which is the only way to convince; and, if that does not do, try to change the conversation, by saying, with good humour, "We shall hardly convince one another, nor is it necessary that we should, so let us talk of something else."

明你本来不喜欢讲故事，而是因为故事简短吸引你讲。与人交谈时最忌讳以自我为中心，永远不要用你自己关心的事或你的私事来引起别人的兴趣，虽然这些对你很有意义，但对别人却很乏味，而且毫不相干；况且，个人无论怎样严密保护隐私都不为过。不论你认为你有什么优秀之处，不要在大家面前装模作样地显摆，也不要像很多人那样在交谈中设法流露这种话口儿来寻找展示它们的机会。假如你真有那些优点，人们一定会发现，无须你自己指出，而且，这样对你更好。永远不要争吵，不要争得面红耳赤，尽管你认为或明知你正确；谦虚冷静地把你的意见说出来，这是唯一能说服人的做法；如果这样还不行，就设法改变话题，心平气和地说："看来我们谁也说服不了谁，也没有必要一定去说服谁，那就让我们谈点别的吧。"

译后语

关于几个细节的处理：

翻译有指导性原则，也常遇到细节，需要斟酌。细节多在词语、短语和句子上。翻译时常需要参照词典，也需要考虑特定语境和译入语习惯。

（1）标题“The Art of Pleasing”的译法

此处将标题译作《取悦于人的艺术》。汉语的“取悦于人”，在一些语境下有贬义，但《现代汉语词典》的解释是：“取得别人的喜欢”，该词本身并无贬义。所以这样处理标题是可以的。

（2）It can hardly be reduced to rules; and your own **good sense and observation** will teach you more of it than I can.

这句话里的 sense 应该是指“感觉”“体会”之类，英语的 good sense 是很自然的搭配，在汉语里用与 good 相应的形容词来修饰“感觉”或“体会”似乎不如原文那样自然，因此，将原文“形容词＋名词”的形式改为“副词＋动词”的形式：“你自己好好体会好好观察，会学到很多，比我能教给你的多。”传达了原文的意义，也是习惯的汉语说法。

（3）**Of all things, banish the egotism out of your conversation**, and never think of entertaining people with your own personal concerns, or private affairs; though they are interesting to you, they are tedious and impertinent to everybody else: **besides that, one cannot**

keep one's own private affairs too secret.

这句话有两处需要说明。句子开头部分,"Of all things, banish the egotism out of your conversation",译为"与人交谈时最忌讳以自我为中心",基本是意译,也用"最忌讳"再现了原文的形式和语气。句子结尾部分,"besides that, one cannot keep one's own private affairs too secret",译为"况且,个人无论怎样严密保护隐私都不为过"。这是对前言的补充。

(4) ... nor labour, as many people do, to give that **turn** to the conversation, which may supply you with an opportunity of exhibiting them.

这里的 turn,词典解释为"措辞",a particular way of describing sth,不妨理解为"暗示"。译文用了比较口语化的"话口儿",将此句译为:"也不要像很多人那样在交谈中设法流露这种话口儿来寻找展示它们的机会。"

(5) Never maintain an argument **with heat and clamour**...

有些很自然的英语短语可以译成很自然的汉语短语,如 but give your opinion **modestly and coolly**,可译为"谦虚冷静地",这两个汉语副词不仅本身是习惯用法,放在一起使用也很自然。但有的短语在英语里很自然,但在汉语里却不一定总能找到合适的且读起来也很自然的短语。如,例句中的"(argue) with heat and clamour",翻译时只好忽略与原文对应的形式,把意思译出来,"永远不要争吵,不要争得面红耳赤",这样译传达了原意。

Samuel Johnson

塞缪尔·约翰逊(1709—1784),英国作家、批评家和词典编纂者,18 世纪伦敦的重要人物。鉴于他是声誉很高的作家和幽默演说家,1775 年牛津大学授予他荣誉博士称号,人们常常称他约翰逊博士。他的 *Dictionary of the English Language* (1755)是第一部收录词条比较全的英语词典,词义精确,引语丰富。他的其他重要著作有 *Rasselas* (1759)、*The Lives of the Poets* (1779—1781)。1773 年,他与朋友游历苏格兰西部诸岛,写了 *Journey to the Western Islands* 一书。后文"Congregational Music"即取自该书,"William Collins"一文选自 *Lives of the Poets*。

Congregational Music

Samuel Johnson

As we sat at Sir Alexander's table, we were entertained, according to the ancient usage of the North, with the melody of the bagpipe. Everything in these countries has its history. As the bagpiper was playing, an elderly gentleman informed us, that in some remote time, the *Macdonalds* of Glengary having been injured, or offended by the inhabitants of *Culloden*, and resolving to have justice or vengeance, came to *Culloden* on a Sunday, where finding their enemies at worship, they shut them up in the church, which they set on fire; and this, said he, is the tune that the piper played while they were burning.

Narrations like this, however uncertain, deserve the notice of a traveler, because they are the only records of a nation that has no historians, and afford the most genuine representation of the life and character of the ancient Highlanders.

聚会音乐

塞缪尔·约翰逊

我们坐在亚历山大爵士的桌旁，主人按照北方古老习俗招待我们听风笛乐。这些地区发生的每件事都有历史。风笛演奏者正在演奏时，一位年长的先生告诉我们，很久很久以前，格伦加里地区的麦克唐纳家人因受到卡洛登居民的伤害或冒犯，决心讨个公道或报仇，在一个礼拜日来到卡洛登，发现他们的敌人正在教堂里做礼拜，便把他们关在里面，放火把教堂烧了；他说，这就是他们被烧的时候风笛手演奏的那支曲调。

这样的故事，尽管难以确定其真伪，但值得旅行者关注，因为对一个没有历史学家的国家，这是它唯一的记录，最真实地反映了古代苏格兰高地人的生活和性格。

译后语

句子组织与信息传递

这篇小文读起来很具美感，很有力量。文章的美感和力量是多种因素作用的结果，其中包括组织严密的句子。此文仅百余字，却讲述了很多事情，特别是第一段的第三句，一位年长的先生用一句话为“我们”讲了一个很久以前发生的故事，来诠释风笛曲的内容：前一个分词结构“having been injured, or offended by the inhabitants of *Culloden*, and resolving to have justice or vengeance”，讲格伦加里地区的麦克唐纳家人为什么来到卡洛登；后一个分词结构 finding their enemies at worship，讲他们为什么把卡洛登居民关在教堂里。这些分词形式和位置安排产生一种效果，即很少的文字提供了密集的信息，读起来紧凑、连贯、有力量，有很强的美感。

第一段首尾衔接，开始说听风笛乐，结尾交代曲子的源头，内容和结构都十分完整。

第二段是作者的评论：当地的这种民间传说对旅行者有价值，通过故事了解古代苏格兰高地人的生活和性格。

William Collins

Samuel Johnson

He now (about 1744) came to London a literary adventurer, with many projects in his head, and very little money in his pocket. He designed many works, but his great fault was irresolution, or the frequent calls of immediate necessity broke his schemes, and suffered him to pursue no settled purpose. A man, doubtful of his dinner, or trembling at a creditor, is not much disposed to abstracted meditation or remote enquiries. He published proposals for a *History of the Revival of Learning*, and I have heard him speak with great kindness of Leo the Tenth, and with keen resentment of his tasteless successor. But probably not a page of the *History* was ever written. He planned several tragedies, but he only planned them. He wrote now and then odes and other poems, and did something, however little.

About this time I fell into his company. His appearance was decent and manly; his knowledge considerable, his views extensive, his conversation elegant, and his disposition cheerful. By degrees I gained his confidence; and one day was admitted to him when he was immured by a bailiff that was prowling in the street.

威廉·柯林斯

塞缪尔·约翰逊

他那会儿(大约1744年)来到伦敦时是个文学冒险者,脑子里有很多计划,而口袋里却没有多少钱。他制订了很多写作计划,但他有一个大毛病:犹豫不决,或者说他的计划常常被迫在眉睫的事情所破坏,使他无法实现既定的目标。一个食不饱腹,或有人讨债时就胆战心惊的人,不会专心致志思考问题,或致力于长远的事情。他发表了一些动议,想撰写一部《学术复兴史》,我听他说过对利奥十世教皇充满善意的话,也听他说过对其粗俗的继任者表示非常愤恨的话。但这部《复兴史》也许连一页也没写出来。他计划写好几部悲剧,但只是计划而已。他偶尔写些颂歌和别的诗,也做了些事情,尽管微不足道。

大约这个时候,我和他有了交往。他仪表端庄,颇有男人气派;他知识渊博,视野开阔,谈吐文雅,性格开朗。我慢慢得到他的信任。有一天,他被正在街上巡查的司法官禁闭,我被准许去看他。

On this occasion recourse was had to the booksellers, who, on the credit of a translation of Aristotle's *Poetics*, which he engaged to write with a large commentary, advanced as much money as enabled him to escape into the country. He shewed me the guineas safe in his hand. Soon afterwards his uncle, Mr. Martin, a lieutenant-colonel, left him about two thousand pounds; a sum which Collins could scarcely think exhaustible, and which he did not live to exhaust. The guineas were then repaid, and the translation neglected.

But man is not born for happiness. Collins, who, while he *studied to live*, felt no evil but poverty, no sooner *lived to study* than his life was assailed by more dreadful calamities, disease and insanity ...

Such was the fate of Collins, with whom I once delighted to converse, and whom I yet remember with tenderness.

在这种场合只好求助出版商，他同意翻译亚里士多德的《诗学》，并写一篇长篇评论，出版商为他预支了稿费，能满足他逃往乡下之需。他给我看了他手中的几尼。不久，他舅舅马丁先生，一个陆军中校，给他留下大约2000英镑，柯林斯觉得这是一笔几乎花不完的钱，他生前确也没有花完。后来他把预支的几尼退给出版商，书也没有翻译。

但人生来不是享福的。柯林斯在为生计而进行研究的时候，除贫穷之外还没有体会过别的弊端。在他还没来得及为从事研究而生活的时候，他却遭遇了更可怕的灾难的打击：疾病和精神失常……

这就是柯林斯的命运，一个我曾与之愉快交谈的人，一个我仍亲切缅怀的人。

译后语

修辞效果

我们在谈上篇《聚会音乐》时说过，它的一个突出特点是句子组织严密，文章充满美感和力量。《威廉·柯林斯》一文的突出特点是成功运用修辞手段，这是使文章产生同样效果的重要因素之一。如：

1. 并列结构(parallel structure)

(1) A man, **doubtful of his dinner, or trembling at a creditor**, is not much disposed to abstracted meditation or remote enquiries.

(2) His appearance was decent and manly; **his knowledge considerable, his views extensive, his conversation elegant, and his disposition cheerful**.

(3) Such was the fate of Collins, **with whom I once delighted to converse, and whom I yet remember with tenderness**.

以上三例中黑体部分皆为并列结构，其功能是产生形式上的平衡和意义表达上的简洁。形式上的平衡给人以美感，意义上的简洁给人以力量。

2. 对比(antithesis)

(1) He now (about 1744) came to London a literary adventurer, **with many projects in his head** and **very little money in his pocket**.

(2) ... and I have heard him **speak with great kindness of** Leo the Tenth, and **with keen resentment of** his tasteless successor.

(3) Collins, who, while he ***studied to live***, felt no evil but poverty, no sooner ***lived to study*** than his life was assailed by more dreadful calamities, disease and insanity...

以上三例中黑体部分皆为对比，对比产生反差，不论形式上或意义上都给人以鲜明感觉，给人留下深刻印象。

翻译时注意到并列结构和对比的形式及其特有的修辞效果，加上恰当处理具体的词语和句子，可以译出较好的文字。

David Hume

大卫·休谟(1711—1776),苏格兰哲学家和历史学家,被认为是西方哲学史和苏格兰启蒙时期最重要的人物之一。他的重要著作有 *Treatise of Human Nature* (1739—1740)和 *History of England* (1754—1762)。后文"Foreign Trade"选自他的 *Essays*。

Foreign Trade

David Hume

If we consult history, we shall find, that in most nations foreign trade has preceded any refinement in home manufactures, and given birth to domestic luxury. The temptation is stronger to make use of foreign commodities which are ready for use, and which are entirely new to us, than to make improvements on any domestic commodity, which always advance by slow degrees, and never affect us by their novelty. The profit is also very great in exporting what is superfluous at home, and what bears no price, to foreign nations whose soil or climate is not favourable to that commodity. Thus men become acquainted with the *pleasures* of luxury, and the *profits* of commerce; and their *delicacy* and *industry* being once awakened, carry them on to farther improvements in every branch of domestic as well as foreign trade; and this perhaps is the chief advantage which arises from a commerce with strangers. It rouses men from their indolence; and, presenting the gayer and more opulent part of the nation with objects of luxury which they never before dreamed of, raises in them a desire of a more splendid way of life than what their ancestors enjoyed. And at the same time,

对外贸易

大卫·休谟

如果我们查阅一下历史，就会发现，在多数国家，对外贸易一直优先于本国产品的改进和发展，从而催生了国内对奢侈生活的追求。使用业已存在的、对我们是全新的外国商品，比改进国内商品具有更大的诱惑力，因为改进总是缓慢的，而且永远不会让我们有新奇感。把国内过剩的和价格低廉的商品出口到土壤或气候不适宜生产这些商品的外国，利润是非常可观的。这样，人们就感受到奢侈生活所带来的快乐和商业所产生的利润；一旦人们的审美情趣和勤奋精神被唤醒，他们就会对内外贸易的各个方面做进一步改进；这也许就是对外贸易所具有的主要优越性。它把人们从好逸恶劳的惰性中唤醒，用从前做梦也想不到的奢侈品来展现这个国家更快乐更富有的一面，并在他们心中唤起一种渴望，渴望比他们先辈享有更美好的生活方式。

the few merchants who possess the secret of this importation and exportation, make great profits; and, becoming rivals in wealth to the ancient nobility, tempt other adventurers to become their rivals in commerce. Imitation soon diffuses all those arts, while domestic manufacturers emulate the foreign in their improvements, and work up every home commodity to the utmost perfection of which it is susceptible. Their own steel and iron, in such laborious hands, become equal to the gold and rubies of the Indies.

同时，熟谙进出口秘密的少数商人也获得巨大利润，在财富方面可与古代贵族相匹敌，也引诱别的冒险家在商业上与他们竞争。国内厂商在改进中与外国厂商竞争，把国内生产的每一种商品改进到尽善尽美的程度，这是可能的，与此同时，通过仿制，所有那些技艺很快得到了普及。在如此勤奋的人们手里，他们的钢铁就等同于东印度群岛的黄金和红宝石。

译后语

译文表达方式应与上下文切合

有时,用英汉词典里现成的译文翻译英语词语并不恰当,放在上下文里不合适。翻译时不求词语表层的对应,而寻找能表达相近意思的表达方式。如:

(1) The temptation is stronger to make use of foreign commodities **which are ready for use**, and which are entirely new to us, than to make improvements on any domestic commodity...

这里的 which are ready for use 是指已经制造出来或已经投放市场的商品,此处将其译为"业已存在的",可指前者,也可指后者,虽然所指比较宽泛,但说法通俗,意思清楚,无歧义。

(2) ... and never **affect** us by their novelty.

英汉词典通常将此类上下文里的 affect 译成"影响""感染"或"打动"等,但将此类词语直接用于此句都不恰当。实际上,这句话的意思可以用以下类似的方式来表达:"而且永远不会让我们有新奇感"等。

(3) ... and their delicacy and **industry** being once awakened ...

《英汉大词典》(陆谷孙主编)对 industry 有一个解释:技能,但仍需结合上下文对其做些补充性的解释,如"制造的技能"。

(4) ... raises in them a **desire** of a more splendid way of life than what their ancestors enjoyed.

虽然 of 之后修饰 desire 的成分很长，但在英语里读起来很自然，并不觉得头轻脚重。但在汉语里，如将一个很长的定语放在“渴望”之前，则有头重脚轻之感。为了避免句子结构失衡，故在翻译 desire 时，将其重复一次：“并在他们心中唤起一种渴望，渴望比他们先辈享有更美好的生活方式。”第一个“渴望”是名词，第二个“渴望”是动词，汉语里常有这种用法。

Gilbert White

吉尔伯特·怀特(1720—1793),英国国教会的神职人员和博物学家,最著名的著作是 *The Natural History and Antiquities of Selborne* (1789)。此书是写给当时英国最重要的动物学家托马斯·彭南特(Thomas Pennant)的书信,信中谈及他在塞尔伯恩地区发现的鸟类和动植物。很多人认为怀特是英国第一个生态学家,是尊重自然界理念的奠基人之一。后文即选自 *The Natural History and Antiquities of Selborne*。

The Bat

Gilbert White

I was much entertained last summer with a tame bat, which would take flies out of a person's hand. If you gave it anything to eat, it brought its wings round before the mouth, hovering and hiding its head in the manner of birds of prey when they feed. The adroitness it showed in shearing off the wings of the flies, which were always rejected, was worthy of observation and pleased me much. Insects seemed to be most acceptable, though it did not refuse raw flesh when offered; so that the notion that bats go down chimneys and gnaw men's bacon seems no improbable story. While I amused myself with this wonderful quadruped, I saw it several times confute the vulgar opinion, that bats, when down on a flat surface, cannot get on the wing again, by rising with great ease from the floor. It ran, I observed, with more dispatch than I was aware of; but in a most ridiculous and grotesque manner.

Bats drink on the wing, like swallows, by sipping the surface, as they play over pools and streams. They love to frequent waters, not only for the sake of drinking, but on account of insects, which

蝙　蝠

吉尔伯特·怀特

去年夏天，一只驯养的蝙蝠很是让我快活了一阵，它竟然会从人的手里叼苍蝇。如果你喂它东西吃，它就会把翅膀兜到嘴的前面，悬停在空中，把头遮起来，像猛禽吃食一样。它剔去苍蝇翅膀（翅膀总是不吃的）时所展现的灵巧很值得一看，我觉得很有意思。它最爱吃昆虫，不过，喂它生肉它也不拒绝；因此，说蝙蝠能从烟囱钻进屋里吃熏肉似乎并不是不可能的。正当我兴致勃勃地观看这个令人赞叹的四足动物时，我看见它一连几次从地板上轻松地飞起，这就推翻了那种通常流行的看法，认为蝙蝠一旦落在平地上就飞不起来。我注意到，它跑得很快，我原来不知道它跑得这么快；但姿势很可笑，怪模怪样的。

蝙蝠和燕子一样，会边飞边喝水，在池塘和小河上玩耍掠过水面时就把水喝了。它们喜欢去有水的地方，不单是为了喝水，也为了吃昆虫，水面上

are found over them in the greatest plenty. As I was going some years ago, pretty late, in a boat from Richmond to Sunbury, on a warm summer's evening, I think I saw myriads of bats between the two places; the air swarmed with them all along the Thames, so that hundreds were in sight at a time.

总有大量的昆虫。几年前一个温暖的夏季的傍晚，时间很晚了，我坐船从里士满去森伯里，一路上看见无数蝙蝠；沿泰晤士河两岸上空成群结队地飞来飞去，有时一次就看见好几百只。

译后语

1. 三个常用动词的翻译：

（1）I was much **entertained** last summer with a tame bat, which would take flies out of a person's hand.

（2）The adroitness it showed in shearing off the wings of the flies, which were always rejected, was worthy of observation and **pleased** me much.

（3）While I **amused** myself with this wonderful quadruped...

英文词典 *Webster's New World Dictionary*（Third College Edition）为这三个动词所做的释义很相近：

entertain: to hold the interest of and give pleasure to; to amuse;

please: to give pleasure to;

amuse: to keep pleasantly or enjoyably occupied or interested.

翻译这几个动词时既要使译文符合原文词义，还要尽量避免使用雷同的词语。以下是这三句话的试译：

（1）去年夏天，一只驯养的蝙蝠很是让我**快活**了一阵，它竟然会从人的手里叼苍蝇。

（2）它剔去苍蝇翅膀（翅膀总是不吃的）时所展现的灵巧很值得一看，我**觉得**很**有意思**。

（3）正当我**兴致勃勃**地观看这个令人赞叹的四足动物时……

2. 两个句子译文的变通：

（1）I saw it several times confute the vulgar **opinion**, that bats, when down on a flat surface, cannot get on the wing again...

此句里的 opinion 和 that 引导的从句是同位关系，后者说了前者的具体内容，将 opinion 译成"意见"或"看法"都可以，然后接着说"认为……"比较自然。如：

> 我看见它一连几次从地板上轻松地飞起，这就推翻了那种通常流行的看法，认为蝙蝠一旦落在平地上就飞不起来。

（2）It ran, I observed, with **more** dispatch **than** I was aware of...

With 短语里的 more than 是比较级形式，翻译时若一方面保持形式的对应同时又要文字像原文那样自然简练，颇觉困难。故做如下变通：

> 我注意到，它跑得很快，我原来不知道它跑得这么快……

Edmund Burke

埃德蒙·伯克(1729—1797),英国辉格党政治家、作家。1765至1794年间任英国议会下议院议员。他因发表支持美国独立的演说和文章而著称。1790年,发表 *Reflections of the Revolution in France*,在书中表达了反对法国大革命中较为极端行为的立场。他认为:"参加政治必须永远反对谋求私利,只允许追求同整体利益相一致的合理的自身利益。"(《简明不列颠百科全书》)这是很好的思想境界,值得学习。后文"Cultivating Generous and Honest Feelings"出自他的 *Thoughts on the Present Discontents*,原标题为"The Arena, 1770",为与文章内容契合,现标题为译者所加。

Cultivating Generous and Honest Feelings

Edmund Burke

I remember an old scholastic aphorism, which says "that the man who lives wholly detached from others must be either an angel or a devil." When I see in any of these detached gentlemen of our times the angelic purity, power, and beneficence, I shall admit them to be angels. In the meantime, we are born only to be men. We shall do enough if we form ourselves to be good ones. It is therefore our business carefully to cultivate in our minds, to rear to the most perfect vigour and maturity, every sort of generous and honest feeling that belongs to our nature. To bring the dispositions that are lovely in private life into the service and conduct of the commonwealth; so to be patriots, as not to forget we are gentlemen. To cultivate friendships, and to incur enmities. To have both strong, but both selected: in the one, to be placable; in the other, immoveable. To model our principles to our duties and our situation. To be fully persuaded, that all virtue which is impracticable is spurious; and rather to run the risque of falling into faults in a course which leads us to act with effect and energy than to loiter out our

培养慷慨正直的感情

埃德蒙·伯克

我记得一句颇富学究气的格言说："完全与别人脱离的人不是天使就是魔鬼。"当我在今天那些与人脱离的有教养的人身上看见天使般的纯洁、力量和仁慈时，我会承认他们是天使。但同时，我们生来只是为了做人。如果我们使自己成为好人，那就很好了。因此，我们要做的是在我们心灵里细心培养本来属于我们本性的慷慨正直的感情，使其具有最完美的活力，达到最成熟的程度。将我们在私生活里表现出来的美好的性情用来为全体公民服务和影响他们的行为；使我们成为爱国者，不至于忘记我们是有教养的人。培育友谊和招致敌意。两个方面都要很强劲，但都是有选择的：一方面，随和，另一方面，坚定。把我们的原则用于工作和环境中去。相信没有实际意义的优点是虚假的；宁可在有效和有力的行动中冒犯错误的危险，

days without blame, and without use. Public life is a situation of power and energy; he trespasses against his duty who sleeps upon his watch, as well as he that goes over to the enemy.

也不整天无所事事、心安理得地闲逛。公共生活是一种充满活力和影响力的环境;执勤疏忽的人和投降敌人的人一样,都是渎职。

译后语

关于两个句子的翻译：

(1) It is therefore our business carefully **to cultivate** in our minds, **to rear** to the most perfect vigour and maturity, every sort of generous and honest feeling that belongs to our nature.

此句里的 to cultivate 和 to rear 意思相近，但各有一个不同的状语：前者的是 in our minds，后者的是 to the most perfect vigour and maturity；两个动词共有一个宾语，即 every sort of generous and honest feeling that belongs to our nature。因此，译文做如下处理：

> 因此，我们要做的是在我们心灵里细心培养本来属于我们本性的慷慨正直的感情，使其具有最完美的活力，达到最成熟的程度。

将 to cultivate 和 to rear 译作一个动词"培养"，并依据汉语习惯重新安排了两个状语的位置。

(2) To cultivate friendships, and to incur enmities. To have both strong, but both selected: in the one, **to be placable**; in the other, **immoveable**.

这两个句子相互联系：to be placable 是指前面的 to cultivate friendships，immovable 是指前面的 to incur enmities。因此，译文做如下处理：

> 培育友谊和招致敌意。两个方面都要很强劲，但都是有选择的：一方面，随和，另一方面，坚定。

William Cowper

威廉·考珀(1731—1800),英国诗人,是当时最受欢迎的诗人之一,也是浪漫诗歌的先驱之一。他以写日常生活和英国乡村风光而改变了18世纪自然诗歌的方向。诗人柯勒律治(Samuel Taylor Coleridge)称他为最好的现代诗人。诗人华兹华斯(William Wordsworth)特别称赞他的诗歌"Yardley-Oak"。他的宗教情结和与约翰·牛顿的联系导致他写了很多优秀作品,使他深深留在人们的记忆中。他的主要作品有:*Olney Hymns*(1779,与约翰·牛顿合作)、*John Gilpin*(1782)、*The Task*(1785);并于1791年出版了荷马史诗《伊利亚特》(*Iliad*)和《奥德赛》(*Odysscy*)的翻译作品。后文均来自*Letter to the Reverend John Newton*。

A Candidate for Parliament

William Cowper

As when the sea is uncommonly agitated, the water finds its way into creeks and holes of rocks, which in its calmer state it never reaches, in like manner the effect of these turbulent times is felt even at Orehard side, where in general we live as undisturbed by the political element, as shrimps or cockles that have been accidentally deposited in some hollow beyond the water mark, by the usual dashing of the waves. We were sitting yesterday after dinner, the two ladies and myself, very composedly, and without the least apprehension of any such intrusion in our snug parlour, one lady knitting, the other netting, and the gentleman winding worsted, when to our unspeakable surprise a mob appeared before the window; a smart rap was heard at the door, the boys halloo'd, and the maid announced Mr. Grenville.

Puss was unfortunately let out of her box, so that the candidate, with all his good friends at his heels, was refused admittance at the grand entry, and referred to the back door, as the only possible way of approach.

议会候选人

威廉·考珀

当海浪异常汹涌时，海水便灌进小湾和岩洞里；海水比较平静时，到不了这些地方。同样，动荡年代的影响甚至在奥列哈德这一方也感觉到了；通常情况下，我们的生活不受政治因素干扰，就像偶尔被海浪冲到水线以上低凹处的小虾和鸟蛤。昨天吃完午饭，两个女眷和我正在温馨的会客厅里静静坐着，根本不担心会有人闯进来。一个女士在织毛活儿，另一个在编织网罩，男士在缠毛线。这时候窗前突然来了一伙人，让我们大吃一惊，接着是急促的敲门声，男孩们"嘿"了一声，女仆人说，格伦维尔先生来了。

不幸的是，帕斯[①]刚从它的盒子里被放出来，因此，议会候选人以及随他而来的朋友们都被拒之正门外，被打发到唯一可进的后门。

① 帕斯是一只猫，议会候选人造访时它正好从盒子里放出来，此时若开大门怕它跑出去，故将议会候选人一伙打发到后门。

Candidates are creatures not very susceptible of affronts, and would rather, I suppose, climb in at a window, than be absolutely excluded. In a minute, the yard, the kitchen, and the parlour, were filled. Mr. Grenville, advancing toward me, shook me by the hand with a degree of cordiality that was extremely seducing. As soon as he and as many more as could find chairs were seated, he began to open the intent of his visit. I told him I had no vote, for which he readily gave me credit. I assured him I had no influence, which he was not equally inclined to believe, and the less, no doubt, because Mr. Ashburner, the draper, addressing himself to me at this moment, informed me that I had a great deal. Supposing that I could not be possessed of such a treasure without knowing it, I ventured to confirm my first assertion, by saying, that if I had any I was utterly at a loss to imagine where it could be, or wherein it consisted. Thus ended the conference. Mr. Grenville squeezed me by the hand again, kissed the ladies, and withdrew. He kissed likewise the maid in the kitchen, and seemed upon the whole a most loving, kissing, kind-hearted gentleman. He is very young, genteel, and handsome. He has a pair of very good eyes in his head, which not being sufficient as it should seem for the many nice and difficult purposes of a senator, he has a third also, which he wore suspended by a riband from his button-hole. The boys halloo'd, the dogs barked, Puss scampered, the hero, with his long train of obsequious followers, withdrew. We made ourselves very merry with the adventure, and in a short time settled into our former tranquility, never probably to be thus interrupted more.

候选人这种人对于受辱不怎么在乎,他们宁肯爬窗而入也不愿意被拒之门外,我想。一会儿工夫,院子、厨房和客厅里都挤满了人。格伦维尔先生朝我走过来,带着极具诱惑的热情和我握手。他和其他能找到座位的人刚一坐下,就开门见山说明来意。我告诉他我没有选票,为此,他立即称赞我。我很恳切地对他说我没有影响力,他就不像刚才那样相信我了,因为这时纺织品商阿什伯纳先生正在对我说话,他说我有很大的影响力,格伦维尔先生无疑就更不相信我的话了。假设说,我若有这样的影响力,我不会不知道的;我小心地证实我刚才的说法:"假如我有任何影响力,我想象不出我的影响力在哪里,或表现在哪方面。"我们的对话就这样结束了。格伦维尔先生又紧紧握了我的手,亲吻两位女士,走了。他在厨房里也亲吻了女佣,看来他基本上是个很有爱心、喜欢亲吻、心地善良的绅士。他很年轻,彬彬有礼,很英俊。他有一双很好看的眼睛,但要达到一个参议员很多不错而又难以达到的目的,两只眼睛看来不够用;他还有第三只,用一条丝带挂在扣眼上。男孩们"嘿"了一声,狗儿叫着,帕斯又蹦又跳,这位英雄和对他献媚取宠的大队人马走了。这段插曲让我们很开心。过了一会儿,我们又像刚才那样安静下来,也许再没有像这样被打扰过。

译后语

1. 比喻

文章的第一句话是比喻，包含一个**隐喻**和一个**明喻**：

"... when the sea is uncommonly agitated, the water finds its way into creeks and holes of rocks" 比喻 "the effect of these turbulent times is felt even at Orehard side"；

"which in its calmer state it never reaches" 比喻 "where in general we live as undisturbed by the political element, as shrimps or cockles that have been accidentally deposited in some hollow beyond the water mark, by the usual dashing of the waves"。

这句话是个主题句(thesis statement)，统领全文，文章其余部分都在说明这个主题。翻译时需理清句中的比喻关系。

2. 理解

理解是做好翻译的前提，正确的翻译基于正确的理解。下面是文章第三段中的一个句子：

I told him I had no vote, for which he readily gave me credit. I assured him I had no influence, which he was not equally inclined to believe, and the less, no doubt, because Mr. Ashburner, the draper, addressing himself to me at this moment, informed me that I had a great deal.

笔者对句中黑体部分是这样理解的：

"... for which he readily gave me credit"，当"我"告诉他"我"没

有选票时，格伦维尔立即称赞我。

“... which he was not equally inclined to believe”，当“我”说“我”没有影响力时，他就不像刚才那样相信“我”了；这句话说明刚才他相信“我”说的话。

“... and the less”，当阿什伯纳先生说“我”有很大的影响力时，格伦维尔就更不相信“我”的话了。

Country Music

William Cowper

My greenhouse is never so pleasant as when we are just upon the point of being turned out of it. The gentleness of the autumnal suns, and the calmness of this latter season, make it a much more agreeable retreat than we ever find it in summer; when, the winds being generally brisk, we cannot cool it by admitting a sufficient quantity of air, without being at the same time incommoded by it. But now I sit with all the windows and the door wide open, and am regaled with the scent of every flower in a garden as full of flowers as I have known how to make it. We keep no bees, but if I lived in a hive I should hardly hear more of their music. All the bees in the neighbourhood resort to a bed of mignonette, opposite to the window, and pay me for the honey they get out of it by a hum, which, though rather monotonous, is as agreeable to my ear as the whistling of my linnets. All the sounds that nature utters are delightful,—at least in this country. I should not perhaps find the roaring of lions in Africa, or of bears in Russia, very pleasing; but I know no beast in England whose voice I do not account musical, save and except always the braying of an ass. The notes of all our birds and

乡村音乐

威廉·考珀

我的温室从未像我们即将从那里撤出时那样舒适。温和的秋阳和静谧的季节使它成了比夏季更加宜人的去处。夏季里，一般来说风很凉爽，我们不能让很多凉气进来，那会给我们带来麻烦。可现在，我坐在温室里，门窗大开，花园里（我尽所能在那里栽满了花）的芬芳让我心旷神怡。我们没有养蜂，可是，即使我住在蜂箱里，听到的蜜蜂吟唱也不会比这里多。附近所有的蜜蜂都飞到窗户对面的木犀草花坛上来采蜜，然后用唱歌回报我，虽然歌声单调，听起来却和我的朱顶雀的叫声一样悦耳。自然界发出的所有声音都让人感觉愉快——至少在这个国家是这样。我感觉，也许非洲狮和俄罗斯熊的吼声不是很好听，但我知道，在英国，除了驴叫，没有一种动物的叫声是不悦耳的。所有鸟类和家禽的鸣叫无一例外让我感觉愉快。我不会想

fowls please me, without one exception. I should not indeed think of keeping a goose in a cage, that I might hang him up in the parlour for the sake of his melody, but a goose upon a common, or in a farm-yard, is no bad performer; and as to insects, if the black beetle, and beetles indeed of all hues, will keep out of my way, I have no objection to any of the rest; on the contrary, in whatever key they sing, from the gnat's fine treble to the bass of the bumble-bee, I admire them all.

到把一只鹅养在笼子里,挂在客厅听它的叫声,但在公共用地上或农家庭院里,鹅并非是很蹩脚的演员。至于昆虫,假如黑甲虫以及各种颜色的甲虫避开我,我对其余的昆虫均无反感;相反,不论它们用什么音调唱歌,从蠓虫的高音到大黄蜂的低音,我都欣赏。

译后语

本文所说的温室可能是为花园培育花木秧苗的地方。因“夏季里，……风很凉爽”，需要关上门窗，保持室温。夏末秋初，育苗工作结束，作者坐在温室里，打开门窗，感受从花园吹来的花香。下面说说关于几个句子的翻译：

（1）My greenhouse is never so pleasant as when we are just upon the point of being turned out of it.

这里所说正是秋天即将到来，“我们”就要从温室里撤出来时的感觉：

我的温室从未像我们即将从那里撤出时那样舒适。

（2）**The gentleness of the autumnal suns, and the calmness of this latter season,** make it a much more agreeable retreat than we ever find it in summer...

此句的主语部分“The gentleness of the autumnal suns, and the calmness of this latter season”可直译为“秋阳的温和与季节的静谧”，但汉语更习惯说“温和的秋阳和静谧的季节”。

（3）... we cannot cool it by admitting a sufficient quantity of air, without being at the same time incommoded by it.

此句直译起来很别扭，为译其意而改动了句子的表述方式：

我们不能让很多凉气进来，那会给我们带来麻烦。

（4）But now I sit with all the windows and the door wide open, and am regaled with the scent of every flower in a garden **as**

full of flowers as I have known how to make it.

这里指温室外面的花园,作者在花园里栽满了花木,句子最后一部分"as full of flowers as I have known how to make it",译成汉语时不大容易弄得很通顺,故将其放在括号里:

可现在,我坐在温室里,门窗大开,花园里(我尽所能在那里栽满了花)的芬芳让我心旷神怡。

William Hazlitt

威廉·黑兹利特(1778—1830),英国作家,以其人文主义散文和文学批评著称,现在被视为英国伟大批评家和伟大散文家,与塞缪尔·约翰逊和乔治·奥威尔齐名。最出名的著作有*Characters of Shakespeare's Plays*(1817—1818)和以亲切笔调写就的*Table-Talk, or, Original Essays*(1821)。后文"On Going a Journey"即出自该书。另一篇"The Pleasures of Reading"则出自*The Plain Speaker*。他同时还是画家,有自画像,为他的朋友查尔斯·兰姆画过肖像,他为父亲作的画像参加过画展。

On Going a Journey

William Hazlitt

One of the pleasantest things in the world is going a journey; but I like to go by myself. I can enjoy society in a room; but out of doors, nature is company enough for me. I am then never less alone than when alone.

The fields his study, nature was his book.

I cannot see the wit of walking and talking at the same time. When I am in the country I wish to vegetate like the country. I am not for criticising hedge-rows and black cattle. I go out of town in order to forget the town and all that is in it. There are those who for this purpose go to watering-places, and carry the metropolis with them. I like more elbow-room and fewer encumbrances. I like solitude, when I give myself up to it, for the sake of solitude; nor do I ask for

a friend in my retreat,
Whom I may whisper solitude is sweet.

谈旅游

威廉·黑兹利特

世界上最快乐的事情之一是旅游，但我喜欢一个人旅游。虽然我欣赏在室内与人相聚；但在野外，大自然足可与我为伴。与我独处相比，此时我更不觉孤独。

田野是他的书房，大自然是他的书。①

我看不出边走边聊有什么意思。我到了乡下，就希望像乡下生活那样悠闲。我不赞成挑剔乡下的树篱和黑色牛群。我离开都市是为了忘记都市和那里的一切。有人为了这个目的而去矿泉疗养地，也就把大都市的东西带去了。我喜欢多一点空间，少一点累赘。我喜欢独享清静，当我沉溺其中时，就是为清静而清静；我不请求

朋友来到我的静僻处，

为了告诉他独享清静是多么甜蜜。②

---

① 引自罗伯特·布龙菲尔德（Robert Bloomfield，1766—1823）的《农夫之子》（*The Farmer's Boy*）。

② 引自威廉·考珀（William Cowper，1731—1800）的《隐居》（*Retirement*）。

The soul of a journey is liberty, perfect liberty, to think, feel, do, just as one pleases. We go a journey chiefly to be free of all impediments and of all inconveniences; to leave ourselves behind, much more to get rid of others. It is because I want a little breathing-space to muse on indifferent matters, where Contemplation

May plume her feathers and let grow her wings,
That in the various bustle of resort
Were all too ruffled, and sometimes impair'd,

that I absent myself from the town for a while, without feeling at a loss the moment I am left by myself. Instead of a friend in a postchaise or in a Tilbury, to exchange good things with, and vary the same stale topics over again, for once let me have a truce with impertinence. Give me the clear blue sky over my head, and the green turf beneath my feet, a winding road before me, and a three hours' march to dinner—and then to thinking! It is hard if I cannot start some game on these lone heaths. I laugh, I run, I leap, I sing for joy. From the point of yonder rolling cloud I plunge into my past being, and revel there, as the sun-burnt Indian plunges headlong into the wave that wafts him to his native shore. Then long-forgotten things, like "sunken wrack and sumless treasuries," burst upon my eager sight, and I begin to feel, think, and be myself again.

旅游的目的就是为了寻求自由，寻求完全的自由，为了随心所欲地去想、去感、去做。我们旅游主要是为了摆脱所有的羁绊和累赘；放下自己的事情，更是为了摆脱别人。这是因为我想要一点喘息空间来思考一些无关紧要的事情，其间“沉思”

可以梳理她的羽毛，让她的翅膀长得丰满；
因为在频繁的迁徙中她的羽翅
被搅得七零八乱，有时还会受到损坏，[①]

因此，我就离开都市一段时间，而且我脱身的那一刻并不感到无所适从。与其和朋友坐在四轮或双轮马车里谈论一些称心的事情，变换方式重复那些陈旧的话题，那就让我无礼一回吧。给我一片湛蓝的天空吧，给我一块绿色的草地吧，让我眼前展现一条弯曲的小路吧，让我走三小时的路程去吃晚饭吧——然后再思考一些事情！在这寂静的荒野里，若不纵情做些活动那是很难的。于是我笑呀，跑呀，跳呀，为了寻开心我唱呀。那边的浮云让我回想起我的过去，并陶醉其中，如同那皮肤晒得黝黑的印度人一头扎进浪里，任其将他漂回故乡的岸边。然后，早已忘怀的事情，像海底的“沉船和无数的珠宝”[②]突然映入我渴求的视线，我又开始感觉、

① 作者根据约翰·弥尔顿(John Milton，1608—1674)的《科马斯》(*Comus*)中的诗句进行了改写。

② 引自莎士比亚(William Shakespeare，1564—1616)的《国王亨利五世》(*The Life of King Henry V*)第1幕第2场。

Instead of an awkward silence, broken by attempts at wit or dull common-places, mine is that undisturbed silence of the heart which alone is perfect eloquence. No one likes puns, alliterations, antitheses, argument, and analysis better than I do; but I sometimes had rather be without them. "Leave, oh, leave me to my repose!" I have just now other business in hand, which would seem idle to you, but is with me "very stuff o' the conscience." Is not this wild rose sweet without a comment? Does not this daisy leap to my heart set in its coat of emerald?

思考,清醒过来。我的寂静不是那种尴尬的寂静,要靠机智和老生常谈来打破。我的寂静是心灵深处不受干扰的寂静,这本身就是完美的表达。没有人比我更喜欢双关语、头韵、对仗,也没有人比我更喜欢论理和分析,但有时我宁愿没有这些。"让我,啊,让我独享安静吧!"[①]我现在正忙着别的事情,这在你看来似乎是清闲,但对于我,这正是"良知的根本"[②]。难道这野玫瑰不是无人品评也自芳吗?难道这雏菊花不正跳进我那绿宝石包裹的心房吗?

---

① 引自托马斯·格雷(Thomas Gray,1716—1771)的诗《奥丁的衰落》(*The Descent of Odin*)。

② 引自莎士比亚的《奥赛罗》(*Othello*)第1幕第2场。

译后语

关于几个句子的翻译：

(1) I am then never less **alone** than when **alone**.

这句话中的alone不是“孤独”，是指独自一人时的清静。此句可理解为：

与我独处相比，此时我更不觉孤独。

(2) There are those who for this purpose go to watering-places, and **carry the metropolis with them**.

句中的“carry the metropolis with them”是指把大都市的东西带去了。

(3) The soul of a journey is liberty...

此句可直译作“旅游的灵魂是自由”，但“旅游的目的就是为了寻求自由”更通俗些。

(4) It is because I want a little breathing-space to muse on indifferent matters, **where** Contemplation

May plume her feathers and let grow her wings,
That in the various bustle of resort
Were all too ruffled, and sometimes impair'd...

这句话里的where是指在muse on的过程中，人格化的Contemplation：

可以梳理她的羽毛，让她的翅膀长得丰满；
因为在频繁的迁徙中她的羽翅

被搅得七零八乱，有时还会损坏……

(5) ... for once let me have a truce with **impertinence**.

这里的 impertinence 是指作者因不愿意与人闲谈而可能表现出来的无礼。

The Pleasures of Reading

William Hazlitt

The last time I tasted this luxury in its full perfection was one day after a sultry day's walk in summer between Farnham and Alton. I was fairly tired out; I walked into an inn-yard (I think at the latter place); I was shown by the waiter to what looked at first like common outhouses at the other end of it, but they turned out to be a suite of rooms, probably a hundred years old—the one I entered opened into an old-fashioned garden, embellished with beds of larkspur and a leaden Mercury; it was wainscoted, and there was a grave-looking, dark-coloured portrait of Charles II hanging up over the tiled chimneypiece. I had *Love for Love* in my pocket, and began to read; coffee was brought in in a silver coffee-pot; the cream, the bread and butter, everything was excellent, and the flavour of Congreve's style prevailed over all. I prolonged the entertainment till a late hour, and relished this divine comedy better even than when I used to see it played by Miss Mellon, as Miss Prue; Bob Palmer, as Tattle; and Bannister, as honest Ben. This circumstance happened just five years ago, and it seems like yesterday.

读书的快乐

威廉·黑兹利特

最近一次享受读书的美感是在夏季一个闷热的日子里我从法纳姆走到奥尔顿以后。当时我很累;我走进一个小旅店的院落(我想是在奥尔顿);侍者把我领到院子另一端的房子,初看起来像普通的附属建筑,原来那是一套客房,大约有一百年的历史了。我进的房间面向一个旧式花园,花园里有飞燕草花坛,还有一尊铅灰色的墨丘利神像;房间装饰着护壁板,壁炉镶着瓷砖,壁炉台上方挂着一幅深色调的查理二世肖像,表情庄严。我衣袋里装着《为爱而爱》,便开始读起来。侍者用银质咖啡壶端来咖啡;还有奶油、面包和黄油,一切都好极了,而康格里夫作品的风味更好。我怀着愉悦的心情一直读到很晚,我喜欢这部神圣喜剧,比我过去所看的由梅隆女士扮演普鲁女士、鲍勃·帕尔默扮演塔特尔、班尼斯特扮演诚实的本的舞台演出还要喜欢。那是五年前的事,就好像发生在昨天一样。

If I count my life so by lustres, it will soon glide away; yet I shall not have to repine, if, while it lasts, it is enriched with a few such recollections!

假如我以五年为单位来计算，我的生命将很快消逝；然而，在我的有生之年，假如能有几次这样的回忆，我将毫无怨言！

译后语

做英汉翻译时，原文的短语搭配和句法结构是关注的重点。短语搭配和句法结构有时可以直译，译文也并不难懂，但读者的反应有不同。双语读者在译文里会看到原文的痕迹，因而理解译者的处理方式；单语读者因为缺乏原文背景，读译文时会有异样的感觉，有的可能感觉新鲜，有的可能不大习惯。但实际情况是，翻译时常有变通。至于如何变，还是取决于译者本人——取决于译者的翻译主张和喜好，以及他的行文方式。因此，不同译者有不同的变通方法。本文译者希望变通时兼顾三个方面，即英语的句子结构、汉语的行文方式以及汉语读者（主要指单语大众读者）的接受心理。所谓照顾原文的句子结构，是指变通时不把原文的句子结构变得面目全非，有所变有所不变；关于汉语的行文方式与汉语读者的接受心理，这二者基本上是一致的，前者是指汉语句子的突出特点——通顺，后者则指读者的心理感受——读起来不别扭。试以下面的句子为例做简要说明：The last time I tasted this **luxury** in its full perfection was one day after **a sultry day's walk** in summer between Farnham and Alton.

这个句子的长短属中等偏长，但句子主谓分明，翻译时先说什么后说什么并不太费思索，也容易再现原文句子的基本结构。但这句话里有一个短语“a sultry day's walk”需要处理好。这个短语虽然只有四个词，但它的意思却难以用一个相应的汉语短语来表达，因此，需对其做些灵活变通。变通的做法是将 sultry 和 summer 联系起来，将名词 walk 变为动词。译文如下：

最近一次享受读书的美感是在夏季一个闷热的日子里我从法纳姆走到奥尔顿以后。

这个译文保持了原文句子主谓分明的结构，从汉语角度看，虽然句子略长，但读起来并不别扭。

又如“I prolonged the entertainment till a late hour...”，如果直译此句，译文可能是“我将这一快乐的心情延续到夜晚”。这样的说法也并不难懂，但如译作“我怀着愉悦的心情一直读到很晚……”可能更符合汉语的说话习惯。

再如“...everything was excellent, and the flavour of Congreve's style **prevailed over all**.”，这个句子里的“prevailed over all”，词典里的解释是“战胜”“压倒”或“占上风”等，但放在上下文里都不协调。因此，如将其译为“更好”，句子变成如下的模样：“……一切都好极了，而康格里夫作品的风味更好。”这样就与前面的“好极了”形成了有效的比较。

另外，lustre 一词等同于 lustrum，意为“五年之期”。

Dorothy Wordsworth

多萝西·华兹华斯(1771—1855),英国作家、诗人,她的作品主要包括书信、日记、诗歌和短篇小说。她是浪漫派诗人威廉·华兹华斯的胞妹,终身未嫁。他们兄妹二人自幼关系亲密,在威廉结婚之后,她仍然与哥哥一家生活在一起。后文出自*Journal*。

The Beggars

Dorothy Wordsworth

A very tall woman, tall much beyond the measure of tall women, called at the door. She had on a very long brown cloak and a very white cap, without bonnet. Her face was excessively brown, but it had plainly once been fair. She led a little bare-footed child about two years old by the hand, and said her husband, who was a tinker, was gone before with the other children. I gave her a piece of bread. Afterwards on my way to Ambleside, beside the bridge at Rydale, I saw her husband sitting by the roadside, his two asses feeding beside him, and the two young children at play upon the grass. The man did not beg. I passed on and about a quarter of a mile further I saw two boys before me, one about 10, the other about 8 years old, at play chasing a butterfly. They were wild figures, not very ragged, but without shoes and stockings. The hat of the elder was wreathed round with yellow flowers, the younger, whose hat was only a rimless crown, had stuck it round with laurel leaves. They continued at play till I drew very near, and then they addressed me with the begging cant and the whining voice of sorrow.

乞丐

多萝西·华兹华斯

一个很高的女人，比一般高女人高出很多，来到门口乞讨。她身穿一件很长的棕色斗篷，头戴一顶很白的鸭舌帽，没戴女帽。她的脸晒得黝黑，但看得出来，那曾经是一张白皙的脸。她手领着一个两岁左右的孩子，光着脚，她说，她丈夫是个修补匠，早就带着其他孩子走了。我给了她一块面包。后来在去安布尔赛德的路上，在赖代尔的桥旁，我看见她丈夫坐在路边，他的两头驴子在旁边吃草，两个小孩在草地上玩耍。这个人没有向我乞讨。我走过去了，走了约四分之一英里，便看见前面有两个小男孩，一个10岁左右，一个8岁左右，正在追逐一只蝴蝶。全然是两个野孩子，衣服不是很破，没穿鞋子，也没穿袜子。大一点的男孩帽子上扎了一圈黄色的花，小一点的戴一个无檐帽，周边插了一圈桂叶。他们一直在玩耍，等我走近时，用乞丐惯用的虚言假语和哭哭啼啼的悲腔跟我搭讪。

I said "I served your mother this morning." (The boys were so like the woman who had called at... that I could not be mistaken.) "O!" says the elder, "you could not serve my mother for she's dead, and my father's on at the next town—he's a potter." I persisted in my assertion, and that I would give them nothing. Says the elder, "Let's away," and away they flew like lightning. They had however sauntered so long in their road that they did not reach Ambleside before me, and I saw them go up to Matthew Harrison's house with their wallet upon the elder's shoulder, and creeping with a beggar's complaining foot. On my return through Ambleside I met in the street the mother driving her asses, in the two panniers of one of which were the two little children, whom she was chiding and threatening with a wand which she used to drive on her asses, while the little things hung in wantonness over the pannier's edge.

我说:“今天早上我接待过你们妈妈了。”(这两个孩子特别像那个上门乞讨的女人……我不会弄错的。)“哎呀!”大一点的男孩说,“你不可能接待过我妈妈的,因为她死了,我爸爸在前面的小镇上——他是个陶工。”我坚持说接待过她了,什么也没给他们。大一点的孩子说:“我们走吧。”他们飞也似的跑了。然而,他们在路上磨蹭的时间太长了,没有在我之前到达安布尔赛德,我看见他们去了马修·哈里森家,大一点的孩子肩上背着挎包,拖着有毛病的乞丐脚慢慢走去。我回来经过安布尔赛德时,在街上看见这位母亲赶着她的驴子,其中一头驮着两个驮筐,那两个孩子就坐在筐里,小家伙们把身子探出筐外肆意打闹,她就责骂他们,用赶驴子的木棍吓唬他们。

译后语

关于几个句子的理解和翻译：

（1）A very tall woman, **tall much beyond the measure of tall women**...

这里 tall much beyond the measure of tall women 形式上是原级，但意义上是比较级，故译作“比一般高女人高出很多”。

（2）Her face was excessively **brown**, but it had plainly once been fair.

一般 brown 指巧克力色、咖啡色，汉语也常说棕色、褐色；这里应该是指被太阳晒黑的颜色，故将此句译作：“她的脸晒得黝黑，但看得出来，那曾经是一张白皙的脸。”

（3）I persisted in my **assertion**, and that I would give them nothing.

这里的 assertion 系指“我”刚才说过的 I served your mother this morning，故将此句译作：“我坚持说接待过她了，什么也没给他们。”

（4）... and I saw them go up to Matthew Harrison's house with their wallet upon the elder's shoulder, and **creeping** with a beggar's complaining foot.

creep 是指小心慢慢走，脚有毛病是假装的，因为前面说过“... and away they flew like lightning”。

Robert Southey

罗伯特·骚塞(1774—1843),英国浪漫派诗人,1813年至1843年间的桂冠诗人。虽然他的诗名被华兹华斯(William Wordsworth)和柯勒律治(Samuel Taylor Coleridge)所掩盖,他的散文一直广受欢迎。他还写了不少传记作品,包括John Bunyan、John Wesley、William Cowper、Oliver Cromwell和Horatio Nelson等人的传记。此外,还有著名的儿童文学作品*The Story of the Three Bears*。后文来自*Life of Nelson*。

Nelson's Departure from Portsmouth

Robert Southey

Early on the following morning he reached Portsmouth; and having dispatched his business on shore, endeavoured to elude the populace by taking a by-way to the beach; but a crowd collected in his train, pressing forward, to obtain a sight of his face: many were in tears, and many knelt down before him, and blessed him as he passed. England has had many heroes; but never one who so entirely possessed the love of his fellow countrymen as Nelson. All men knew that his heart was as humane as it was fearless; that there was not in his nature the slightest alloy of selfishness or cupidity; but that, with perfect and entire devotion, he served his country with all his heart, and with all his soul, and with all his strength; and, therefore, they loved him as truly as and fervently as he loved England. They pressed upon the parapet, to gaze after him when his barge pushed off, and he was returning their cheers by waving his hat. The sentinels, who endeavoured to prevent them from trespassing upon this ground, were wedged among the crowd; and an officer, who, not very prudently upon such an occasion, ordered

纳尔逊[①]驶离朴次茅斯

罗伯特·骚塞

他第二天早晨很早就到了朴次茅斯，处理完岸上的事务就设法避开当地群众取小路来到海边。可是，他身后聚集了一大群人，前拥后挤，为了一睹他的风采；很多人热泪盈眶，他走过时很多人跪下为他祝福。英格兰有过很多英雄，但没有一个像纳尔逊那样深受同胞的爱戴。人们都知道，正像他有一颗无畏的心一样，他还有一颗仁慈的心；在他的品性里没有掺杂丝毫的自私或贪婪，而是怀着百分之百的忠诚，全心全意、竭尽全力为他的国家服务。因而，人们真心地、热诚地爱戴他，就像他爱戴英格兰那样。当他的专用艇驶离港口时，人们挤在低矮的护墙上目送他，他挥动帽子回应人们的欢呼。哨兵们阻止人们拥进这块空地，但他们被挤进人群。有一个军官，在这种场合下很不明智地命令哨兵

① 纳尔逊(1758—1805)，英国著名海军统帅，因其战功卓著，被视为英国民族英雄。

them to drive the people down with their bayonets, was compelled speedily to retreat; for the people would not be debarred from gazing, till the last moment, upon the hero—the darling hero of England!

用刺刀把人们赶下去，但他却被迫急忙退了回去，因为直到最后也不能阻止人们瞻仰这位英雄——这位深受人们爱戴的英格兰民族英雄！

译后语

1. 关于标题“Nelson's Departure from Portsmouth”

可译作《纳尔逊驶离朴次茅斯》，似也可译作《纳尔逊驶离朴次茅斯的时刻》，因为文章讲述的是纳尔逊离开港口时的情景。

2. ... but never one who so **entirely** possessed the love of his fellow countrymen as Nelson.

句中的 entirely 一般是“完全地”“彻底地”的意思，此处对这个副词做了处理：“但没有一个人像纳尔逊那样深受同胞的爱戴”。

3. ... there was not in his nature the slightest **alloy** of selfishness or cupidity...

此处的 alloy 为名词，意为“掺杂物”，应该将它译出来：“在他的品性里没有掺杂丝毫的自私或贪婪”。此处使用了汉语的动词“掺杂”。

Charles Lamb

查尔斯·兰姆(1775—1834),英国散文家和文学批评家,写有诗歌、小说和剧本,1808 年出版 *Specimens of English Dramatic Poets Who Lived about the Time of Shakespeare*,奠定了他作为批评家的地位。他与姐姐玛丽·兰姆合写了著名的儿童读物 *Tales from Shakespeare* (1807)。1820 年以后,他开始为 *London Magazine* 撰稿,后结集为 *Essays of Elia* (1823)。后文"The Old Margate Hoy"取自 *Last Essays of Elia*(1833)。

The Old Margate Hoy

Charles Lamb

All this time sat upon the edge of the deck quite a different character. It was a lad, apparently very poor, very infirm, and very patient. His eye was ever on the sea, with a smile: and, if he caught now and then some snatches of these wild legends, it was by accident, and they seemed not to concern him. The waves to him whispered more pleasant stories. He was as one, being with us, but not of us. He heard the bell of dinner ring without stirring; and when some of us pulled out our private stores—our cold meat and our salads—he produced none, and seemed to want none. Only a solitary biscuit he had laid in; provision for the one or two days and nights, to which these vessels then were oftentimes obliged to prolong their voyage. Upon a nearer acquaintance with him, which he seemed neither to court nor decline, we learned that he was going to Margate, with the hope of being admitted into the Infirmary there for sea-bathing. His disease was a scrofula, which appeared to have eaten all over him. He expressed great hopes of a cure; and when we asked him, whether he had any friends where he was going, he replied, "he *had* no friends."

古老的马盖特客船

查尔斯·兰姆

甲板边缘上坐着一个很特别的人，是个小伙子，看上去很穷，很弱，也很有耐心。他总是微笑看着大海；假如他不时听见一些怪异传奇的片段，那只是偶然而已，而且似乎也与他无关。海浪给他讲述着让他更快活的故事。他作为一个乘客与我们同行，但却不是我们当中的一员。他听见开饭的铃声，却无动于衷；我们一些人拿出各自的食物——冷肉和沙拉，他什么也没拿出来，似乎他什么也不想吃。他只准备了一块家常小甜饼作为一两天的干粮，这些船只常常不得不航行这么长时间。有一个比较接近他的人，这个人他既不讨好也不疏远，从这人那里我们得知他是去马盖特，希望住进那里的医院以便洗海水浴。他患的是淋巴结核，看样子结核已经蚕食了他的全身。他迫切希望把病治好。当我们问他所去之处是否有朋友时，那人说："他没有朋友。"

译后语

一、关于文字：

这段二百余字的小文使人不厌读。主人公是个很平常的人物，但作家要写他，因为他的行为给作家留下难忘的印象，虽身患重病却不悲观，作为病人不卑不亢。只几个简单的细节便塑造了一个能让人感知的鲜活形象：很穷，很弱，但不烦躁，也不悲观；总是带着微笑看大海；听见开饭的铃声却无动于衷；原来他身患疾病，希望去医院得到救治。文字简单平实，不加修饰，也许就是从这简单平实的叙述中读者可以窥见作者的个人气质和审美追求。另有几处修辞因素顺便提一下：

1. 倒装。文中有几个句子是倒装的，产生增强印象的修辞效果，如：

(1) All this time **sat upon the edge of the deck** quite a different character.（谓语前置）

(2) The waves **to him** whispered more pleasant stories.（介词短语前置）

(3) **Upon a nearer acquaintance with him**... we learned that he was going to Margate...（介词短语前置）

2. 具有句子效果的短语。用几个短语表达了需要完整句子表达的内容，行文简洁，如：

(1) It was a lad, **apparently very poor**, very infirm, and very patient.

(2) He was as one, being with us, **but not of us**.

(3) Only a solitary biscuit he had laid in; **provision for the one or two days and nights**...

二、关于译文：

翻译时无须对原文做特别处理，只随其平实的叙述逐句行文即可。倒装句酌情而定，该简洁的务必简洁。下句：

Upon a nearer acquaintance with him, which he seemed neither to court nor decline, we learned that he was going to Margate, with the hope of being admitted into the Infirmary there for sea-bathing.

为使译文通顺，做了如下处理：

有一个比较接近他的人，这个人他既不讨好也不疏远，从这人那里我们得知他是去马盖特，希望住进那里的医院以便进行海水浴。

最后一句："... and when we asked him, whether he had any friends where he was going, he replied, "he *had* no friends."" 含蓄地表达了作者对他的关切之情。

Washington Irving

华盛顿·欧文(1783—1859),美国早期作家,被誉为美国文学之父。最著名的著作有 *A History of New York* (1809)、*The Sketch Book of Geoffrey Crayon, Gent* (1819—1820)。后者简称 *The Sketch Book*,收入了 33 篇短文,大部分为英国见闻,也有少数是以美国为背景的。其中包括被认为是最早的美国短篇小说的"The Legend of Sleepy Hollow"和"Rip Van Winkle"。这两个故事都是在民间传说的基础上写就的。*The Sketch Book* 是第一部享有国际声誉的美国文学作品。此外,欧文还著有文学论文等。他晚年主要从事传记文学创作,有 *Mahomet and His Successors* (1850)和五卷本的 *The Life of George Washington* (1855—1859)。后文均选自 *The Sketch Book*。

Poets' Corner

Washington Irving

I passed some time in Poets' Corner①, which occupies an end of one of the transepts or cross aisles of the abbey. The monuments are generally simple; for the lives of literary men afford no striking themes for the sculptor. Shakespeare and Addison have statues erected to their memories; but the greater part have busts, medallions, and sometimes mere inscriptions. Notwithstanding the simplicity of these memorials, I have always observed that the visitors to the abbey remained longest about them. A kinder and fonder feeling takes place of that cold curiosity or vague admiration with which they gaze on the splendid monuments of the great and the heroic. They linger about these as about the tombs of friends and companions; for indeed there is something of companionship between the author and the reader.

---

① Poets' Corner 也作Poet's Corner，这里依据原文写作 Poets' Corner。

诗人角[1]

华盛顿·欧文

我在诗人角逗留了一阵,诗人角位于教堂里一个耳堂的末端,或者说是侧廊交叉的地方。纪念碑一般很简单,因为文人的生活没有为雕塑家提供特别引人注目的主题。莎士比亚和艾迪生都有纪念塑像,但其他多是半身塑像和嵌壁纪念牌,有的只是铭文牌。尽管这些纪念的标志物很简单,但我总是注意到参观者在这里逗留的时间最长。他们亲切和爱戴的感情油然而生,而没有通常注视伟人和英雄的精致纪念碑时那种冷漠的好奇心和茫然的钦佩感。他们在这里逗留就像走在朋友和伴侣的坟墓之间一样,因为在作家和读者之间确有一种伴侣的感觉。

---

① 诗人角:威斯敏斯特教堂(也译作西敏寺大教堂,Westminster Abbey)的一部分,此处有许多英国著名作家和诗人的坟墓或纪念碑。葬在此处的作家和诗人有乔叟(Chaucer)、勃朗宁(Browning)、丁尼生(Tennyson)、狄更斯(Dickens)、哈代(Hardy)、吉卜林(Kipling)。此外,还有莎士比亚(Shakespeare)、弥尔顿(Milton)、拜伦(Byron)、雪莱(Shelley)和许多其他人的纪念碑。——《牛津英美文化词典》

Other men are known to posterity only through the medium of history, which is continually growing faint and obscure; but the intercourse between the author and his fellow men is ever new, active and immediate. He has lived for them more than for himself; he has sacrificed surrounding enjoyments, and shut himself up from the delights of social life, that he might the more intimately commune with distant minds and distant ages. Well may the world cherish his renown; for it has been purchased, not by deeds of violence and blood, but by the diligent dispensation of pleasure. Well may posterity be grateful to his memory; for he has left it an inheritance, not of empty names and sounding actions, but whole treasures of wisdom, bright gems of thought and golden vein of language.

其他的人，后人只是通过历史媒介才知道的，而历史正在变得越来越微弱，越来越模糊；但作家和他的同胞之间的交流总是新鲜的、积极的、直接的。他为他们而生活，胜于为他自己；他牺牲周围的快乐，规避社会生活的乐趣，这样他就可能与遥远的智者和遥远的年代进行更加亲密的感情交流。但愿世界能很好地珍惜作家的名声，因为这名声不是通过诉诸暴力和导致流血的业绩得来的，而是通过坚持不懈地给予人们快乐而取得的。但愿后世心怀感激之情记住他，因为他给后世留下一份遗产，这遗产不是空洞的名声和夸张的行为，而是完整的智慧宝藏、闪亮的思想精华和美好的语言风格。

译后语

这是一篇见闻，文字朴实，不加修饰，语言风格很突出。

文中有两个非限定性定语从句，翻译时也做了非限定性处理：

(1) I passed some time in Poets' Corner, which occupies an end of one of the transepts or cross aisles of the abbey.

我在诗人角逗留了一阵，诗人角位于教堂里一个耳堂的末端，或者说是侧廊交叉的地方。

(2) Other men are known to posterity only through the medium of history, which is continually growing faint and obscure;

其他的人，后人只是通过历史媒介才知道的，而历史正在变得越来越微弱，越来越模糊；

最后一个句子里有好几个并列结构，翻译时也做了相应处理：

Well may posterity be grateful to his memory; for he has left it an inheritance, not of empty names and sounding actions, but whole treasures of wisdom, bright gems of thought and golden vein of language.

但愿后世心怀感激之情记住他，因为他给后世留下一份遗产，这遗产不是空洞的名声和夸张的行为，而是完整的智慧宝藏、闪亮的思想精华和美好的语言风格。

The Stage Coach

Washington Irving

In the course of a December tour in Yorkshire, I rode for a long distance in one of the public coaches, on the day preceding Christmas. The coach was crowded, both inside and out, with passengers, who, by their talk, seemed principally bound to the mansions of relations or friends, to eat the Christmas dinner. It was loaded also with hampers of game, and baskets and boxes of delicacies; and hares hung dangling their long ears about the coachman's box, presents from distant friends for the impending feast. I had three fine rosy-cheeked boys for my fellow-passengers inside, full of the buxom health and manly spirit which I have observed in the children of this country. They were returning home for the holidays in high glee, and promising themselves a world of enjoyment. It was delightful to hear the gigantic plans of the little rogues, and the impracticable feats they were to perform during their six weeks' emancipation from the abhorred thraldom of book, birch, and pedagogue.

公共马车

华盛顿·欧文

12月在约克郡旅行期间，我曾乘坐一辆公共马车走过很长一段路程。那是圣诞节的前一天，马车里里外外挤满了乘客，从他们的谈话听得出，好像主要是去亲戚朋友家吃圣诞晚餐的。马车上还有装着野味的大篮子，盛着佳肴的筐子和盒子；马车夫的座厢周围挂着野兔，长长的耳朵耷拉下来——都是远方朋友为即将来临的盛宴送的礼物。车里和我做伴的乘客有三个长得很漂亮的男孩，面色红润，身体丰健，尽显男子气概，这是我在这个国家的孩子们身上都能看到的。他们正高高兴兴回家度假，期待着无限的欢乐。这些小家伙们谈论着在六周的假期里，从讨厌的书本、桦鞭和老师的束缚下解放出来，要实施宏大的计划并完成不切实际的业绩。听到这些，真是让人心情愉快。

They were full of anticipations of the meeting with the family and household, down to the very cat and dog; and of the joy they were to give their little sisters by the presents with which their pockets were crammed; but the meeting to which they seemed to look forward with the greatest impatience was with Bantam, which I found to be a pony, and, according to their talk, possessed of more virtues than any steed since the days of Bucephalus. How he could trot! how he could run! and then such leaps as he would take—there was not a hedge in the whole country that he could not clear.

They were under the particular guardianship of the coachman, to whom, whenever an opportunity presented, they addressed a host of questions, and pronounced him one of the best fellows in the world. Indeed, I could not but notice the more than ordinary air of bustle and importance of the coachman, who wore his hat a little on one side, and had a large bunch of Christmas greens stuck in the buttonhole of his coat. He is always a personage full of mighty care and business, but he is particularly so during this season, having so many commissions to execute in consequence of the great interchange of presents ...

Perhaps it might be owing to the pleasing serenity that reigned in my own mind, that I fancied I saw cheerfulness in every countenance throughout the journey. A stage coach, however, carries animation always with it, and puts the world in motion as it whirls along. The horn, sounded at the entrance of a village, produces a general bustle. Some hasten forth to meet friends; some with bundles

他们期待见到父母、家人乃至小猫小狗，期待看见自己塞满口袋的礼物会给小妹妹们带来怎样的喜悦；不过，他们最迫不及待要见的是“班塔姆”[1]，我发现原来是一匹矮脚马，据他们说，这匹小马比布塞弗勒斯[2]以来的任何骏马优点都多。它小跑时那么帅气！它快跑时那么迅速！还有它跳跃时的那个姿势——全英国没有一个树篱是它跳不过去的。

孩子们是由马车夫特别监护的，一有机会，他们就向他提出很多问题，并说他是世界上最好的人之一。的确，我不由得注意到马车夫非同寻常的劳碌神色和显得很重要的样子，他歪戴着帽子，上衣扣眼里插着一大束圣诞节的冬青枝叶。他一向是个热心和忙碌的重要人物，在这个季节里更是如此，因为他受到很多人的委托，替他们来回传递礼物……

也许是因为我的心境喜悦安详，一路上，我在每一张脸上看见的都是快活。不管怎样，公共马车总是充满生机，它沿途急速行进时，把所有的人都调动起来。马车一到村口，喇叭一响，全村就热闹了。有的人赶紧跑来迎接朋友，有的人赶忙拿着包

① Bantam，词典里有解释，一是指爪哇产矮脚鸡，性好斗；二是指矮小而勇猛好斗的人。这里采取音译，下半句“原来是一匹矮脚马”对其做了解释，意思清楚。

② 布塞弗勒斯，亚历山大大帝的战马的名称。

and band-boxes to secure places, and in the hurry of the moment can hardly take leave of the group that accompanies them. In the meantime, the coachman has a world of small commissions to execute. Sometimes he delivers a hare or pheasant; sometimes jerks a small parcel or newspaper to the door of a public house; and sometimes, with knowing leer and words of sly import, hands to some half-blushing, half-laughing housemaid an odd-shaped billet-doux from some rustic admirer. As the coach rattles through the village, every one runs to the window, and you have glances on every side of fresh country faces and blooming giggling girls. At the corners are assembled juntos of village idlers and wise men, who take their stations there for the important purpose of seeing company pass; but the sagest knot is generally at the blacksmith's, to whom the passing of the coach is an event fruitful of much speculation.

袱和圆筒纸板盒来占位子，因一时忙乱而来不及和送行的人们告别。与此同时，马车夫有人们托付的一大堆事情要办。有时他去送一只野兔或野鸡；有时往酒馆门口扔去一个小包或一卷报纸；有时会意地斜睨着半羞半笑的女仆，说些诡秘而含蓄的话，然后递给她一封某村的崇拜者写来的样子奇怪的情书。马车咕隆咕隆穿过村子时，人们就都跑上来，你会发现充满活力的乡下人和面容红润的女孩子们咯咯笑着从车窗往里看。街角聚集着一群闲来无事和消息灵通的村民，他们守在那里的重要目的，就是观看旅客经过；但是最有见识的一群人则待在铁匠铺里，对他们来说，马车路过是一件大事，可以引发许多猜想。

（与卞建华合译）

译后语

一、关于原文

《公共马车》写作者在英国的见闻，从文体上看，归于游记，应属散文。文章以公共马车为线索，写车上放假回家的学生和节日里探亲访友的乘客，写马车进村后，纯朴的村民欢迎、观看马车的情景，生动描绘了圣诞来临的节日里，人们的喜悦心情。文字简单，文笔轻松，但却展现了栩栩如生的场面，塑造了生动的人物形象。例如：

（1）... but the meeting to which they seemed to look forward with the greatest impatience was with Bantam, which I found to be a pony, and, according to their talk, possessed of more virtues than any steed since the days of Bucephalus.

纯真的少年谈到自己喜爱的东西时常常夸张，爱用绝对化的词语，对自己喜爱的宠物更是如此，孩子们是可爱的。

（2）How he could trot! how he could run! and then such leaps as he would take—there was not a hedge in the whole country that he could not clear.

这是作者转述孩子们赞叹小马的语言，从其简单而又恰到好处的措辞，我们体会他们为小马感到自豪的心情。

（3）He is always a personage full of mighty care and **business**, but he is particularly so during this season, having so many commissions to execute in consequence of the great interchange of presents...

在圣诞节期间，马车夫因为受人之托，为人传送礼物，表现出关心、热心的样子；此处的 business，参考译文译成“忙碌”，也应该有“身负重任”的意思。这是对马车夫心理的准确描写。

(4) As the coach rattles through the village, every one runs to the window, and you have glances on every side of fresh country faces and blooming giggling girls.

这句话一方面写了乡下人对路过马车的好奇，也写了节日里喜庆的气氛。

总之，在人物心理和环境气氛的描绘上，作者对事物准确的把握，运用文字上的驾轻就熟，都是应该学习和借鉴的。

二、关于译文

关于本文的翻译有几个方面需要做些解释：

本文属于散文体旅游札记。翻译时，力求理解原文内容，把握其朴实无华的文字风格，在词汇、句法和语篇各个层面上传达出原文的特征，使译文具有和原文类似的艺术感染力。本着这一目的，在译文处理上做了一些变通：

1. 转换

由于英汉两种语言之间的差异，翻译很难做到也不应该追求字、词、句形式上的对应。因此，翻译过程中，常有变通，如必要的转换：

(1) It was loaded also with hampers of game, and baskets and boxes of delicacies; and hares hung dangling their long ears about the coachman's box, presents from distant friends for the impending feast.

> 马车上还有装着野味的大篮子，盛着佳肴的筐子和盒子；马车夫的座厢周围挂着野兔，长长的耳朵耷拉下来——

都是远方朋友为即将来临的盛宴送的礼物。

原文中 It was loaded with 后面是三个名词短语 hampers of game、baskets and boxes of delicacies 和 hares hung dangling their long ears，译文在语态上做了变通，并将分词结构"hares hung dangling their long ears about the coachman's box"单独译成一个小句，在同位语"present ..."前加上"都是"二字，使译文语义更加明确，符合汉语的表达习惯。

(2) They were returning home for the holidays in high glee, and promising themselves a world of enjoyment.

他们正高高兴兴回家度假，期待着无限的欢乐。

这里，原文中的介词短语 for the holidays 和 in high glee 转换成汉语的"度假"和"高高兴兴(地)"。promising themselves a world of enjoyment 译为"期待着无限的欢乐"。

(3) The horn, sounded at the entrance of a village, produces a general bustle.

马车一到村口，喇叭一响，全村就热闹了。

这句译文用通俗的汉语表达，融会了原文的意思和语气，表层形式虽有变化，内容与原文类似。

(4) As the coach rattles through the village, every one runs to **the window**, and **you have glances on every side** of fresh country faces and blooming giggling girls.

马车咕隆咕隆穿过村子时，人们就都跑上来，你会发现充满活力的乡下人和面容红润的女孩子们咯咯笑着从车窗往里看。

原文中的 you have glances on every side 指的是马车上的乘客

透过车窗看到马车周围的人们。这里将 the window 和 you have glances on every side 合译为"你会发现……从车窗往里看",将 fresh country faces and blooming giggling girls 传译为"充满活力的乡下人和面容红润的女孩子们咯咯笑着",较为形象。

2. 调整与重组

英语句法重句子结构的完整和逻辑上的合理;汉语句法关系主要靠词序和语义关系,追求达意。换言之,英语句子通常以主谓结构为主干,以谓语动词为中心,借助分词、介词、连词、关系代词、关系副词等连接手段,把句子的各个语法成分层层搭架;汉语一般通过多个动词的连用或流水句式,按照时间顺序和事理推移的方式,把事情一件件交代清楚。英语的前置或后置修饰成分能使限定的概念准确严密,但也增加了翻译的难度。这篇文章里有不少长句,翻译长句子,应先理出句子的主要轮廓;其次,辨清句子的主从结构,找出各分句之间的从属关系,然后逐一翻译各分句,统观全句,再做调整、润色等。例如:

(1) **It was delightful to hear** the gigantic plans of the little rogues, and the impracticable feats they were to perform during their **six weeks' emancipation** from the abhorred thraldom of book, birch, and pedagogue.

这些小家伙们谈论着在六周的假期里,从讨厌的书本、桦鞭和教师的束缚下解放出来,要实施宏大的计划并完成不切实际的业绩。听到这些,真是让人心情愉快。

英语一般是先概括后分解、先统论后叙述,而汉语往往相反。这里,将做实际主语的不定式结构提前,单独译成主谓宾结构的句子,将定语"six weeks'"译成状语"在六周的假期里",emancipation

转换成动词"解放出来",并将 It was delightful to hear 放在句末,翻译成"听到这些,真是让人心情愉快"。使语义重心落在句子后半部,符合汉语的行文习惯。

(2) They **were full of anticipations of** the meeting with the family and household, down to the very cat and dog; and of the joy they were to give their little sisters by the presents **with which their pockets were crammed**; but the **meeting to which** they seemed to look forward with the greatest impatience was with Bantam, which I found to be a pony, and, according to their talk, possessed of more virtues than any steed since the days of **Bucephalus**.

他们期待见到父母、家人乃至小猫小狗,期待看见自己塞满口袋的礼物会给小妹妹们带来怎样的喜悦;不过,他们似乎最迫不及待要见的是"班塔姆",我发现原来是一匹矮脚马,据他们说,这匹小马比布塞弗勒斯以来的任何骏马优点都多。

这里将 were full of anticipations of 译为"期待",将定语从句 with which their pockets were crammed 译成"塞满口袋的",将名词 meeting 转换为动词"见",将 to which 引导的定语从句译为"他们似乎最迫不及待要",将 which 引导的非限制性定语从句译成一个独立的主谓宾句,并采用了音译、注释、增补的方法传译 Bucephalus 这一专有名词,使译文上下连贯、衔接自然、层次清楚。

(3) Sometimes he delivers a hare or pheasant; sometimes jerks a small parcel or newspaper to the door of a public house; and sometimes, **with knowing leer and words of sly import**, hands to **some half-blushing, half-laughing housemaid** an odd-shaped billet-doux

from some rustic admirer.

有时他去送一只野兔或野鸡;有时往酒馆门口扔去一个小包或一卷报纸;有时会意地斜睨着半羞半笑的女仆,说些诡秘而含蓄的话,然后递给她一封某村的崇拜者写来的样子奇怪的情书。

按照原文的时间和逻辑顺序,将介词短语充当的伴随情况状语 with knowing leer and words of sly import 分开译为"会意地斜睨着……"和"说些诡秘而含蓄的话……",将"some half-blushing, half-laughing housemaid"译为"半羞半笑的女仆",插入其中,并增补了"然后"一词,使句子逻辑清晰,行文自然。

总之,整体上,译文没有在形式上拘泥于原文,为了再现原文韵味,在理解的基础上,采用了转换、增减、调整与重组等手段,努力保持原文的意蕴。

Dulce Domum

Washington Irving

We had passed for some time along the wall of a park, and at length the chaise stopped at the gate. It was in a heavy magnificent old style, of iron bars, fancifully wrought at top into flourishes and flowers. The huge square columns that supported the gate were surmounted by the family crest. Close adjoining was the porter's lodge, sheltered under dark fir trees, and almost buried in shrubbery.

The postboy rang a large porter's bell, which resounded through the still, frosty air, and was answered by the distant barking of dogs, with which the mansion house seemed garrisoned. An old woman immediately appeared at the gate. As the moonlight fell strongly upon her, I had a full view of a little primitive dame, dressed very much in the antique taste, with a neat kerchief and stomacher, and her silver hair peeping from under a cap of snowy whiteness. She came curtseying forth, with many expressions of simple joy at seeing her young master. Her husband, it seemed, was up at the house keeping Christmas eve in the servants' hall; they could not do without him, as he was the best hand at a song and story in the household.

回家真好

华盛顿·欧文

我们沿花园围墙走了一阵，马车最后在大门口停下。那是老式的铁栅门，样子很厚重很讲究，铁栅顶端锻有漂亮的花饰。支撑铁门的巨大方柱的上面冠以家族纹章。铁门旁是门卫的小房，房顶上方被幽森的冷杉遮挡，下面几乎被灌木丛掩埋。

马车驭者敲响大门铃，铃声在寂静寒冷的空中回响，随之从远处传来狗的叫声，看来这座大宅院有狗驻守。一个老妇人立即出现在门口。当月光明亮地照在她身上，我眼前所见俨然是一个古代的娇小女人，身穿古式的衣服，颈上围着一条小巧的方巾，胸前戴一件兜饰，雪白的帽子下面露着银发。她行屈膝礼走过来，说了很多因看见年轻主人而感到高兴的话。好像是她的丈夫，正在仆人的餐厅里忙着过圣诞夜的事情；人们没有他不行，因为他在这个家里唱歌讲故事都是一把好手。

My friend proposed that we should alight and walk through the park to the hall, which was at no great distance, while the chaise should follow on. Our road wound through a noble avenue of trees, among the naked branches of which the moon glittered as she rolled through the deep vault of a cloudless sky. The lawn beyond was sheeted with a slight covering of snow, which here and there sparkled as the moon beams caught a frosty crystal; and at a distance might be seen a thin transparent vapour, stealing up from the low grounds and threatening gradually to shroud the landscape.

My companion looked around him with transport. "How often," said he, "have I scampered up this avenue, on returning home on school vacations! How often have I played under these trees when a boy! I feel a degree of filial reverence for them, as we look up to those who have cherished us in childhood. My father was always scrupulous in exacting our holidays, and having us around him on family festivals. He used to direct and superintend our games with the strictness that some parents do the studies of their children. He was very particular that we should play the old English games according to their original form; and consulted old books for precedent and authority for every 'merrie disport'; yet I assure you there never was pedantry so delightful. It was the policy of the good old gentleman to make his children feel that home was the happiest place in the world; and I value this delicious home feeling as one of the choicest gifts a parent could bestow."

我的朋友建议我们下车，穿过花园直奔仆人的餐厅走过去，好在距离不远，马车可以在后面跟着。我们沿一条宽敞的林间大路蜿蜒前行，月亮在晴朗高远的天空移动，月光透过光秃秃的树枝闪闪发亮。那面的草坪盖着一层薄薄的雪，月光照到霜样的结晶时，有些地方便闪烁亮光；远处隐约可见一层透明的薄雾从低矮的地面缓缓升起，眼看就要将周围变成一片朦胧的景色。

我的旅伴激动地四下张望着说："假期回家时我在这条路上跑过不知多少趟呀！小时候我在这些树下玩过不知多少回呀！我对它们总怀有一种亲子般的崇敬之情，正如我们小时候抬头仰望那些关爱我们的人一样。假期里，我的父亲对我们要求很严格，节日家庭聚会时一定要我们在他的身边。他总是指导监督我们做游戏，那股严格劲儿就和一些父母指导和监督他们孩子学习一样。他特别要求我们按照原有的形式做英国古老的游戏，为了寻找范例而查阅古书，为了每一次'娱乐'而咨询权威；但是，我可以向你保证，从来没有过如此墨守成规而又让人快活的人。这个可爱的老绅士总是让他的孩子们感觉家是世界上最幸福的地方；我珍惜这一甜蜜的家的感觉，把它看作父母给我们的最好的礼物之一。"

We were interrupted by the clamour of a troop of dogs of all sorts and sizes, "mongrel, puppy, whelp and hound, and curs of low degree," that, disturbed by the ring of the porter's bell, and the rattling of the chaise, came bounding, open-mouthed, across the lawn.

"—The little dogs and all,

Tray, Blanch, and Sweetheart—see, they bark at me!"

cried Bracebridge, laughing. At the sound of his voice, the bark was changed into a yelp of delight, and in a moment he was surrounded and almost overpowered by the caresses of the faithful animals.

我们被一群品种各异、大小不一的狗的叫声打断了，“杂种狗、小狗崽、幼犬和猎犬，还有不太凶狠的恶犬”[①]。它们被门铃声和马车声惊动，张着大嘴，从草坪上跳跃着跑过来。

这些小狗，脱雷、布兰奇、史威塔，

瞧，它们都在向我狂吠！[②]

布雷斯布里奇边笑边嚷着说。听见他的声音，狗的吠声变成一阵欢快的叫声。顷刻间，他被狗包围了，差点儿被这些忠诚的动物充满爱意的动作拥倒了。

---

① 此引语出自英国诗人奥利弗·戈德史密斯（1728—1774）的诗《疯狗的挽歌》。

② 此引语出自莎士比亚戏剧《李尔王》第3幕第6场。

译后语

关于文章标题，“Dulce Domum”原是一首歌曲的名字，英裔加拿大作曲家罗伯特·S. 安布罗斯（Robert Steele Ambrose，1824—1908）所作，意为“Sweetly at Home”，此处译为《回家真好》。

阅读英语时，如能经常对英汉两种语言的表达方式和句子结构进行比较，常常会发现，我们用英语写作或做汉英翻译时，感觉棘手的一些概念在英语经典作家的笔下往往变得很简单、很自然，而且很生动。阅读美国作家华盛顿·欧文的作品就有这种感觉。例如：

（1）It was in a heavy magnificent old style, of iron bars, **fancifully wrought at top into flourishes and flowers**.

这句话的后半部分 fancifully wrought at top into flourishes and flowers 是说“铁栅顶端锻有漂亮的花饰”，这个表达方式看起来很简单，但 work（锻）的过去分词形式的选择和介词短语 at top 的位置安排都是很有讲究的，除轻重音节的排列和节奏的效果外，很能唤起读者的想象。

（2）She came curtseying forth, with many expressions of simple **joy** at seeing her young master.

这里 with 短语中的 joy 一词有连接作用，对于前面的 expressions 具有修饰功能，后面的 at 短语道出“joy”产生的原因。这一小词使整个句子显得既自然又紧凑。

（3）He used to direct and superintend our games with the strictness that some parents **do the studies of their children**.

在这个语境里,do the studies of their children 是指前面所说 to direct and superintend 指导和监督,它不仅起了代替作用,并为全句创造了一种简洁明快的风格。

(4) At the sound of his voice, **the bark was changed into a yelp of delight**.

狗的叫声从警觉到“欢快”的变化,the bark was changed into a yelp of delight,写得很巧妙很自然,如能在英语阅读或英汉翻译过程中经常做类似的比较,可以增加对英语的感性认识,培养语感。这是学习英语的有效途径,也对提高汉英翻译能力有帮助。

Jane Taylor

简·泰勒(1783—1824),英国诗人、小说家,诗歌作品有 *Original Poems for Infant Minds*(1804—1805)两卷本诗集,收录她和姐姐安(Ann)以及别的诗人的作品,还有 *Rhymes for the Nursery* (1806)、*Hymns for Infant Minds* (1808),以上两本诗集也是与别人合集的作品。她最出名的诗歌是“Star”,也称“Twinkle, Twinkle, Little Star”,后配上一个法国曲调而流行于世。此外还有小说 *Display* (1814)。后文选自 *Contributions of Q. Q.* 。

A Young Lady's Education

Jane Taylor

Well! ... my education is at last finished: indeed it would be strange, if, after five years' hard application, anything were left incomplete. Happily that is all over now; and I have nothing to do, but to exercise my various accomplishments.

Let me see! —as to French, I am mistress of that, and speak it, if possible, with more fluency than English. Italian I can read with ease, and pronounce very well: as well, at least, and better, than any of my friends; and that is all one need wish for in Italian. Music I have learned till I am perfectly sick of it. But, now that we have a grand piano, it will be delightful to play when we have company. I must still continue to practice a little;—the only thing, I think, that I need now to improve myself in. And then there are my Italian songs! which everybody allows I sing with taste, and as it is what so few people can pretend to, I am particularly glad that I can.

My drawings are universally admired; especially the shells and flowers; which are beautiful, certainly; besides this, I have a decided

一个年轻女士的教育

简·泰勒

啊！……我的教育终于完成了：假如经过五年的勤奋学习，还有未学完的课程，那就真的奇怪了。幸运的是，所有的课程都结业了，除了练习已学完的各个科目，我没有要做的事情了。

让我看看！关于法语，我已经很熟练地掌握了，我讲法语可能比英语还流利。意大利语，我读起来很容易，而且发音很好——比我任何朋友的发音都好，至少和他们一样好；一个人学习意大利语所希望的莫过于此。音乐么，我一直学到腻烦了为止。可是，我们现在既然有了一架三角钢琴，当我们有几个人在一起的时候弹一弹那是很惬意的事情。我必须继续练习练习，我想，这是我现在唯一需要提高的科目。然后就是我唱的意大利歌曲！大家都承认我唱得有味道，而且，因为很少有人能自称做到这点，让我感到特别高兴的是，我能。

我的绘画受到普遍赞赏，特别是贝壳和花卉，当然都画得很漂亮；此外，我对各种精巧的装饰品

taste in all kinds of fancy ornaments.

And then my dancing and waltzing! in which our master himself owned that he could take me no farther!—just the figure for it certainly; it would be unpardonable if I did not excel.

As to common things, geography, and history, and poetry, and philosophy, thank my stars, I have got through them all! so that I may consider myself not only perfectly accomplished, but also thoroughly well informed.

Well, to be sure, how much have I fagged through; the only wonder is that one head can contain it all.

都表现出明显的品位。

然后是我的舞蹈和华尔兹！在这方面，我们的老师自己也承认，他教不了我了！当然，我就是跳舞蹈的身材；假如我不能做得出类拔萃，那倒是不可原谅的。

至于普通科目，地理呀、历史呀、诗歌呀、哲学呀，庆幸我的好运气，我都通过了！因此，我不妨把自己看作很有造诣，而且知识面很宽。

啊，诚然，我已经付出很多辛苦；唯一让人感到惊奇的是，一个人的脑袋竟然能盛下这么多东西。

译后语

下面说说几个单词意思的确定与翻译：

（1）**Well**! ... my education is at last finished:

（2）**Well**, to be sure, how much have I fagged through; the only wonder is that one head can contain it all.

以上两句里的 well 是感叹词，《牛津高阶英汉双解词典》（以下词语的英语解释皆出自此词典）说："used to express surprise, anger or relief"。第一个句子表达 relief，第二个句子表达 surprise。因此，这两个 well 都可以用"啊"来表达。

（3）**Happily** that is all over now...

Happily 意思是 by good luck，和 fortunately 是同义词，译成"幸运的是"比较合适。

（4）... and I have nothing to do, but to exercise my various **accomplishments**.

根据不同上下文，accomplishment 可有几个解释。在这里，意思是 the successful completing of sth，具体指"已学完的各个科目"。

（5）... as to French, I am **mistress** of that...

这里 mistress 指 a woman who is highly skilled in sth，此句可译作"关于法语，我已经很熟练地掌握了"。

（6）Italian I can read with ease, and pronounce very well: **as well**, at least, and better, than any of my friends;

这里的 as well 与常规用法不同，通常是 as well as，这里可能是

省略了第二个 as,按这样理解,将译文做如下处理:

"意大利语,我读起来很容易,而且发音很好——比我任何朋友的发音都好,至少和他们一样好。"

(7) And then there are my Italian songs! which everybody **allows** I sing with taste, and as it is what so few people can **pretend to**, I am particularly glad that I can.

这里的 allows 意为 to admit that sth is true, pretend to 意为"to claim to be, do or have sth, especially when this is not true",相当于汉语类似"自称"的意思。

(8) And then my dancing and waltzing! in which our master himself **owned** that he could take me no farther!

这个句子里的 owned 与上句的 allows 相同,意为"承认"。

(9) ... thank my **stars**, I have got through them all!

此句里的 stars 指命运、运气(此词与星相有关,指根据人出生时的星象预测人的未来)。

Thomas De Quincey

托马斯·德昆西(1785—1859),英国散文家和评论家,为多家杂志写了大量散文,后人整理成多卷本文集出版。德昆西在大学时开始吸食鸦片,到1817年达到严重程度。后来他把自己吸食鸦片的经历写下来,1821年开始陆续在《伦敦杂志》(*London Magazine*)上发表。当时查尔斯·兰姆正在该杂志连载他的 *Essays of Elia*,据说德昆西引起的轰动盖过兰姆。1822年,以 *Confessions of an Opium-Eater* 为书名结集出版,以此闻名英国文坛。后文"A London Waif"摘自该书。

A London Waif

Thomas De Quincey

Towards nightfall I went down to Greek Street, and found, on taking possession of my new quarters, that the house already contained one single inmate,—a poor, friendless child, apparently ten years old; but she seemed hunger-bitten; and sufferings of that sort often make children look older than they are. From this forlorn child I learned that she had slept and lived there alone for some time before I came; and great joy the poor creature expressed when she found that I was in future to be her companion through the hours of darkness. The house could hardly be called large,—that is, it was not large on each separate storey; but, having four storeys in all, it was large enough to impress vividly the sense of its echoing loneliness; and, from the want of furniture, the noise of the rats made a prodigious uproar on the staircase and hall; so that, amidst the real fleshly ills of cold and hunger, the forsaken child had found leisure to suffer still more from the self-created one of ghosts. Against these enemies I could promise her protection; human companionship was in itself protection; but of other and more needful

一个伦敦孤苦女孩

托马斯·德昆西

天快黑的时候，我来到希腊大街，当我住进新地方时，发现里面已经有一个人—— 一个可怜无助的孩子，看样子有10岁，似乎饿得够呛了；挨饿的孩子看上去常常比实际年龄大。这个孤苦伶仃的孩子告诉我，在我到来之前，她在这里已经住了一段时间，就一个人睡在这里；当她知道我以后黑夜里要和她做伴时，可怜的小家伙非常高兴。这幢房子称不上很大，就是说，单看每一层并不大，但房子一共有四层，也不小了，足以让人感觉到里面回荡着孤独静寂的气氛；因为没有家具，老鼠就在楼梯和门厅里闹腾，声音很大；因此，这个被遗弃的孩子一边忍受着肉体的寒冷和饥饿，同时还有闲暇想象出鬼魂来折磨自己。我答应保护她免受这些敌人的伤害；有人相依为伴这本身就是保护，但至于其他方面以及她更需要的东西，唉！我就无能为力了。

aid I had, alas! little to offer. We lay upon the floor, with a bundle of law-papers for a pillow, but with no other covering than a large horseman's cloak; afterwards, however, we discovered in a garret an old sofa-cover, a small piece of rug, and some fragments of other articles, which added a little to our comfort. The poor child crept close to me for warmth, and for security against her ghostly enemies. When I was not more than usually ill, I took her into my arms, so that, in general, she was tolerably warm, and often slept when I could not...

Whether this child were an illegitimate daughter of Mr. Brunell, or only a servant, I could not ascertain; she did not herself know; but certainly she was treated altogether as a menial servant. No sooner did Mr. Brunell make his appearance than she went below-stairs, brushed his shoes, coat, etc.; and, except when she was summoned to run upon some errand, she never emerged from the dismal Tartarus of the kitchens to the upper air until my welcome knock towards nightfall called up her little trembling footsteps to the front door. Of her life during the daytime, however, I knew little but what I gathered from her own account at night; for, as soon as the hours of business commenced, I saw that my absence would be acceptable; and, in general, therefore, I went off and sat in the parks or elsewhere until the approach of twilight.

我们躺在地板上，用一捆法律文件当枕头，除了一件骑手穿的大斗篷没有别的东西可盖；后来我们在一个小阁楼里发现了一件旧沙发罩，一小块地毯，还有一些别的物件的残片，这几样东西让我们感觉舒服些。可怜的孩子爬过来凑近我，为了暖和，也为了不受她的那些鬼魂的伤害。要是我不病得特别厉害，就把她搂在怀里，这样，一般情况下，她不至于冻得受不了，我睡不着觉时她却常常能够进入梦乡……

这个孩子究竟是布鲁内尔先生的私生女，还是他的佣人？我说不准，她自己也不清楚；但她肯定是被当作一个做粗活的佣人来对待的。布鲁内尔先生一露面，她就赶紧跑到楼下，给他擦皮鞋、刷上衣，等等。除非主人差遣她去做什么事情，她是不会从那地狱般昏暗的厨房里出来到上面透透气的，直到傍晚我敲门时（这让她心情愉快），她才双腿颤抖着迈着小步来到前门。然而，她白天是怎么度过的，我不大知道，也只是夜里她自己对我说的那点情况而已；因为，她开始十沾时，我看得出来，我要是离开，她还是能够接受的，所以，一般情况下，我就走开，到公园里或别的地方去坐坐，傍晚时分再回来。

译后语

1. 关于几个单词的翻译：

（1）a poor, **friendless** child

这里的 friendless 意为“没有朋友的”，一个 10 岁的小女孩，在这种境况下，谈不上有朋友，即使曾经有过童年伙伴，也帮不了她，不如译作“没有亲友的”或“无助的”更恰当；关于 poor，译作“可怜的”比较合适，符合文章作者看见她时的心情，故不妨将这个短语译作“一个可怜无助的孩子”。

（2）第一段里有两个句子使用了介词 against，“**Against** these enemies I could promise her protection...”和“The poor child crept close to me for warmth, and for security **against** her ghostly enemies.”。against 是一个普通的介词，在这两处都是“避免”或“防止”的意思，这里将其分别译为“可怜的孩子爬过来凑近我，为了暖和，也为了不受她的那些鬼魂的伤害。”

（3）...but certainly she was treated altogether as a **menial** servant.

形容词 menial 指所做的工作并不重要，也无需技巧，工资也低，故将 a menial servant 译为“做粗活的佣人”。

（4）... for, as soon as the hours of business commenced, I saw that my absence would be acceptable...

此句和上句“Of her life during the daytime, however, I knew little but what I gathered from her own account at night...”联系着，

故将此句译作"……因为，她开始干活时，我看得出来，我要是离开，她还是能够接受的……"

2. 关于一个长句的翻译：

... and, except when she was summoned to run upon some errand, she never emerged from the dismal Tartarus of the kitchens to the upper air until my welcome knock towards nightfall called up her little trembling footsteps to the front door.

翻译时需弄清这句话里几个部分的关系："and, except when she ... never..."（除非……她是不会……直到……她才……）。

译为：

除非主人差遣她去做什么事情，她是不会从那地狱般昏暗的厨房里出来到上面透透气的，直到傍晚我敲门时（这让她心情愉快），她才双腿颤抖着迈着小步来到前门。

Frederick Marryat

弗雷德里克·马里亚特(1792—1848),英国小说家,与狄更斯(1812—1870)同时代。1806 年参加英国皇家海军,有 25 年的海上生活经历。1830 年开始全职写作,他是英国航海故事的先驱作家,作品受马克·吐温、康拉德和海明威等作家的推崇。代表作品有半自传小说 *Mr. Midshipman Easy* (1836)、儿童故事 *The Children of the New Forest* 等。后文即出自 *Mr. Midshipman Easy*。

Naval Politeness

Frederick Marryat

When Jack Easy had gained the deck he found the sun shining gaily, a soft air blowing from the shore, and the whole of the rigging and every part of the ship loaded with the shirts, trousers, and jackets of the seamen, which had been wetted during the heavy gale, and were now hanging up to dry; all the wet sails were also spread on the booms or triced up in the rigging, and the ship was slowly forging through the blue water. The captain and first lieutenant were standing on the gangway in converse, and the majority of the officers were with their quadrants and sextants ascertaining the latitude at noon. The decks were white and clean, the sweepers had just laid by their brooms, and the men were busy coiling down the ropes. It was a scene of cheerfulness, activity, and order, which lightened his heart after the four days of suffering, close air, and confinement, from which he had just emerged.

The captain, who perceived him, beckoned to him, asked him kindly how he felt; the first lieutenant also smiled upon him, and many of the officers, as well as his messmates, congratulated him upon his recovery.

海军的礼貌

弗雷德里克·马里亚特

杰克·伊赛来到甲板上，他发现那里阳光明媚，微风从海岸徐徐吹来，索具[1]上及船上各处挂满了水兵们的衬衫、裤子和夹克，都是在飓风里被海水打湿的，现在挂出来晾晒；湿漉漉的船帆也都摊在帆桁上，或吊在绳索上，船在蓝色的海水里缓缓穿行。舰长和舰务官正站在甲板舷梯上说话，多数军官正在用四分仪和六分仪测定中午时分舰船所在位置的纬度。甲板洁白干净，打扫者刚刚把扫帚放起来，水兵们正忙着盘绕绳子。这是一幅欢快、忙碌而有序的景象。杰克憋在空气窒闷的船舱里，整整受了四天罪，现在刚刚出来。看到这种景象，他感到舒心。

舰长看见他便举手打招呼，关切地问他感觉如何；舰务官也冲他微笑，很多军官以及他的战友们都祝贺他康复。

---

① 索具包括支撑桅杆的固定支索和用于升降及收放风帆的活动吊索在内的所有绳缆。

The captain's steward came up to him, touched his hat, and requested the pleasure of his company to dinner in the cabin. Jack was the essence of politeness, took off his hat, and accepted the invitation. Jack was standing on a rope which a seaman was coiling down; the man touched his hat and requested he would be so kind as to take his foot off. Jack took his hat off his head in return, and his foot off the rope. The master touched his hat and reported twelve o'clock to the first lieutenant—the first lieutenant touched his hat and reported twelve o'clock to the captain—the captain touched his hat and told the first lieutenant to make it so. The officer of the watch touched his hat, and asked the captain whether they should pipe to dinner—the captain touched his hat, and said, "If you please."

The midshipman received his orders—and touched his hat—which he gave to the head boatswain's mate, who touched his hat, and then the calls whistled cheerily.

"Well," thought Jack, "politeness seems to be the order of the day, and every one has an equal respect for the other." Jack stayed on deck; he peeped through the ports, which were open, and looked down into the deep blue wave; he cast his eyes aloft, and watched the tall spars sweeping and tracing with their points, as it were, a small portion of the clear sky, as they acted in obedience to the motion of the vessel; he looked forward at the range of carronades which lined the sides of the deck, and then he proceeded to climb one of the carronades, and lean over the hammocks to gaze on the distant land.

舰长手下的服务员走到他跟前，举手碰了一下帽子，请他光临在房舱里举行的午餐。杰克是非常懂礼貌的人，他摘下帽子，接受了邀请。杰克踩在一个水兵正在缠绕的绳子上；水兵举手碰了一下帽子，很抱歉请他把脚移开。杰克随即摘下帽子，把脚从绳子上移开。航行舰长举手碰了一下帽子，向舰务官报告此时是中午 12 点；舰务官举手碰了一下帽子，向舰长报告时间是中午 12 点；舰长举手碰了一下帽子，告诉舰务官认定这个时间，并将其记入航海日志。值班长举手碰了一下帽子，请示舰长是否应该吹哨开饭；舰长举手碰了一下帽子，说："请便。"

海军军官候补生接到命令，举手碰了一下帽子，又把命令传给大副；大副举手碰了一下帽子，然后响起了欢快的哨声。

"看来讲礼貌是最重要的事，"杰克想，"人们互相尊重，一视同仁。"杰克仍站在甲板上。他透过打开的舷窗，往下看着深蓝色的海浪；他又抬起头来看上面，高高桅杆的尖顶似乎正随着船身的移动掠过并追踪一小块晴朗的天空；他看见前面沿甲板舷侧排列的臼砲，然后爬上其中一门，将身子探过吊床凝视远处的陆地。

"Young gentleman, get off those hammocks," cried the master, who was officer of the watch, in a surly tone.

Jack looked round.

"Do you hear me, sir? I'm speaking to you," said the master again.

Jack felt very indignant, and he thought that politeness was not quite so general as he supposed.

“年轻的先生，离开吊床那儿。”航行舰长，他是值班长，粗鲁地喊道。

杰克四下看了看。

“你听见了吗，先生？说你呢。”航行舰长又说。

杰克很气愤。他想，情况并非如他所想，不是人人都懂礼貌。

译后语

本文取自小说 *Mr. Midshipman Easy*，描写早期英国皇家海军士兵、官兵之间在语言和举止方面表现的礼貌，一种自觉的文明行为，值得学习，值得提倡，它体现了对他人的理解与尊重。

有两点需要说明：

（1）文中第三段有一个 touched his hat 的动作，因为这是表示礼貌的标志性动作，作者有意突出这个鲜明的形象，故多次使用同样的说法，没有变换词语，没有变换说法。译者也遵照原文，没有做任何变换，清一色的"举手碰了一下帽子"。

（2）文中第三段里还有一句话，"... the captain touched his hat and told the first lieutenant **to make it so**"，应弄清其中 to make it so 的意思。小说 *Mr. Midshipman Easy* 描写 19 世纪初期英国海军在海上的活动，那时是用仪器观测太阳以确定时间，据悉一天测量三次，日出测一次，中午测一次，日落测一次。测定的时间经船长认可后记入航海日志。所以将此句译成如下模样："舰长举手碰了一下帽子，告诉舰务官认定这个时间，并将其记入航海日志。"

John Gibson Lockhart

约翰·吉布森·洛克哈特(1794—1854),苏格兰文学评论家、传记作家,瓦尔特·司各特爵士的女婿。他最著名的作品是 *Memoirs of the Life of Sir Walter Scott* (1837—1838),普遍认为是继苏格兰作家詹姆斯·博斯韦尔(James Boswell)写的 *The Life of Samuel Johnson* (1791)之后的一部伟大传记。后文所说的 Sir Walter 就是瓦尔特·司各特(Sir Walter Scott,1771—1832),苏格兰小说家和诗人,作者的岳父。司各特被尊称为苏格兰历史小说之父,1814 年出版第一部历史小说 *Waverley*,此后写了大量作品,包括 *Guy Mannering* (1815)、*Rob Roy* (1818)和 *Ivanhoe* (1820)等。后文取自 *Memoirs of the Life of Sir Walter Scott*。

The Death of Sir Walter

John Gibson Lockhart

As I was dressing on the morning of Monday, the 17th of September, Nicolson came into my room, and told me that his master had awoke in a state of composure and consciousness, and wished to see me immediately. I found him entirely himself, though in the last extreme of feebleness. His eye was clear and calm—every trace of the wild fire of delirium extinguished. "Lockhart," he said, "I may have but a minute to speak to you. My dear, be a good man—be virtuous—be religious—be a good man. Nothing else will give you any comfort when you come to lie here." He paused, and I said, "Shall I send for Sophia and Anne?" "No," said he, "don't disturb them. Poor souls! I know they were up all night—God bless you all." With this he sunk into a very tranquil sleep, and, indeed, he scarcely afterwards gave any sign of consciousness, except for an instant on the arrival of his sons. They, on learning that the scene was about to close, obtained a new leave of absence from their posts, and both reached Abbotsford on the 19th. About half-past one p.m., on the 21st of September, Sir Walter breathed his last, in

瓦尔特爵士之死

约翰·吉布森·洛克哈特

9月17日，星期一早晨，我正在穿衣服，尼科尔森进来了，告诉我他的主人醒了，神情镇静，神志清醒，希望立即见我。虽然他身体极度虚弱，但我发现他状态如常，眼睛明亮，眼神安详——丝毫也没有那种神志不清时眼神恍惚的迹象。“洛克哈特，”他说，“我也许只有一分钟的时间和你说说话。我亲爱的，做一个好人——为人要讲道德，信教要虔诚——做一个好人。等你将来躺在这里时，没有别的东西会让你感到安慰。”他停下了，我说：“要我找人把索菲亚和安妮叫来吗？”“不用了，”他说，“别打扰她们了。怪可怜的！我知道她们一夜没睡——上帝保佑你们大家。”说完他又安静地睡了。此后几乎没再看出他有任何意识，只是在他的儿子们到来时有一点清醒。他们听说他快不行了，便又请假离开工作，哥俩于19日回到阿伯茨福德。9月21日下午1点半，瓦尔特爵士停止呼吸，当时

the presence of all his children. It was a beautiful day—so warm that every window was wide open, and so perfectly still that the sound of all others most delicious to his ear, the gentle ripple of the Tweed over its pebbles, was distinctly audible as we knelt around the bed, and his eldest son kissed and closed his eyes.

他的孩子们都在身边。那天天气很好，很暖和，窗户都打开了，外面非常安静，周围人们发出的声音会让他感觉温馨。我们围着他的床榻跪着，他的大儿子吻合他的眼睛时，特威德河水的微波流过卵石滩时发出的潺潺声清晰可辨。

译后语

这篇文章属传记，因纪实，文字既简单又简洁，且生动，适合学习英语的人阅读和模仿。其文字的简单和简洁，除表现在句子的组织外，还表现在动词（包括动词搭配）的选择和介词短语的使用上。

下面例句里的动词都是常用动词，很简单，与文章的叙事风格很协调，不但意思准确，而且语气得体。

（1）Nicolson came into my room, and told me that...

（2）I found him entirely himself...

（3）My dear, be a good man—be virtuous—be religious—be a good man.

（4）Nothing else will give you any comfort when you come to lie here.

（5）I know they were up all night—

翻译这些动词也应选择简单简洁的汉语常用词，行文上力求与原文风格相近。

英语介词有时具有动词功能，能很好地表现人和事物的状态，而且节约文字。培养使用英语介词短语的意识对学习英语写作和汉英翻译都有帮助。例如：

（1）... his master had awoke in a state of composure and consciousness...

……（告诉我）他的主人醒了，神情镇静，神志清醒……

(2) ... on the arrival of his sons...

……在他的儿子们到来时……

(3) ...on learning that the scene was about to close...

(他们)听说他快不行了……

(4) ... in the presence of all his children...

……当时他的孩子们都在身边……

(5) ... the gentle ripple of the Tweed over its pebbles, was distinctly audible...

……特威德河水的微波流过卵石滩时发出的潺潺声清晰可辨……

John Henry Newman

约翰·亨利·纽曼(1801—1890),是英国基督教圣公会牛津运动领袖(Oxford Movement),后来改奉天主教,成为天主教会领导者,19世纪英国宗教历史上的一个重要人物,他同时也从事文学创作。少年时代就大量阅读了瓦尔特·司各特(Walter Scott)和罗伯特·索锡(Robert Southey)的小说,14岁开始读托马斯·潘恩(Thomas Paine)和大卫·休谟(David Hume)的著作。他的主要作品有自传 *Apologia Pro Vita Sua* (1865—1866)、*Grammar of Assent* (1870)和诗歌 *The Dream of Gerontius* (1865)。后文"The Classics"出自 *Grammar of Assent*,"Definition of a Gentleman"出自 *Idea of a University*。

The Classics

John Henry Newman

Let us consider, too, how differently young and old are affected by the words of some classic author, such as Homer or Horace. Passages, which to a boy are but rhetorical common-places, neither better nor worse than a hundred others which any clever writer might supply, which he gets by heart and thinks very fine, and imitates, as he thinks, successfully, in his own flowing versification, at length come home to him, when long years have passed, and he has had experience of life, and pierce him, as if he had never known them, with their sad earnestness and vivid exactness. Then he comes to understand how it is that lines, the birth of some chance morning or evening at an Ionian festival, or among the Sabine hills, have lasted generation after generation, for thousands of years, with a power over the mind, and a charm, which the current literature of his own day, with all its obvious advantages, is utterly unable to rival. Perhaps this is the reason of the mediaeval opinion about Virgil, as of a prophet or magician; his single words and phrases, his pathetic half lines, giving utterance, as the voice of Nature herself,

古典文学

约翰·亨利·纽曼

让我们也考虑一下,像荷马或贺拉斯这样的古典作家的言语对年轻人和老年人产生怎样迥然不同的影响。有一些在学童看来语言平淡无奇的段落,与任何聪明的作家所能写的上百篇别的东西不相上下,他将它们背下来,认为写得不错,并且以为在他自己写的流畅的诗文里模仿得很成功;最后,很多年过去了,他有了生活阅历,这些文字的真谛他才理解,并突然以其悲伤的诚实感和生动的准确性深深打动了他,似乎他以前从来没读过这些文字。然后,他渐渐懂得,这些某个早晨或晚上在古希腊爱奥尼亚人的节日或在萨宾山区偶得的诗行,以其震撼心灵的力量和他那个时期的文学(尽管有明显的优点)完全无法与之媲美的魅力,是如何一代接一代地传颂了几千年。也许,因此才有了中世纪对维吉尔的评价:他犹如一个预言家或魔术师;他的单个的词和单个的短语,以及他那带有感伤情调的半行的诗句,就像大自然自己的声音一样,

to that pain and weariness, yet hope of better things, which is the experience of her children in every time.

表达着那种痛苦和厌倦，也表达着追求更加美好事物的希望，而这也正是每一个时代大自然之子的经验。

译后语

“The Classics”，根据陆谷孙主编的《英汉大词典》，意为古典文学，主要指古希腊、古罗马文学。此处作为文章标题，“The Classics”不妨译作《古典文学》。这篇文章讲了一个重要道理——读者因年龄和阅历不同会对古典文学有不同的感受。

文章只有四句话，除第一句外，其余三句都很长，第二句最长，78 个词，句子结构也复杂，为翻译提供了思考空间。

Passages, which to a boy are but rhetorical common-places, neither better nor worse than a hundred others which any clever writer might supply, which he gets by heart and thinks very fine, and imitates, as he thinks, successfully, in his own flowing versification, at length come home to him, when long years have passed, and he has had experience of life, and pierce him, as if he had never known them, with their sad earnestness and vivid exactness.

理解这样的长句需先弄清它的结构。这句话的主语是 passages，它有两个谓语，come home to him 和 and pierce him，“主语＋谓语”构成句子的主干结构。passages 有两个较长的定语从句，第一个为“which to a boy are but rhetorical common places, neither better nor worse than a hundred others which any clever writer might supply”，第二个为“which he gets by heart and thinks very fine, and imitates, as he thinks, successfully, in his own flowing versification”，第一个从句里的 a hundred others 又带一个定语从句，which any clever writer might supply。这些从句都是用来修饰主语的成

分。再看句子的两个谓语，一个是 come home to him，它带两个状语从句，“when long years have passed, and he has had experience of life”；另一个是 and pierce him，它带一个“with phrase, with their sad earnestness and vivid exactness”，和一个以 as if 引导的从句，as if he had never known them。对句子做这样的分解有利于弄清句子的构造，以显示其纷繁的枝叶是如何附着在它的主干上。（文章的第三句和第四句也是长句子，可以用同样的方式对其结构做分析）如何将这个错综复杂的英语句子译成自然通顺的汉语句子，原则上是以句子的主语和谓语为出发点来考虑其他附属成分在句中的位置，哪些跟着主语，哪些跟着谓语，哪个先说，哪个后说，要安排好，将它们围绕句子主干结构有机地组织起来。当然，不同译者会采用不同处理方式。

译者翻译这句话时考虑了三点。一是主语 passages（段落）放在什么位置好，也就是这句话如何开头好。它的位置有两个选择：（一）“有一些在学童看来语言平淡无奇的段落”；（二）“有一些段落在学童看来语言平淡无奇”。这两个译文都可以嵌入句中，而且读起来也通顺。但第一个译文里的“段落”前面有一个定语“有一些在学童看来语言平淡无奇的”，这样作为主语的“段落”就被置于强调的位置上（emphatic position），比第二个译文显得更突出，故选择了第一个译法。

译者考虑的第二点是关于“这些文字的真谛他才理解”这句话里动宾倒置的问题，因为其正常的语序应该是“他才理解这些文字的真谛”。将动宾倒置是考虑到与后面“深深打动了他”的衔接，因为其逻辑主语是“这些文字”（passages），或“这些文字的真谛”。

第三点，关于 sad earnestness and vivid exactness 的译法。按照字面将其译作“悲伤的诚实感和生动的准确性”，这在汉语有些不自然，也还说得通。

Definition of a Gentleman

John Henry Newman

Hence it is, that it is almost a definition of a gentleman, to say he is one who never inflicts pain. This description is both refined and, as far as it goes, accurate. He is mainly occupied in merely removing the obstacles which hinder the free and unembarrassed action of those about him; and he concurs with their movements rather than takes the initiative himself. His benefits may be considered as parallel to what are called comforts or conveniences in arrangements of a personal nature: like an easy chair or a good fire, which do their part in dispelling cold and fatigue, though nature provides both means of rest and animal heat without them. The true gentleman in like manner carefully avoids whatever may cause a jar or a jolt in the minds of those with whom he is cast; all clashing of opinion, or collision of feeling, all restraint, or suspicion, or gloom, or resentment; his great concern being to make every one at their ease and at home. He has his eyes on all his company; he is tender towards the bashful, gentle towards the distant, and merciful toward the absurd; he can recollect to whom he is speaking; he guards against unseasonable allusions, or topics which may irritate; he is

什么样的人是有修养的人

约翰·亨利·纽曼

因此,可以说,他是一个从不让别人感到痛苦的人,这几乎就是关于有修养的人的定义。这样描述是精练的,而且,就其本身而言,也是准确的。他主要致力于为周围的人们排除障碍,以便让他们自由自在地活动;他附和他们的行动,而不是自己采取主动。他这样做的好处相当于为人们之间带来舒适和便利:就像一把安乐椅或温暖的壁炉,能驱散寒冷和疲倦,尽管没有这些,大自然也能提供休息和增加体温的方法。同样,一个真正有修养的人总是小心翼翼地避免给与他志同道合的人们的心理造成刺激或震惊,比如意见分歧,感情不和,种种制约,或疑心,或愁绪,或怨恨。他最关心的是让人们精神放松,感觉舒服。他随时留意和他在一起的人们;他对羞怯者温柔,对疏远者和蔼,对荒谬者仁慈;他知道正在和谁说话;他注意不说不合时宜的含沙射影的话,也不涉及可能惹人恼火的话题;他

seldom prominent in conversation, and never wearisome. He makes light of favours while he does them, and seems to be receiving when he is conferring. He never speaks of himself except when compelled, never defends himself by a mere retort, he has no ears for slander or gossip, is scrupulous in imputing motives to those who interfere with him, and interprets everything for the best. He is never mean or little in his disputes, never takes unfair advantage, never mistakes personalities or sharp sayings for arguments, or insinuates evil which he dare not say out. From a long sighted prudence, he observes the maxim of the ancient sage, that we should ever conduct ourselves towards our enemy as if he were one day to be our friend. He has too much good sense to be affronted at insults, he is too well employed to remember injuries, and too indolent to bear malice. He is patient, forbearing, and resigned, on philosophical principles; he submits to pain, because it is inevitable, to bereavement, because it is irreparable, and to death, because it is his destiny. If he engages in controversy of any kind, his disciplined intellect preserves him from the blundering discourtesy of better, though less educated minds; who, like blunt weapons, tear and hack instead of cutting clean, who mistake the point in argument, waste their strength on trifles, misconceive their adversary, and leave the question more involved than they find it. He may be right or wrong in his opinion, but he is too clear-headed to be unjust; he is as simple as he is forcible, and as brief as he is decisive.

与人交谈时很少突出自己，也从不表示厌倦。他对自己做的好事则是轻描淡写，本来是在给予，看上去却像是在受人之恩。除非不得已，他从不谈论自己，也从不为了替自己辩护而反驳别人；他不听流言蜚语，对于妨碍他的人，他不轻易说人家动机不良，他解释任何事情总是往最好处想。与人有了争端，他从不表现小气刻薄，从不乘人之危，从不为了争辩而误解别人的人格或尖利的言辞，或者暗示那些他不敢说出口的邪恶的事情。他从有远见的审慎的观点出发，遵守古代圣贤的座右铭：我们应该这样对待我们的敌人，好像他终有一天会成为我们的朋友。他很明智，不因受辱而感到被冒犯，他忙于自己的事情，不对自己所受的伤害耿耿于怀，也懒于为此而心怀恶意。在关涉哲学原则上，他表现耐心、宽容、和顺。他正视痛苦，因为痛苦不可避免；他忍受丧亲之痛，因为失去的亲人不可挽回；他屈从于死亡，因为死亡是他最终的归宿。假如他卷入纷争，他那训练有素的智力使他避免犯那些智力虽强但缺乏教育的人们常有的粗鲁和失礼——那些人如同粗钝的刀斧，乱劈乱砍，而不是整整齐齐地切割；他们曲解论点，在枝节问题上浪费精力；他们误解对手，把问题弄得越来越复杂。而他的意见可能是对的，也可能是错的，但是他的头脑非常清醒，不至于不公正。正像他强劲一样，他很单纯；正像他果断一样，他很直率。

译后语

本文选自英国19世纪作家约翰·亨利·纽曼(1801—1890)的关于大学教育问题的讲演和论文集 *The Idea of a University Defined and Illustrated* (1873),讨论关于人的修养问题。人的修养问题是文明社会里人们关心的重要问题,也是不同文化里人们的共同话题。在这个问题上,人们的共同语言比较多,共同概念比较多。但在讨论这个问题时的表达方式上——词汇、短语或句式的使用上——不同语言各有其独特之处。这篇文章从正反两个方面讨论什么样的人是有修养的人,其表达方式值得研究,能给我们以启示,能让我们认识什么是好的符合习惯说法的英语。比如:

(1) His benefits may be considered as **parallel to** what are called comforts or conveniences in arrangements of a personal nature...

这句话里的 parallel to 意思是 very similar,相当于汉语的"相似""类似"。如 a parallel career(相似的职业)、parallel development(相似的发展状况)等。此外,译文对这句话里的 his benefits 做了一点扩展,如果将其字对字地直译成"他的好处",没有把意思说透,实际是"他这样做的好处"。

(2) cause a **jar** or a **jolt** in the minds 中,jar 为 an unpleasant shock,jolt 为"a sudden strong feeling, especially of shock or surprise",相当于汉语的"刺激"或"震惊"。

(3) clashing of opinion,动词 to clash 有一个意思是 to argue or

disagree seriously，就是我们常说的“意见分歧”；再看 collision of feeling，collision 意为 a strong disagreement，这里的 collision of feeling 译为“感情不和”合适。

（4）He makes light of favours while he does them…“他对自己做的好事则是轻描淡写”，即他没有把自己做的好事看得很重要。

（5）takes unfair advantage 和汉语的“乘人之危”的意思类似。

（6）“he… is scrupulous in **imputing** motives to those who interfere with him…”中，动词 to impute 的意思是“to say，often unfairly，that sb is responsible for sth”，相当于汉语的“归咎于……”“把……强加于……”。对这句话做了如下处理：“对于干扰他的人，他不轻易说他们动机不良……”。

这里仅举几个例子，意在说明，好的英语作家写的东西里，总有让我们感到新鲜和轻巧的表达方式，几乎每个词、每个搭配、每个句子都值得琢磨，琢磨他们为什么这样说，我们读的时候有什么感觉。在阅读中（主要是通过阅读）不厌其烦地做这种思考和体悟，很有好处。

James Frederick Ferrier

詹姆斯·弗雷德里克·费里尔(1808—1864),苏格兰哲学家。1842年至1845年任爱丁堡大学教授,1845年起任安德鲁大学教授,直至逝世。主要著作有 *The Institutes of Metaphysic* (1854)、*The Theory of Knowing and Being* (1854)、*Lectures on Greek Philosophy*,语言风格朴素而富有魅力。*Lectures on Greek Philosophy* 是用英语介绍希腊哲学的最好著作之一。后文即出自该书。

The True End of Man

James Frederick Ferrier

The philosophy of the Cyrenaic school, founded by Aristippus, proceeds on the assumption that happiness is, in point of fact, the good, the supreme good, or chief end of man; and this assumption, so far from being discountenanced by the philosophy of Socrates, is involved in that philosophy as one of its most vital principles. Viewed as a matter of fact, we must admit that his own happiness, whatever it may consist in, or whatever may be the means to be employed in the attainment, is the end which each individual has most at heart, and at which he ultimately aims. This is the end after which all men most eagerly strive. Happiness is the goal which, consciously or unconsciously, we are all struggling to reach. Milton has written two epic poems in which he commemorates our fallen and our restored condition. He has written "Paradise Lost" and "Paradise Regained". But the true epic of humanity—the epic which is in a constant course of evolution from the beginning until the end of time, the epic which is daily poured forth from the heart of the whole human race, sometimes in rejoicing paeans, but oftener amid woeful lamentation, tears, and disappointed hopes—what is it but Paradise sought for?

人生的真正目的

詹姆斯·弗雷德里克·费里尔

亚里斯提卜创建的昔兰尼学派哲学认为，事实上，幸福是人所追求的好的、至高无上的或主要的目的；这个认识，非但没有遭到苏格拉底哲学的反对，而是作为它的最重要的原则之一融入其中。鉴于人要追求幸福是事实，我们必须承认，他自己的幸福，不论其本质特征可能是什么，也不论采取什么方式去获得，是每个人心中最重视的目的，是每个人最终追求的目标。这是所有的人最渴望达到的目的。幸福是我们所有的人有意无意努力实现的目标。弥尔顿写了两部史诗，纪念我们堕落和复原的状况。他写了《失乐园》和《复乐园》。但人类真正的史诗——从时间的开始到时间的终结一直处于发展过程的史诗，全人类每天每日发自内心的史诗，有时是欢乐的赞歌，但更多的是悲伤、眼泪和失望——除了我们所追求的乐园还能是什么呢？

译后语

1. 关于文章标题的翻译：

"The True End of Man"可直译为《人的真正目的》，但不妨将 Man 扩展为"人生"，《现代汉语词典》对"人生"的解释是"人的生存与生活"，因此将标题译作《人生的真正目的》是可以的。

2. 关于第一句话里的"proceeds on the assumption that..."

"on the assumption that..."一般译为"基于……的假设"，如果与文章下一句里的"viewed as a matter of fact"联系起来看，这里所谈的是一种观点，与其依据字面意思译成"假设"，不如译成"认为"更确切。因此，将"The philosophy of the Cyrenaic school, founded by Aristippus, proceeds on the assumption that happiness is..."译为"亚里斯提卜创建的昔兰尼学派哲学认为……"。

3. 关于第二句话里的 Viewed as a matter of fact：

这里 Viewed as a matter of fact 是把前一句里所表达的意思，即"happiness is, in point of fact, the good, the supreme good, or chief end of man"，看作一个事实，为了翻译方便，不妨将其扩展为 With that viewed as a matter of fact 或 Considering that as a matter of fact 等，因此可将这个短语译为"鉴于人要追求幸福是事实，我们必须承认……"。

4. 文中的 Paradise sought for 带有神学色彩，作者所倡导的是精神上的圣洁的幸福，有别于亚里斯提卜的幸福观。

Charles Dickens

查尔斯·狄更斯(1812—1870),英国维多利亚时期伟大的现实主义小说家,作品享有极高声誉。进入20世纪,他的文学天赋得到广泛认可,其小说一直广受欢迎。主要作品有:*The Posthumous Papers of the Pickwick Club* (1836—1837)、*The Adventures of Oliver Twist* (1837—1839)、*The Old Curiosity Shop* (1840—1841)、*David Copperfield* (1849—1850)、*Great Expectations*(1860—1861)等。随后的选文即出自 *The Old Curiosity Shop*。

The Widow at the Grave

Charles Dickens

She was looking at a humble stone which told of a young man who had died at twenty three years old, fifty-five years ago, when she heard a faltering step approaching, and looking round saw a feeble woman bent with the weight of years, who tottered to the foot of that same grave and asked her to read the writing on the stone. The old woman thanked her when she had done, saying that she had had the words by heart for many a long, long year, but could not see them now.

"Were you his mother?" said the child.

"I was his wife, my dear."

She the wife of a young man of three-and-twenty! Ah, true! It was fifty-five years ago.

"You wonder to hear me say that," remarked the old woman, shaking her head. "You're not the first. Older folk than you have wondered at the same thing before now. Yes, I was his wife. Death doesn't change us more than life, my dear."

"Do you come here often?" asked the child.

墓旁的寡妇

查尔斯·狄更斯

她在看一块简陋的墓碑，上面写的是关于 55 年前死去的一个年轻人，终年 23 岁。正在这时，忽然听见一阵踉跄的脚步声越来越近，回头看时，只见一个身体虚弱的妇人，岁月压弯了身子，正摇摇晃晃朝同一座坟墓走过来。老人请她把碑文读给她听，她读完，老人道了谢，说很多年来她都能记住碑文，可现在看不见了。

“你是他母亲吗?”女孩问。

“我是他妻子，亲爱的孩子。”

她，一个 23 岁年轻人的妻子！啊，没错！那是 55 年前的事了。

“听我这么说你感到惊讶吧，”老妇人摇着头说，“你不是头一个。比你年岁大的人从前对这事也是感到惊讶。是的，我是他妻子。他的死并没有改变我们的关系，还和他生前一样，亲爱的。”

“你常来这里吗?”女孩问。

"I sit here very often in the summer-time," she answered. "I used to come here once to cry and mourn, but that was a weary while ago, bless God!"

"I pluck the daisies as they grow, and take them home," said the old woman after a short silence. "I like no flowers so well as these, and haven't for five and fifty years. It's a long time, and I'm getting very old!"

Then growing garrulous upon a theme which was new to one listener though it were but a child, she told her how she had wept and moaned and prayed to die herself, when this happened; and how when she first came to that place, a young creature strong in love and grief, she had hoped that her heart was breaking as it seemed to be. But that time passed by, and although she continued to be sad when she came there, still she could bear to come, and so went on until it was pain no longer, but a solemn pleasure, and a duty she had learned to like. And now that five-and-fifty years were gone, she spoke of the dead man as if he had been her son or grandson, with a kind of pity for his youth, growing out of her own old age, and an exalting of his strength and manly beauty as compared with her own weakness and decay; and yet she spoke about him as her husband too, and thinking of herself in connexion with him, as she used to be and not as she was now, talked of their meeting in another world, as if he were dead but yesterday, and she, separated from her former self, were thinking of the happiness of that comely girl who seemed to have died with him.

“夏天我常在这里坐，”她答道，“曾经有一阵我常来这里哭泣，哀悼，可是，唉，岁月悠悠，那是很久以前的事了，感谢上帝！”

“雏菊开花时我就摘些带回家，”老妇人沉默一会儿说，“别的花都不像这些花让我喜欢，55年没有摘过了。很久了，我现在也很老了。”

她喋喋不休地谈着一个话题，但对这个听者来说却很新鲜，尽管她只是个孩子。老妇人告诉她，当时她是如何地哭泣呀，哀悼呀，甚至祈求自己一死了事；她，一个怀着强烈爱恋和深深悲痛的年轻女子，头一次来到这个地方时，她的心似乎碎了，她也希望她的心真的碎了。但那一阵子过去了，虽然她来这里时心情还是悲痛，可她能够忍受，她还是来，直到她的感觉不再是痛苦，而是一种庄重的喜悦和严肃的责任，她逐渐喜欢起这种感觉。现在，55个年头已经过去了，她怀着因年迈而对他英年早逝的遗憾，以及比之自己的虚弱和衰老而对他的坚强意志和男子之美的赞美，在谈论死者时似乎他是她的儿子或孙子；然而，她也将他当作丈夫来谈，而且想到昔日自己和他在一起的生活（现已不复存在），她便谈起他们将在另一个世界相会，那情景好像他昨日刚刚死去，而她，似乎告别了此前的自己，正在感受着那个似乎已经随他而去的秀丽女孩的幸福。

译后语

文中人物对话语言和作者叙述语言风格不同，前者句子简单，意思明了，很符合说话人的身份，如：

（1）“Were you his mother?”said the child.

“I was his wife, my dear.”

（2）“I sit here very often in the summer-time,”she answered. “I used to come here once to cry and mourn, but that was a weary while ago, bless God!”

翻译这些对话，需拿准意思，掌握好语气，使译文与原文相符。作者的叙述语言句子比较长，比较复杂，翻译时常需重新组织。还有一些表达方式，包括搭配、短语和句式，很自然的英语，听起来很舒服，但译成汉语时要取得同样效果挺费思索，如：

（3）... and looking round saw a feeble woman **bent with the weight of years,** who tottered to the foot of that same grave...

这里 bent with the weight of years 是说长年累月的哀伤和煎熬把一个秀丽的年轻女子变成一个伺偻老妇。英语的 years 和汉语的“岁月”相似，让人产生联想，故将此短语译作“岁月压弯了身子”，符合原文意思。

（4）“I used to come here once to cry and mourn, but that was a **weary while** ago, bless God!”

此句里的 weary 与 while 搭配，直译比较困难，weary 实是老妇人的感觉。

(5) Then growing garrulous upon a theme which was new to one listener though it were but a child, she told her how she had wept and moaned and prayed to die herself, when this happened...

这是一个主从复合句，其中 she told her 部分为主句，主句前面的分词结构为状语，因为此状语涵盖内容较多，翻译时若保持原文形式有困难，故做如下变通：

她喋喋不休地谈着一个话题，但对这个听者来说却很新鲜，尽管她只是个孩子。她告诉她，当时她是如何地哭泣呀、哀悼呀，甚至祈求自己一死了事……

(6) she spoke of the dead man as if he had been her son or grandson, with a kind of pity for his youth, growing out of her own old age, and an exalting of his strength and manly beauty as compared with her own weakness and decay...

此句关键在于译好 with 短语，因其很长也较复杂，译成汉语时要浓缩内容、压缩长度，否则会把译文句子弄得很累赘。如：

……她怀着因年迈而对他英年早逝的遗憾，以及比之自己的虚弱和衰老而对他的坚强意志和男子之美的赞美，在谈论死者时似乎他是她的儿子或孙子……

Benjamin Jowett

本杰明·乔伊特(1817—1893),英国古典学者、神学家、教育家,1842年开始在牛津大学巴利奥尔学院(Balliol College, Oxford)任教,1855年被任命为"钦定希腊语教授"(Regius Professorship of Greek),1870年起任该学院院长。他以译介柏拉图作品闻名。著有 *The Epistles of St. Paul* (1855),译著有柏拉图的 *Dialogue*、亚里士多德的 *Politics* 等。后文"Socrates Under Sentence of Death Hears the Voice of the Laws of Athens"出自 *Translation of the Crito*,"Last Words on Plato"出自 *Introduction to the Laws of Plato*。

Socrates Under Sentence of Death Hears the Voice of the Laws of Athens

Benjamin Jowett

Has a philosopher like you failed to discover that our country is more to be valued and higher and holier far than mother or father or any ancestor, and more to be regarded in the eyes of the gods and of men of understanding? also to be soothed, and gently and reverently entreated when angry, even more than a father, and either to be persuaded, or if not persuaded, to be obeyed? And when we are punished by her, whether with imprisonment or stripes, the punishment is to be endured in silence; and if she lead us to wounds or death in battle, thither we follow as is right; neither may any one yield or retreat or leave his rank, but whether in battle or in a court of law, or in any other place, he must do what his city and his country order him; or he must change their view of what is just: and if he may do no violence to his father or mother, much less may he do violence to his country.

被判死刑的苏格拉底听见雅典法律的声音

本杰明·乔伊特

像你这样的哲学家难道没有发现我们的国家远比母亲或父亲或任何先辈更有价值、更崇高、更神圣,在诸神和理智的人们心目中更受到重视吗?而且,在她生气时,安慰她,温柔地、尊敬地对待她,甚至胜于对待父亲,或者劝说她,假如劝说不成,或者服从她吗?当她惩罚我们时,或者监禁,或者鞭打,我们要默默忍受;如果她带领我们去战斗并负伤或牺牲,我们就跟着她去战斗,这是正确的;谁也不能屈服,或者退却,或者脱离队伍,然而,不论在战场上或法庭上,或任何别的地方,任何人都必须执行他的城市和他的国家的命令;不然,他就得改变他们对于正义的观点:假若他不能冒犯他的父母,他就更不能冒犯他的国家。

译后语

本文是一个段落，两个句子。第一句是反问句(rhetorical question)，“Has a philosopher like you failed to discover that...”，而且很长，翻译时应先处理好各组成成分，如在 our country is more to be valued and higher and holier 中，more、higher 和 holier 是三个并列的形容词比较级，more to be valued 形式上与后二者不同，翻译时须予以注意。句子里还有好几个 to be 的被动形式，如 to be regarded、to be soothed、to be obeyed 等，连续出现，因为主句谓语动词 to discover 带一个宾语从句，从句主语是 country，这几个成分需处理好。这里译文多将其变为主动形式，读来通顺自然。朗读时，句尾的“吗”应读升调，凡因逗号和顿号而停顿的地方都应读升调。

Last Words on Plato

Benjamin Jowett

And so having brought into the world "noble children", he rests from the labours of authorship. More than two thousand two hundred years have passed away since he returned to the place of Apollo and the Muses. Yet the echo of his words continues to be heard among men, because of all philosophers he has the most melodious voice. He is the inspired prophet or teacher who can never die, the only one in whom the outward form adequately represents the fair soul within; in whom the thoughts of all who went before him are reflected and of all who come after him are partly anticipated. Other teachers of philosophy are dried up and withered—after a few centuries they have become dust; but he is fresh and blooming, and is always begetting new ideas in the minds of men. They are one-sided and abstract; but he has many sides of wisdom. Nor is he always consistent with himself, because he is always moving onward, and knows that there are many more things in philosophy than can be expressed in words, and that truth is greater than consistency. He who approaches him in the most reverent spirit shall reap most of the fruit of his wisdom; he who reads him by the light

最后评说柏拉图

本杰明·乔伊特

这样，他给世界带来了“高尚的孩子”之后，便停止了著述。自从他回到阿波罗和缪斯诸女神的地方，两千二百多年已经过去了。然而，他的话继续在人们中间回响着，因为，在所有哲学家里，他的声音最悦耳。他是受神灵启示的永垂不朽的预言家或导师，他外在的形体充分体现了内在的美丽灵魂；他既反映了先前所有人的思想，也部分地预见了后来所有人的思想，在这些方面，他是独一无二的。别的哲学导师们已经枯萎了，几个世纪之后他们都变成了尘埃；但他犹如鲜花，仍在盛开，而且，总是在人们头脑里孕育新的思想。那些哲学导师们是片面的、抽象的，他则具有多方面的智慧。他并不总是前后一致，因为他一直在前进；而且他知道，在哲学里，有很多概念是无法用语言表达的；他也知道，真理比一致性更伟大。怀着敬意对待他的人会收获他绝大部分的智慧果实，只凭借古人的评

of ancient commentators will have the least understanding of him.

We may see him with the eye of the mind in the groves of the Academy, or on the banks of the Ilissus, or in the streets of Athens, alone or walking with Socrates, full of those thoughts which have since become the common possession of mankind. Or we may compare him to a statue hid away in some temple of Zeus or Apollo, no longer existing on earth, a statue which has a look as of the God himself. Or we may once more imagine him following in another state of being the great company of heaven which he beheld of old in a vision. So, "partly trifling, but with a certain degree of seriousness", we linger around the memory of a world which has passed away.

论去阅读他的人是不会理解他的。

我们不妨想象他在学园[①]的树林里,或在伊利萨斯河岸上,或在雅典的街道上,独自思考或与苏格拉底边散步边讨论那些后来成为人类共同财富的思想。或者,我们不妨把他比作曾经隐于现已不复存在的宙斯神庙或阿波罗神庙里的塑像,一座具有庙中之神的那种神态的塑像。或许,我们不妨再次想象他以另一种生命形态追随他很久以前在幻想中所看见的天国众神。因此,“多少带点轻慢,但也怀着某种程度的严肃的感情”[②],我们流连于一个已逝世界的记忆里。

① 柏拉图在雅典的讲学处。

② 引自柏拉图的《会饮篇》。

译后语

关于英语介词短语 full of 的翻译：

文章的第二段有四个句子，前三句都是以“We/we may”起始的排比句：“We may see him...”“Or we may compare him...”“Or we may once more imagine him...” 其中第一句“We may see him with the eye of the mind in the groves of the Academy, or on the banks of the Ilissus, or in the streets of Athens, alone or walking with Socrates, **full of** those thoughts which have since become the common possession of mankind.”翻译时需做斟酌。

首先关于语序。这个句子可以分为两部分：We may see him with the eye of the mind 为句子主体部分，其余皆为状语部分（含一个定语从句 which have since become the common possession of mankind）。若按原文语序翻译此句，以“我们不妨想象他……”开始，接着翻译状语部分，所得译文句子也还通顺易懂，且与第一段最后一句“he... will have the least understanding of him”意义上的衔接也紧密。若颠倒语序，按汉语多数情况下先说状语的习惯，以“当他在……时”开始，最后说句子主体部分“我们不妨想象他……”，这样比较符合汉语读者的阅读习惯，并且因其与后面的两个“我们不妨”距离较近，其排比效果（即与后两句共同产生的语篇效果）也许略好些；其缺点是，不如原文与上文的衔接紧密。

关于介词短语 full of，《牛津高阶英汉双解词典》（第 7 版）的解释为 Thinking or talking a lot about a particular thing，并附例句

“He was full of his new job and everything he’d been doing.”译为“他滔滔不绝地谈他的新工作和所做的一切。”借鉴这个定义来翻译文中的 full of those thoughts 合适:“……思考或……讨论那些后来成为人类共同财富的思想。”译文并对“alone or walking with Socrates, full of those thoughts”做了整饬,将 alone 和 full of those thoughts 译为“独自思考问题”,将“walking with Socrates, full of those thoughts”译为“与苏格拉底边散步边谈论……”。虽然句子比较长,也比较复杂,但读起来通顺,也清楚地表达了原文的意思。

James Anthony Froude

詹姆斯·安东尼·弗劳德(1818—1894),英国历史学家,1892年任牛津大学近代史钦定讲座教授。早期为杂志写过评论和历史论文,偶尔也写关于宗教方面的文章。后集中精力撰写12卷的历史巨著《从沃尔西陷落到击败西班牙无敌舰队的英国历史》(*History of England from the Fall of Wolsey to the Defeat of the Spanish Armada*),历时20年,至1870年全部出齐,影响深远。后文即出自该书。他被视为英国19世纪最伟大的散文家之一。

The End of the Middle Age

James Anthony Froude

For, indeed, a change was coming upon the world, the meaning and direction of which even still is hidden from us, a change from era to era. The paths trodden by the footsteps of ages were broken up; old things were passing away, and the faith and the life of ten centuries were dissolving like a dream. Chivalry was dying; the abbey and the castle were soon together to crumble into ruins; and all the forms, desires, beliefs, convictions of the old world were passing away, never to return. A new continent had risen up beyond the western sea. The floor of heaven, inlaid with stars, had sunk back into an infinite abyss of immeasurable space; and the firm earth itself, unfixed from its foundations, was seen to be but a small atom in the awful vastness of the universe. In the fabric of habit in which they had so laboriously built for themselves, mankind were to remain no longer.

And now it is all gone—like an unsubstantial pageant faded; and between us and the old English there lies a gulf of mystery which the prose of the historian will never adequately bridge.

中世纪的终结

詹姆斯·安东尼·弗劳德

因为世界的确在发生变化，虽然其意义和方向甚至仍不为我们所知，但这是跨时代的变化。时代的脚步所踩踏出来的道路已被破坏；旧事物正在消失，十个世纪的信仰和生活梦幻般烟消云散。骑士制度正在死亡，大修道院和城堡很快就要一起变成废墟；旧世界所有的存在形式、欲望、信仰和信念正在消失，一去不复返。在西面大洋的彼岸一个新大陆已然出现。布满星辰的苍穹已经沉入无限辽阔的深渊；而坚固的地球本身，当它脱离它的根基时，看上去不过是茫茫宇宙中一个微小的原子。人类已不再生活在他们为自己辛勤建立起来的习惯结构里。

现在一切都不复存在，如同一个虚幻的华丽场景黯然消失；在我们和过去的英国人[①]之间横着一道神秘的鸿沟，历史学家的乏力的文字不足以将其填平。

① 指16世纪欧洲宗教改革运动之前的英国人。

They cannot come to us, and our imagination can but feebly penetrate to them. Only among the aisles of our cathedrals, only as we gaze upon their silent figures sleeping on their tombs, some faint conceptions float before us of what these men were when they were alive; and perhaps in the sound of church bells, that peculiar creation of mediaeval age, which falls upon the ear like the echo of a vanished world.

他们不可能来到我们这里，而我们只能对他们做一些渺远的想象。只有在教堂的侧廊里，只有当我们注视他们静眠于坟墓上的塑像时，也许，当教堂的大钟（中世纪的特殊产物）敲响，如同已逝的世界的回响传到我们耳际时，我们才影影绰绰知道他们生前的身份。

译后语

美国20世纪散文家E.B.怀特主张写作时多用动词和名词。他说:"用名词和动词写作,而不是用形容词和副词。一般情况下,是名词和动词赋予好的作品以强韧和色彩,而不是它们的辅助成分。"(Write with nouns and verbs, not with adjectives and adverbs. In general, however, it is nouns and verbs, not their assistants, that give to good writing its toughness and color.)这篇文章有这个特点,名词多,动词多。文章不足300字,除像new和old几个常用形容词外,真正意义上的形容词只有silent (figures)、faint (conceptions)和peculiar (creation)等,副词也只有laboriously、feebly和perhaps等,所占总字数的比例很小。名词和动词多,一是因为写历史,注重写实,无需渲染;二是作者选择这样写。题材的特点和作者的选择有机结合,使文章充实有力。

翻译这篇文章,推敲并准确翻译其中的名词和动词是重要一环,能基本上体现其历史题材写实的特点。但对多义的名词应根据上下文确定其意义。如:chivalry在这里不是指男人对女人的彬彬有礼,应是中世纪的骑士制度;aisles不是教堂坐席之间的通道,应是指大教堂的侧廊。类似的情况应结合上下文多查词典来确定词义。

文章最后一句需略做说明:

Only among the aisles of our cathedrals, only as we gaze upon their silent figures sleeping on their tombs, some faint conceptions float before us of what these men were when they were alive; and perhaps in the sound of church bells, that peculiar creation of mediaeval age, which falls upon the ear like the echo of a vanished world.

这句话的主句是 some faint conceptions float before us，前面有两个状语成分 Only among the aisles of our cathedrals 和 only as we gaze upon，主句之后的“and perhaps in the sound of...”也应是状语成分。所以，在译文里先说了这三个状语成分，然后再说主句：

> 只有在教堂的侧廊里，只有当我们注视他们静眠于坟墓上的塑像时，也许，当教堂的大钟（中世纪的特殊产物）敲响，如同已逝的世界的回响传到我们耳际时，我们才影影绰绰知道他们生前的身份。

Thomas Hughes

托马斯·休斯(1822—1896),英国作家。1834 年,他 12 岁时进了英格兰中部小镇的拉格比公学(Rugby School,建立于 1567 年)。他以学校生活为背景写了 *Tom Brown's Schooldays* (1857),后文“Coaching to School”为其中一部分。他创作的文学作品还有 *The Scouring of the White Horse* (1859)和 *Tom Brown at Oxford* (1861)。此外还写了数量较多的非虚构作品。

Coaching to School

Thomas Hughes

Tom stands up on the coach and looks back at his father's figure as long as he can see it; and then the guard, having disposed of his luggage, comes to an anchor, and finishes his buttonings and other preparations for facing the three hours before dawn; no joke for those who minded cold, on a fast coach in November, in the reign of his late Majesty.

I sometimes think that you boys of this generation are a deal tenderer fellows than we used to be. At any rate you're much more comfortable travellers, for I see every one of you with his rug or plaid, and other dodges for preserving the caloric, and most of you going in those fuzzy, dusty, padded first-class carriages. It was another affair altogether, a dark ride on the top of the Tally-ho, I can tell you, in a tight Petersham coat, and your feet dangling six inches from the floor. Then you knew what cold was, and what it was to be without legs, for not a bit of feeling had you in them after the first half-hour. But it had its pleasures, the old dark ride. First there was the consciousness of silent endurance, so dear to every

乘坐马车去上学

托马斯·休斯

汤姆站在马车上朝后看着父亲的身影，直到看不见为止；管车人安置好他的行李，然后就座，扣上衣扣，并做好其他准备，迎接黎明前三小时的旅程；但在已故陛下统治时期，11 月里乘坐快捷马车，这对怕冷的人可不是闹着玩的。

我有时想，你们这一代孩子们比我们从前娇气多了。无论怎么说，你们现在出行舒服多了；我看你们每人都有暖膝厚毯，方格花呢披肩以及别的御寒保暖的东西，而且，你们多数人乘坐带柔软灰色坐垫的头等四轮马车。从前，黑夜里坐在四匹马拉的快捷马车上，穿着紧身呢子大衣，双脚耷拉着，离车厢地板六英寸，我跟你们说吧，那可就完全不同了。那时你才知道什么叫冷，你才知道没有腿是什么滋味，因为半个小时之后你的腿就失去了知觉。但是，从前夜间坐车也有它的乐趣。首先是默默忍耐的意识，每个英国人都很珍视这一点，即站出来

Englishman,—of standing out against something, and not giving in. Then there was the music of the rattling harness, and the ring of the horses' feet on the hard road, and the glare of the two bright lamps through the steaming hoar frost, over the leaders' ears, into the darkness; and the cheery toot of the guard's horn, to warn some drowsy pikeman or the ostler at the next change; and the looking forward to daylight—and last, but not least, the delight of returning sensation in your toes.

Then the break of dawn and the sunrise, where can they be ever seen in perfection but from a coach roof? You want motion and change and music to see them in their glory; not the music of singing men and singing women, but good silent music, which sets itself in your own head, the accompaniment of work and getting over the ground.

The Tally-ho is past St. Alban's, and Tom is enjoying the ride, though half-frozen. The guard, who is alone with him on the back of the coach, is silent, but has muffled Tom's feet up in straw, and put the end of an oat-sack over his knees. The darkness has driven him inwards, and he has gone over his little past life, and thought of all his doings and promises, and of his mother and sister, and his father's last words; and has made fifty good resolutions, and means to bear himself like a brave Brown as he is, though a young one. Then he has been forward into the mysterious boy-future, speculating as to what sort of place Rugby is, and what they do there, and calling up all the stories of public schools which he

勇敢面对而不屈服的意识。然后是挽具发出的叮当声和马蹄踏着坚硬路面发出的哒哒声合奏出的悦耳的声音，以及两盏车灯的明亮的光，透过朦胧的白色霜雾，从领跑马匹的耳朵上方照亮前面的黑暗；还有管车人吹的欢快的喇叭声，提醒在下一个换乘车站打瞌睡的看守或马夫；以及人们对于曙光的期盼——最后一点，但并非最不重要的一点，就是脚趾恢复知觉时的快乐。

然后是破晓和日出，要不是从马车顶上，哪儿还能看见它们那完美的景象呢？你需要在动态和变化中并伴随着音乐才能看见它们的辉煌——不是歌唱者的音乐，而是你头脑里那动听的无声的音乐，是工作和行进过程中的伴奏。

马车过了圣奥尔本教堂，汤姆虽然快冻僵了，还是很喜欢这次马车之旅。管车人陪着汤姆坐在马车后部，他默不作声，用麦秸盖住汤姆的双脚，用燕麦袋的一端盖住他的双膝。夜间的黑暗让汤姆关注自己，他回顾着以往的短暂生活，想到他做过的和答应过的所有的事情，想到他的妈妈和姐姐，以及上路前父亲说的话；他立下很多好的志向，他是布朗家的人，虽然年纪还小，但他要表现得像一个勇敢的布朗①。然后，他想到男孩子陌生的未来，猜测拉格比是个什么样的地方，人们在那里做些什么，也想起了假期里从大一点的男孩子那里听到的

① 汤姆全名为 Tom Brown，故有此说。

has heard from big boys in the holidays. He is choke full of hope and life, notwithstanding the cold, and kicks his heels against the back-board, and would like to sing, only he doesn't know how his friend the silent guard might take it ...

And now they begin to see, and the early life of the country-side comes out; a market-cart or two, men in smock-frocks going to their work, pipe in mouth, a whiff of which is no bad smell this bright morning. The sun gets up, and the mist shines like silver gauze. They pass the hounds jogging along to a distant meet, at the heels of the huntsman's back, whose face is about the colour of the tails of his old pink, as he exchanges greetings with coachman and guard. Now they pull up at a lodge, and take on board a well-muffled-up sportsman, with his gun-case and carpet-bag. An early up-coach meets them, and the coachmen gather up their horses, and pass one another with the accustomed lift of the elbow, each team doing eleven miles an hour, with a mile to spare behind if necessary. And here comes breakfast.

"Twenty minutes here, gentlemen," says the coachman, as they pull up at half past seven at the inn-door.

关于此类公学的故事。虽然天气很冷，他还是满怀希望，充满活力，用鞋后跟车座下的后挡板，而且还想唱歌，只是不知道他的朋友、那个沉默的管车人会怎么想……

现在他们看得见了，乡村早晨的情景显现出来了；有一两辆市场上常见的手推车，身穿长工作服去上班的男人，他们嘴里叼着烟斗，在明朗的早晨烟味倒并不难闻。太阳冉冉升起，雾霭映着阳光有如银色的薄纱。前面有一群猎犬跟在猎人身后慢慢跑着奔向远处的猎场，猎人的脸色和他身上那件旧外套的红色差不多，马车从猎犬身边经过时，猎人和车夫以及管车人互致问候。现在他们把车停在一个小舍门前，一个裹得严严实实的狩猎者带着他的枪套和毛毡旅行包上了车。一辆早发的上行马车与他们相遇，车夫们拉紧缰绳，擦身而过时习惯性地翘起胳膊肘以示致意，每组马匹一个小时跑十一英里，必要时多跑一英里。现在到了吃早餐的地方。

“二十分钟，先生们。”七点半他们把车停在小旅馆门前时马车夫说。

译后语

这篇文章里有几个句子翻译时变换了表达方式，在此说明。

(1) Tom stands up on the coach and looks back at his father's figure **as long as he can see it...**

这个句子里的状语从句"as long as he can see it..."直译的意思是"只要他看得见它（身影）……"。就这个从句本身，这样译是可以的，但若将其和主句部分的译文放在一起时听起来不免有点别扭："汤姆站在马车上朝后看着父亲的身影，只要他看得见它……"汉语习惯上不这样说。这里的参考译文将从句做了变通，试译如下：

> *汤姆站在马车上朝后看着父亲的身影，直到看不见为止……*

(2) At any rate you're much more comfortable **travelers**...

这句话可直译为"无论怎么说，你们是更舒服的旅行者……"，译文准确无误，只是汉语通常不这样说。若将其译成"无论怎么说，你们现在出行舒服多了……"更好些。将原文的名词 travelers 变为汉语的动词"出行"。

(3) ... and his father's **last words**...

这里的 last words 是指父亲送儿子上车时最后说的话，不妨译作"临别时父亲说的话"，但汉语的"临别"二字容易产生多种联想。故将其译作"以及上路前父亲说的话"。

(4) ... and pass one another **with the accustomed lift of the elbow...**

这里的“with the accustomed lift of the elbow...”可能是车夫在路上相遇时一种礼貌的示意。为了明示这个习惯动作的意思，译文增加了“以示致意”几个字：他们“擦身而过时习惯性地翘起胳膊肘以示致意……”

Henry Walter Bates

亨利·沃尔特·贝茨(1825—1892),英国博物学家,1848年来到巴西亚马孙河口上的帕拉采集昆虫标本,并沿亚马孙河流域调查。他在巴西待了十一年,共采集14700多个标本。1859年回到英国,1863年发表两卷本的《亚马孙河上的博物学家》(*The Naturalist on the River Amazons*),后文为书中的一部分。

A Naturalist's Day in the Tropics

Henry Walter Bates

We used to rise soon after dawn, when Isidoro would go down to the city, after supplying us with a cup of coffee, to purchase the fresh provisions for the day. The two hours before breakfast were devoted to ornithology. At that early period of the day the sky was invariably cloudless (the thermometer marking 72 or 73 Fahr.); the heavy dew or the previous night's rain, which lay on the moist foliage, becoming quickly dissipated by the glowing sun, which, rising straight out of the east, mounted rapidly towards the zenith. All nature was fresh, new leaf and flower-buds expanding rapidly. Some mornings a single tree would appear in flower amidst what was the preceding evening a uniform green mass of forest—a dome of blossom suddenly created as if by magic. The birds were all active; from the wild-fruit trees, not far off, we often heard the shrill yelping of the Toucans. Small flocks of parrots flew over on most mornings, at a great height, appearing in distinct relief against the blue sky, always two by two, chattering to each other, the pairs being separated by regular intervals; their bright colours, however, were not apparent at that height. After breakfast we devoted the

一个博物学家在热带丛林里的一天

亨利·沃尔特·贝茨

我们经常天刚亮就起来，伊西多罗给我们准备好咖啡，然后进城购买一天的新鲜食品。早饭前的两个小时都用来研究鸟类。那段时间，天空总是清澈无云（气温计显示华氏72度或73度）；挂在湿漉漉的绿叶上的露水或昨夜的雨水，很快就被从东方轰然而起又很快朝当空移动的炽热的太阳驱散。大自然变得十分清新，新叶和花蕾迅速展开。有时早晨，本来前天晚上还是绿油油的树林里有一棵树便开了花，圆形的树冠突然神奇般地被鲜花覆盖。鸟儿都活跃起来，从不远的野生果树里常常传来巨嘴鸟短促的尖叫声。多数早晨都有小群的鹦鹉从高空飞过，身影清晰地映衬着蓝天，总是成双结对，相互说着悄悄话，隔一会儿就有一对飞过；然而，在那样的高度，它们鲜艳的颜色并不十分明显。吃完早饭，

hours from 10 a.m. to 2 or 3 p.m. to entomology; the best time for insects in the forest being a little before the greatest heat of the day. We did not find them at all numerous, although of great variety as to species... After several years' observation, I came to the conclusion that the increase of these creatures was checked by the close persecution of insectivorous animals, which are excessively numerous in this country. The check operates at all periods of life—on the eggs, the larvae, and the perfect insects.

The heat increased rapidly towards two o'clock (92 and 93 Fahr.), by which time every voice of bird or mammal was hushed; only in the trees was heard at intervals the harsh whirr of a cicada. The leaves, which were so moist and fresh in early morning, now become lax and drooping; the flowers shed their petals. Our neighbours, the Indian and Mulatto inhabitants of the open palm-thatched huts, as we returned home fatigued with our ramble, were either asleep in their hammocks or seated on mats in the shade, too languid even to talk. On most days in June and July a heavy shower would fall some time in the afternoon, producing a most welcome coolness. The approach of the rain-clouds was after a uniform fashion very interesting to observe. First, the cool sea-breeze, which commenced to blow about ten o'clock, and which had increased in force with the increasing power of the sun, would flag and finally die away. The heat and electric tension of the atmosphere would then become almost insupportable. Languor and uneasiness would seize on every one, even the denizens of the forest betraying it by their motions. White clouds would appear in the east and gather into cumuli, with an increasing blackness along their lower portions.

从上午十点到下午两三点是我们研究昆虫的时间，树林里适合昆虫活动的最佳时间是一天里气温达到最热之前的一小会儿。虽然昆虫的种类繁多，但每一种的数量并不太多。经过几年的观察，我得出这样的结论：昆虫的数量不能增加是因为它们遭到食虫动物的侵害，而在这个国家里这种动物的数量很大。在昆虫生命的各个阶段，从卵、幼虫到成虫，这种抑制增长的现象都有发生。

下午接近两点时气温迅速上升（达到华氏92度至93度），此时鸟儿和哺乳动物都安静下来，只偶尔从树丛里传来一只知了的尖叫声。早晨湿漉漉、鲜灵灵的树叶现在都在打蔫儿，花瓣也在往下掉。当我们拖着疲惫的双腿回来时，我们的邻居，那些住在棕榈树叶屋顶小屋里的印第安和穆拉托居民们，不是在吊床上睡觉，就是在阴凉里的草垫上坐着，懒洋洋的，连话也不愿意说。在六、七月，多数下午会下很大的阵雨，给人们带来舒适的凉意。雨云来的时候有个规律，注意观察很有意思。首先，大约在十点钟，一阵凉爽的海风开始吹来，风力随着阳光强度的增加而加大，然后逐渐减弱，最后消失。于是，大气的高温和电压变得难以忍受。大家都是无精打采，焦躁不安，连树林里的动物也躁动起来。东边开始出现白云，白云逐渐变成积云，积云下端越来越黑。

The whole eastern horizon would become almost suddenly black, and this would spread upwards, the sun at length becoming obscured. Then the rush of a mighty wind is heard through the forest, swaying the tree-tops; a vivid flash of lightning bursts forth, then a crash of thunder, and down streams the deluging rain. Such storms soon cease, leaving bluish-black, motionless clouds in the sky until night. Meantime all nature is refreshed; but heaps of flower-petals and fallen leaves are seen under the trees. Towards evening life revives again, and the ringing uproar is resumed from bush and tree. The following morning the sun again rises in a cloudless sky, and so the cycle is completed; spring, summer, and autumn, as it were, in one tropical day...

In Europe, a woodland scene has its spring, its summer, its autumn, and its winter aspects. In the equatorial forests the aspect is the same or nearly so every day in the year: budding, flowering, fruiting, and leaf shedding are always going on in one species or other. The activity of birds and insects proceeds without interruption, each species having its own separate times; the colonies of wasps, for instance, do not die off annually, leaving only the queens, as in cold climates; but the succession of generations and colonies goes on incessantly. It is never either spring, summer, or autumn, but each day is a combination of all three. With the day and night always of equal length, the atmospheric disturbances of each day neutralising themselves before each succeeding morn; with the sun in its course proceeding midway across the sky, and the daily temperature the same within two or three degrees throughout the year—how grand in its perfect equilibrium and simplicity is the march of Nature under the equator!

突然间，整个东边地平线上变成黑压压的一片，黑云向上扩散，最终把太阳遮住。然后，便听见树林里刮起大风，吹得树梢东摇西摆；一道明亮的闪电划破天空，跟着轰然一声霹雳，大雨倾盆而下。这样的暴雨很快就过去了，但蓝黑色的乌云仍停留在天空，一动不动，直到夜里。此时，大自然变得清新如洗，但树下满是飘落的花瓣和树叶。将近傍晚又恢复了活力，丛林里又传来响亮的喧嚣声。第二天早晨太阳又在万里无云的天空升起，从而完成了一个循环。可以说，在热带丛林里，一天经历了春、夏、秋三个季节。……

在欧洲，树林里有春、夏、秋、冬四季各异的景象。在赤道森林，不论是哪一种植物，一年里景象天天相同或几乎相同——吐芽，开花，结果，落叶，一年不断，总在进行。各种鸟和昆虫的活动从不间断，每一种都有它自己的活动时间。例如黄蜂，其群落就不像在寒冷气候里那样每年都相继死去，只剩下蜂工，而是群落和世代的更替持续不断地进行。那里从来不是春、夏、秋三季分明，而是每天都有这三者合一的景象。由于白天和黑夜总是一样长，每天大气的扰动到第二天黎明前就销声匿迹，太阳总是按照自己的轨道从天空中间划过，一年之中每天的气温相同，相差不过两三度。在赤道地区，大自然的步伐如此平衡，如此简单，真是太美妙了。

译后语

这是一篇描述自然现象的文章，作者用文字把他多年的观察和研究记录下来，告诉人们他在热带丛林里都看见了什么。他所叙述的事情都是他的所见所闻，因而都是客观而真实的，这里没有想象、创造和夸张。这一客观而如实的描述决定了文章朴实的气韵和风格。

谈到具体的翻译，可能有两方面的因素影响翻译的操作：一是对文章气韵和风格的体会和把握，二是对词语和句子的翻译和组织。在很大程度上，第一个问题更重要，更应该引起译者的关注。因为它直接影响词语和句子的翻译，因为译者可以以此为准绳制约其对文章细节的处理。好的做法是反复阅读原文，领悟和体验作者的行文风格和特色，分析文章内容和文字风格之间的联系，对文章有个总体把握，这对译者处理具体的语句有帮助。

这篇译文总体上想尽量贴近原文风格，对具体语句做了相应处理，结合几个例句的翻译说明一下。

(1) The leaves, which were so moist and fresh in early morning, now become **lax and drooping**...

这里的 lax and drooping 是很简单很形象的表达方式，和汉语常说的“打蔫儿”或“蔫了”相似。

早晨湿漉漉、鲜灵灵的树叶现在都在打蔫儿……

(2) The approach of the rain-clouds was **after a uniform fashion** very interesting to observe.

“... after a uniform fashion”是说雨云每次都是以固定的方式到来，这里将其译成“规律”。

雨云来的时候有个规律，注意观察很有意思。

(3) The whole eastern horizon would become almost suddenly black, and this would spread upwards, the sun at length **becoming obscured**.

becoming obscured 为被动形式，译文变换了语态。

突然间，整个东边地平线上几乎突然间就变成黑压压的一片，黑云向上扩散，最终把太阳遮住。

(4) ... the colonies of wasps, for instance, do not die off annually, leaving only the queens, as in cold climates...

这句话是说，黄蜂在寒冷气候里每年死一回，只留下蜂王，但在热带黄蜂不是这样。

例如黄蜂，其群落就不像在寒冷气候里那样每年都相继死去，只剩下蜂王……

Lord George Sanger

乔治·桑格勋爵(1825—1911),英国 19 世纪大马戏团经理,著有 *Seventy Years of a Showman's Life*(《马戏生涯 70 年》,1903)。后文即取自该书。

A Fair and a Fire

Lord George Sanger

I have reason to remember that particular Stepney Fair... There was an enormous rope factory on one side of the green, an establishment that extended over a piece of ground running quite into the country, and on the last day of the fair this was suddenly discovered to be on fire. It was just towards dusk when the flames were first seen, and in a very little time they had made tremendous headway. The excitement was intense, the people flocking from the fair to witness the fire and to render what assistance they could. With the pleasure seekers went the showmen, one and all, to give what aid was possible, and an extraordinary scene was the result. There was no time to take off dresses, and amid the flying sparks, and in and about the burning buildings, could be seen clowns, knights in armour, Indian chiefs, jugglers in tights and spangles, rope walkers in fleshings—in fact, all the characters of the fair in full dress, striving with might and main to combat the flames. Here would be seen clown, pantaloon, harlequin, and demon passing buckets from hand to hand, while at another point was the feeble parish engine, manned by sweating Saracens, Crusaders, Roman

一场娱乐和一场大火

乔治·桑格勋爵

我有理由记得那个斯特普尼游乐场……在绿地的一侧有一家很大的制绳厂，所占地盘一直延伸到郊外。就在那次娱乐活动的最后一天，工厂突然着火了。快到傍晚的时候，有人看见火苗，一会儿的工夫，火势已经蔓延开了。当时的气氛很紧张，人们一窝蜂似地从游乐场来到现场，希望尽己所能帮助做点什么。演员们也跟游客一起去了，全体出动，也想提供点力所能及的帮助，结果，一个不同寻常的场景出现了。只见在漫天飞舞的火花之中，在大火熊熊的厂房内外，丑角演员、身披盔甲的武士、印第安酋长、身穿紧身衣佩戴闪亮饰物的杂耍演员、穿着肉色紧身服的走钢索演员——实际上，游乐场的全体演员，全副戏装(因为来不及脱掉)，都在竭尽全力与大火进行战斗。这边是丑角演员、身着花色服装的滑稽演员和鬼角演员们在传递水桶，那边是汗流满面的撒拉森人、十字军战士、古罗马

gladiators, and such-like, pumping as though their very lives depended on their exertions. Up on the building, running along beams with crowbars and hatchets, were the tight-rope walkers, vaulters, and acrobats, whose training enabled them to go where no other persons could possibly have clambered, breaking away roofs and walls to prevent the spread of the fire. Over all was the glow of the flames lighting up the faces of the dense multitude that surged and swung and shouted its approval of the efforts of the motley-garbed show-folk to check the advance of the enemy.

It was a picture that would have delighted a painter of weird scenes, though he might have despaired of ever putting its wavering lights and shadows and the strange characters glancing through them effectively on canvas. I know it impressed itself indelibly on my memory, as in my Hamlet dress I took my share of work with the others in checking the roaring flames. At last our efforts told, and we did check them, but not until enormous damage had been done. A big part of the works was, however, saved, and so pleased were the authorities at the spirit the showmen had exhibited that they gave orders for the fair to continue another day to help make up any losses we had sustained through leaving our booths to become fire fighters.

We did rare business on the extra day, for the story of the fire had spread, and the public came in crowds to view the scene and to patronize the showmen who had worked so well.

斗士,凡此种种,用一辆十分单薄的教区消防车在拼命抽水,好像他们的命运取决于他们出力多少似的。再看房顶上,只见走钢丝者、跳跃表演者和杂技演员手持撬棍和斧头在房梁上奔跑,他们接受过这种训练,可以去别人无法攀登的地方,他们拆掉屋顶,推倒墙头,以阻止火势蔓延。现场一片火光照在密集的人群的脸上,他们群情激奋,如波涛涌动,为那些拼命阻止敌人前进的身着花哨服饰的演员们高声喝彩。

这是一个能让擅长描绘奇异场面的画家感到欢欣鼓舞的画面,虽然他也许对自己是否能够把那些不停晃动的光和影以及那些瞥视光影的奇怪人物画出来感到无能为力。当我穿着哈姆雷特的服装和其他人一起阻止咆哮的火焰蔓延时,我知道,这个画面在我的记忆中留下了不可磨灭的印象。最后,我们的努力奏效了,虽然火势被阻止,但已经造成巨大的破坏。然而,工厂的很大一部分保住了,有关部门对演员们所表现出来的精神感到非常欣慰,他们下令让娱乐活动延长一天,以补偿我们因离开表演棚去参加灭火所承受的损失。

加演的那一天我们的生意格外好,因为灭火的事情一传开,人们就成群结队地来现场观看,并且纷纷解囊帮助我们这些灭火时表现出色的演员。

译后语

1. 翻译好动词

这是一篇描写救火的文章，是一个活动的画面，与叙事文和说理文不同，这里用了比较多的动词和动词词组来描写具体生动的场面，翻译时把这些动词和动词词组处理好很重要。如："the people **flocking** from the fair""the feeble parish engine, **manned** by sweating Saracens...""breaking away roofs and walls""the dense multitude that surged and swung and shouted its approval"，等等。

2. 翻译好被动语句

文章里有几个被动语态的句子，如：

(1) ... and on the last day of the fair this was suddenly **discovered to be on fire**.

工厂突然着火了。

(2) It was just towards dusk when **the flames were first seen**...

快到傍晚的时候，有人看见火苗……

(3) ... but not until **enormous damage had been done**.

虽然火势被阻止，但已经造成巨大的破坏。

以上几个被动形式的英语句子，在译文里都变成了主动的形式，这倒不是一成不变的原则，主要是考虑汉语读者读起来自然、通顺，易于接受。这里的汉语译文有的是属于省略行事主语，如"工厂突然着火了"，"虽然火势被阻止，但(大火)已经造成巨大的破坏。"有的是属于增加行事主语，如"快到傍晚的时候，**有人**看见火苗。"

3. 原文重组

翻译时常有对原文进行重组的情况，但一定是有理由，一定是为了某种目的。如：

There was no time to take off dresses, and amid the flying sparks, and in and about the burning buildings, could be seen clowns, knights in armour, Indian chiefs, jugglers in tights and spangles, rope walkers in fleshings—in fact, all the characters of the fair in full dress, striving with might and main to combat the flames.

> 只见在漫天飞舞的火花之中，在大火熊熊的厂房内外，丑角演员、身披盔甲的武士、印第安酋长、身穿紧身衣佩戴闪亮饰物的杂耍演员、穿着肉色紧身服的走钢索演员——实际上，游乐场的全体演员，全副戏装（因为来不及脱掉），都在竭尽全力与大火进行战斗。

这段译文对原文做了一点调整。因为原文的上一句"... **and** an extraordinary scene was **the result**"译成"……**结果**，一个不同寻常的场景出现了"，接下来的场面描写，先是宏观，再是细节，这样处理与上文衔接紧密；原文的第一句话 There was no time to take off dresses 译成"因为来不及脱掉服装"放在"全副戏装"之后的括号内，对其做一个说明，一气呵成完成一个场面的描写，效果是好的。

4. 火势描写的翻译

文章里有一处描写了大火："It was just towards dusk when the flames were first seen, and in a very little time **they had made tremendous headway.**"这里将其译作"……没过一会儿，火势已经蔓延开了。"有一个汉语英译的例子可供借鉴。《红楼梦》第一回讲葫芦

庙因和尚炸供不小心着火的情形，有一句话："彼时虽有军民来救，**那火已成了势**，如何救得下？"霍克斯(David Hawkes)将其译作"... and though the firemen came to put it out, by the time they arrived **the fire was well under way** and long past controlling..."。这两个英语句子对大火的描写都很好，可供借鉴。

Thomas Henry Huxley

托马斯·亨利·赫胥黎(1825—1895),英国生物学家,教育家,达尔文"进化论"在英国的主要支持者。通过演讲以及关于科学、哲学、宗教、政治的论文与著作,他对英国思想界具有重要影响,如"The Physical Basis of Life"(1868)、"On the Hypothesis that Animals are Automata"(1874)和专著 *Ethics and Evolution* (1893)。从文学角度,他是说明文和论说文的大师。1869年,他创造了"agnostic"(不可知论)一词。后文选自他的 *Last Sermons*。

A Game of Chess

Thomas Henry Huxley

Suppose it were perfectly certain that the life and fortune of every one of us would, one day or other, depend upon his winning or losing a game at chess.

Don't you think that we should all consider it to be a primary duty to learn at least the names and the moves of the pieces; to have a notion of a gambit, and a keen eye for all the means of giving and getting out of check? Do you not think that we should look with a disapprobation amounting to scorn, upon the father who allowed his son, or the state which allowed its members, to grow up without knowing a pawn from a knight?

Yet it is a very plain and elementary truth, that the life, the fortune, and the happiness of every one of us, and, more or less, of those who are connected with us, do depend upon our knowing something of the rules of a game infinitely more difficult and complicated than chess. It is a game which has been played for untold ages, every man and woman of us being one of the two players in a game of his or her own. The chess-board is the world, the pieces are the phenomena of the universe, the rules of the game are what

一盘棋

托马斯·亨利·赫胥黎

假设有一天我们每个人的生活和命运肯定要取决于他在棋盘上的输赢。

那么,他至少应该学会棋子的名称和棋步,知道开局让棋法,要有敏锐的眼光能看出将局和摆脱将局的方法,难道你不认为我们应该把这看作是基本的责任吗?假如一个父亲允许儿子或一个国家允许国民长大后连什么是卒什么是马也分不清,难道你不认为我们应该对这样的父亲或国家表示不满甚至轻蔑吗?

然而,我们每个人以及那些和我们多少有着联系的人们的生活、命运和幸福,的确取决于我们是否了解一个远比下棋更加困难和复杂的游戏的规则,这是一个简单的、基本的道理。这是一个人们已经玩过无数岁月的游戏,我们每一个男人或女人都是他或她的游戏中对垒的一方。棋盘就是这个世界,棋子就是宇宙中的各种现象,而游戏规则就

we call the laws of Nature.

The player on the other side is hidden from us. We know that his play is always fair, just, and patient. But also we know, to our cost, that he never overlooks a mistake, or makes the smallest allowance for ignorance. To the man who plays well, the highest stakes are paid, with that sort of overflowing generosity with which the strong shows delight in strength. And one who plays ill is checkmated—without haste, but without remorse.

My metaphor will remind some of you of the famous picture in which Retzsch has depicted Satan playing at chess with man for his soul. Substitute for the mocking fiend in that picture, a calm, strong angel who is playing for love, as we say, and would rather lose than win—and I should accept it as an image of human life.

是我们所谓的自然法则。

游戏的另一方我们看不见。我们知道他在游戏的过程中一直是公平、公正和有耐心的。可是我们付出了代价之后才知道，他从不忽略一个错误，或者说他绝不原谅无知。游戏玩得好的人，得到最高的奖赏，而且是以强者对于力量表现出喜悦时的那种豪爽的方式奖给他的。而游戏玩得差的人则慢慢地、无情地被将死。

我的比喻会让一些人想起雷茨施①的那幅名画，画的是撒旦为了摄取人的灵魂在与人下棋。用一个面容安详、性格坚强的天使代替画中那个嘲弄人的魔鬼吧，正如我们常说的，这个天使是为了爱而下棋，而且宁可输而不赢，我认为这才是人类生活的图景。

① 雷茨施(Moritz Retzsch，1779—1857)，德国画家。

译后语

从英语翻译到汉语，可以保留原文的句法特色，也可以采用汉语的叙述方式，这要看译者的意图。

《一盘棋》是一篇论说文，翻译要把文章的道理说清楚，让读者好懂，好接受，译者在构句时，有意向汉语习惯句式倾斜。从英语向汉语过渡，句式需做变通。

第二段里有两个反问句，在英语里，疑问词一般出现在句首，如第一句：

Don't you think that we should all consider it to be a primary duty to learn at least the names and the moves of the pieces; to have a notion of a gambit, and a keen eye for all the means of giving and getting out of check?

在汉语里，疑问词一般出现在句尾，如：

> 那么，他至少应该学会棋子的名称和棋步，知道开局让棋法，要有敏锐的眼光能看出将局和摆脱将局的方法，难道你不认为我们应该把这看作是基本的责任吗？

译文里疑问词的位置不同，但仍然是反问句。同时，原文的语序被反转过来，这主要是因为英语先行代词 it 的关系。变通以后的汉语句子把原文里的句法特色化解了。

第二句的情况一样，尽管没有先行代词 it，疑问词的位置变了，语序被反转了。

在第四段里，有一个翻译起来颇费思索的句子：

To the man who plays well, the highest stakes are paid, **with** that sort of overflowing **generosity** with which the strong shows delight in strength.

句子前半部分的意思好理解，也不难翻译，“游戏玩得好的人，得到最高的奖赏”；困难出现在由 with 起始的句子后半部分里的 generosity。这个词兼顾后面的 the strong（即 the strong shows delight in strength with generosity）和前面的 the man（即 the man... are paid the highest stakes with that sort of overflowing generosity）。所以，我们把这个 with phrase 作为一种方式来译，又把“奖”字作为动词重复了一次，就成了下面的样子：“而且是以强者对于力量表现出喜悦时的那种豪爽的方式奖给他的。”这不妨也算是句子的变通吧。

最后一段的最后一句也顺便说明一点。

Substitute for the mocking fiend in that picture, a calm, strong angel who is playing for love, as we say, and would rather lose than win—and I should accept it as an image of human life.

其祈使动词 Substitute 的直接宾语是“a calm, strong angel who... would rather lose than win”，因为这个直接宾语较长，固将 for the mocking fiend in that picture 提前。由于这个原因，这句可以有两种处理方法：

> 用一个面容安详、性格坚强的天使代替画中那个嘲弄人的魔鬼吧，正如我们常说的，这个天使是为了爱而下棋，而且宁可输而不赢，我认为这才是人类生活的图景。

或：

换掉画中那个嘲弄人的魔鬼，代之以一个面容安详、性格坚强的天使，众所周知，她是为了爱而下棋，而且宁可输而不赢，我认为这才是人类生活的图景。

Walter Bagehot

沃尔特·巴奇霍特(1826—1877),英国作家,初做律师,后进入他父亲的海运公司和银行工作。为多家杂志撰写经济、政治、历史和文学方面的文章。做过《经济学家》杂志编辑,是《英国宪法》作者。*Lombard Street*(《伦巴第街》,1873)是一部关于他那个时代伦敦金融中心伦巴第街的著作。后文是其中一个片段。

The Old Private Banker

Walter Bagehot

I can imagine nothing better in theory or more successful in practice than private banks as they were in the beginning. A man of known wealth, known integrity, and known ability is largely entrusted with the money of his neighbours. The confidence is strictly personal. His neighbours know him, and trust him because they know him. They see daily his manner of life, and judge from it that their confidence is deserved. In rural districts, and in former times, it was difficult for a man to ruin himself except at the place in which he lived; for the most part he spent his money there, and speculated there if he speculated at all. Those who lived there also would soon see if he was acting in a manner to shake their confidence. Even in large cities, as cities then were, it was possible for most persons to ascertain with fair certainty the real position of conspicuous persons, and to learn all which was material in fixing their credit. Accordingly the bankers who for a long series of years passed successfully this strict and continual investigation, became very wealthy and very powerful.

从前的私人银行家

沃尔特·巴奇霍特

我想象不出比刚开始时的私人银行在理论上更好、在实践上更成功的行业。一个在财富、人品和能力方面都很知名的人,他的邻居们多把钱托付给他保管。这种信任完全是个人之间的。他的邻居们了解他,因为了解而信任他。他们每天看见他怎样生活,并由此判断他们对他的信任是值得的。从前,在农村地区,一个人不大容易损坏自己的名声,除非是在他居住的地方;通常他在那里花钱,在那里做风险交易——假如他做风险交易的话。住在那里的人们很快就看出来他的行为是否动摇了他们对他的信任。甚至在大城市里——就那时城市规模而言——对大多数人来说,完全有可能弄清楚那些引人注目的人的真实状况,并了解决定他们信誉的所有物质状况。于是,那些多年来成功地通过了人们严格的持续调查的银行家们就变得非常富有,非常有影响。

The name "London Banker" had especially a charmed value. He was supposed to represent, and often did represent, a certain union of pecuniary sagacity and educated refinement which was scarcely to be found in any other part of society. In a time when the trading classes were much ruder than they now are, many private bankers possessed a variety of knowledge and a delicacy of attainment which would even now be very rare. Such a position is indeed singularly favourable. The calling is hereditary; the credit of the bank descends from father to son: this inherited wealth soon brings inherited refinement. Banking is a watchful, but not a laborious trade. A banker, even in large business, can feel pretty sure that all his transactions are sound, and yet have much spare mind. A certain part of his time, and a considerable part of his thoughts, he can readily devote to other pursuits. And a London banker can also have the most intellectual society in the world if he chooses it. There has probably very rarely ever been so happy a position as that of a London private banker; and never perhaps a happier.

"伦敦银行家"这个称号具有特别诱人的价值。他应该代表而且的确常常代表了某种结合,即在钱财方面所表现的精明和在教育方面所表现的教养的结合,这种现象在社会的其他人群里很少见。有一个时期,商人阶层比现在的商人要粗鲁得多,而很多私人银行家却具有多方面的知识和精巧的业绩,这即使是现在也不多见。这一状况的确是特别令人赞许的。这种职业是世袭的,银行的信誉由父亲传给儿子:随着这笔继承的财富而来的很快便是继承的教养。银行工作是一个小心谨慎的工作,但并不是费时费力的行业。即使是大银行家,他也很有把握,觉得他所有的交易都做得很稳妥,仍然有多余的脑力考虑别的事情。他可以把一部分时间和相当大的一部分脑力,随时用在其他的追求上。一个伦敦银行家,假如他想的话,也可以拥有世界上最具才智的社交圈。也许历来就很少有过像伦敦私人银行家那样称心如意的境况,而且比那更称心的境况从来就没有过。

译后语

这一段文字描述和分析英国早期银行家的经营情况和人文素质，因为是写实，用词、造句皆根据所表达内容的需要，文笔务实、自然。多读这样的文字对于提高英语写作和翻译尤其有帮助。

以下是几处译文的说明。

1. 关于"Nothing +形容词比较级"

在英语里，句子的否定意义多用谓语动词+not 的形式来表达，也常用带否定意义的代词来表达，如 nothing 和 none。这两种表达方法，我们在阅读中常常见到，在写作里也常常使用。但 nothing 后面用形容词比较级做定语却是值得用心学习的句式，比如：

I can **imagine nothing better in theory or more successful in practice than** private banks as they were in the beginning.

这里的"nothing better in theory or more successful in practice than..."，是很好的英语表达方法，用得十分恰当、自然，应该学会使用。其句子结构并不复杂，翻译起来也不困难，但需将译文的语序和逻辑弄清楚，以再现原文句子的简洁和表现力。

2. 关于英语句子的重复现象

英语里的重复现象表现出两种相反的倾向。有时作者不要重复，是从审美角度考虑，如：Carolyn cries openly at times, Michael struggles not to.

有时作者要重复，是为了取得某种修辞效果，如：

(1) **His neighbours know him**, and trust him because **they know**

him.

这里是为了强调,译文要考虑再现这一效果:

他的邻居们了解他,因为了解而信任他。

(2) ... for the most part **he** spent his money there, and **speculated there** if **he speculated at all**.

……通常他是在那里花钱,在那里做风险交易——假如他做风险交易的话。

3. 省略句式"... and never perhaps a happier."

这是一个省略句式,同时其完整的形式也是一个副词前置的倒装句。就这个例句而言,汉译文应该是一个完整的句子:

……而且比那更称心的境况从来就没有过。

4. 表达方式的差异

英汉两种语言在表达同样意思时,或常常使用不同的表达方式,如:

... it was difficult for a man to ruin himself except at the place in which he lived...

这句话与汉语的习惯说法略有不同,汉语可以说:一个人在他居住的地方容易损坏自己的名声。阅读或翻译时需注意到这个差别。但按照原文语序直译也是可以的,这样在形式上能与原义更贴切。

5. 关于 position 的翻译

这篇文章有三处用了 position:

(1) ... it was possible for most persons to ascertain ... **the real position** of conspicuous persons...

(2) Such a **position** is indeed singularly favourable.

(3) There has probably very rarely ever been so happy a **posi-**

tion…

根据上下文，position 是指 situation，《牛津高阶英汉双解词典》（第六版）这样解释："the situation that sb is in, especially when it affects what they can or cannot do"，据此，译文里将 position 译成"状况""境况"等。

6. 值得再斟酌的译文

文中第二段里的"… many private bankers possessed **a variety of knowledge** and **a delicacy of attainment**"，其中的 a variety of knowledge 和 a delicacy of attainment 为名词短语的平行结构，翻译成汉语时需将其变成"形容词＋名词"的形式，前者并不困难，后者很费思索。attainment 的单数形式一般译为"成绩""成就"等，而如何处理 delicacy 才能与它修饰的名词构成合理的搭配，符合汉语表达习惯，深感力不从心。暂且将其译作"精巧的业绩"，仍觉牵强，有待再斟酌。

Henry Kingsley

亨利·金斯利(1830—1876),英国著名作家查尔斯·金斯利(Charles Kingsley,1819—1875)的弟弟,他在短暂的一生里写了 20 部小说,有 *Geoffrey Hamlyn* (1859)、*The Hillyars and the Burtons* (1865)、*Ravenshoe* (1861)等,其中 *Ravenshoe* 是他最好的作品,后文即选自该书。

The Children at a Wedding

Henry Kingsley

I waited till the procession had gone in, and then I found that the tail of it was composed of Gus, Flora, and Archy, with their nurse. If a bachelor is worth his salt, he will make himself useful. I saw that nurse was in distress and anxious, so I stayed with her.

Archy was really as good as gold till he met with his accident. He walked up the steps with nurse as quiet as possible. But even at first I began to get anxious about Gus and Flora. They were excited. Gus wouldn't walk up the steps; but he put his two heels together, and jumped up them one at a time, and Flora walked backwards, looking at him sarcastically. At the top step but one Gus stumbled; whereupon Flora said, "Goozlemy, goozlemy, goozlemy."

And Gus said, "You wait a minute, my lady, till we get into church," after which awful speech I felt as if I was smoking in a powder magazine.

I was put into a pew with Gus, and Flora, and Archy. Nurse, in her modesty, went into the pew behind us.

I am sorry to say that these dear children, with whom I had no

婚礼上的孩子们

亨利·金斯利

等参加婚礼的队伍进了教堂，我才发现走在最后的是格斯、弗洛拉、阿尔奇，还有他们的保姆。一个单身汉要想受人尊敬，就要让自己成为有用的人。我看见保姆忧心忡忡的样子就留下来陪她。

阿尔奇在出事之前乖极了。他跟保姆上台阶时要多安静有多安静。但一开始我就担心格斯和弗洛拉。他们挺激动的。格斯上台阶时不是一步一步往上走，而是两个脚后跟并拢一级一级往上跳；弗洛拉则转过身来倒着上，带着讥笑的神情看着他。还差一级台阶就到头时，格斯绊倒了，弗洛拉说："好哟，好哟，好哟！"

格斯说："你等着吧，我的小姐，进了教堂再说。"听了这句可怕的话，我感觉好像我正在弹药库里吸烟似的。

我和格斯、弗洛拉和阿尔奇一起被安排坐在一个包厢里。保姆谦让，坐在我们身后的包厢里。

这些宝贝孩子们（从前我不认识）太淘气了，我

previous acquaintance, were very naughty. The ceremony began by Archy getting too near the edge of his hassock, falling off, pitching against the pew door, bursting it open, and flying out among the free seats, head foremost. Nurse, a nimble and dexterous woman, dashed out, and caught him up, and actually got him out of the church door before he had time to fetch his breath for a scream. Gus and Flora were left alone with me.

Flora had a great scarlet and gold church service. As soon as she opened it, she disconcerted me by saying aloud, to an imaginary female friend, "My dear, there is going to be a collection; and I have left my purse on the piano."

At this time, also, Gus, seeing that the business was well begun, removed to the further end of the pew, sat down on the hassock, and took from his trousers' pocket a large tin trumpet.

I broke out all over in a cold perspiration as I looked at him. He saw my distress, and putting it to his lips, puffed out his cheeks. Flora administered comfort to me. She said, "You are looking at that foolish boy. Perhaps he won't blow it, after all. He mayn't if you don't look at him. At all events, he probably won't blow it till the organ begins; and then it won't matter so much."...

I wish those dear children (not meaning them any harm) had been, to put it mildly, at play on the village green, that blessed day.

When I looked at Gus again, he was still on the hassock, threatening propriety with his trumpet. I hoped for the best. Flora had her prayer-book open, and was playing the piano on each side of

很抱歉这么说他们。仪式一开始，阿尔奇因为跪在太靠垫子边缘的地方而掉了下来，撞在包厢门上，把门撞开，一头扎进外面空座位中间。保姆动作敏捷，冲出去一把抓住他，还没等他来得及叫唤就把他弄到教堂门外了。包厢里只剩下了格斯、弗洛拉和我。

弗洛拉做了一个非常精彩的礼拜仪式。她一开始就对一个想象出来的女性朋友大声说："我亲爱的，一会儿要举行募捐的，我把钱包留在钢琴上了。"她这么一说可把我弄糊涂了。

这时，格斯见婚礼仪式已经开始，便挪到包厢最远的一端，坐在跪垫上，从裤子口袋里掏出一个挺大的镀锡喇叭。

我看着他时出了一身冷汗。他看见我焦虑的样子，便把喇叭放在嘴唇上，鼓起了嘴巴。弗洛拉安慰我说："你在看着那个傻孩子，他也许不会吹的。你要是不看他，他也许就不吹了。反正风琴开始演奏前他也许不会吹的，那就不要紧了。"……

说得好听一点，我真希望在那个幸福的日子里这些宝贝孩子（不是在说他们的坏话）正在乡村草地上玩耍。

我再看格斯时，他仍坐在跪垫上，要吹喇叭胡闹。但愿他别那样。弗洛拉打开祈祷书，用手指在书的两个页面上做出弹钢琴的样子。过了一会儿，

it, with her fingers. After a time she looked up at me, and said out loud—

"I suppose you have heard that Archy's cat has kittened?"

I said, "No."

"Oh, yes, it has," she said. "Archy harnessed it to his meal cart, which turns a mill, and plays music when the wheels go round; and it ran downstairs with the cart; and we heard the music playing as it went; and it kittened in the wood-basket immediately afterwards; and Alwright says she don't wonder at it; and no more do I; and the steward's-room boy is going to drown some. But you mustn't tell Archy, because, if you do, he won't say his prayers; and if he don't say his prayers, he will—etc., etc." Very emphatically, and in a loud tone of voice.

This was very charming. If I could only answer for Gus, and keep Flora busy, it was wildly possible that we might pull through. If I had not been a madman, I should have noticed that Gus had disappeared.

He had. And the pew door had never opened, and I was utterly unconscious. Gus had crawled up, on all fours, under the seat of the pew, until he was opposite the calves of his sister's legs, against which calves, *horresco referens*, he put his trumpet and blew a long shrill blast. Flora behaved very well and courageously. She only gave one long, wild shriek, as from a lunatic in a padded cell at Bedlam, and then, hurling her prayer-book at him, she turned round and tried to kick him in the face.

她看着我,大声说:“我想,你可能听说阿尔奇的猫生小猫咪了吧?”

我说:“没有呀。”

“咳,生了,她生了。”她说,“阿尔奇把她套在饭车上,车就转圆圈,轱辘一转就响音乐;猫随车下了楼;车下去时我们听见音乐了;然后猫就在木板筐里生了一窝小猫咪;阿尔赖特说她并不感到惊讶,我也不感到惊讶;管家的孩子要扔到水里淹死几只。可你不许告诉阿尔奇,你要告诉他,他就不祈祷了;他要是不祈祷,他就会——怎么怎么样。”她特别强调这一点,说话声音还很大。

这真是太好了。我要是能对格斯负责,也能让弗洛拉忙着,我们很可能就平安无事了。我若不是很愚蠢的话,本来是可以注意到格斯已经消失了。

他是消失了。包厢门从来没有打开过,因此我完全没有意识到。格斯从包厢座位底下爬上来了,一直爬到他妹妹小腿肚子跟前,提起这件事让我不寒而栗,他把喇叭口对着她的腿肚子嗡儿地吹了一声,声音又尖又长。弗洛拉表现很好,也很勇敢。她只是尖着嗓子拉长声猛地一叫,好像精神病院软壁病房里患者的叫声,然后,她拿起祈祷书朝他扔了过去,又转身冲他的脸踢去。

This was the culminating point of my misfortunes. After this, they behaved better ... Gus only made an impertinent remark about Flora's garters, and Flora only drew a short, but trenchant, historical parallel between Gus and Judas Iscariot.

我的不幸遭遇到此已经达到高潮。此后，他们表现好些了……格斯只是针对弗洛拉的吊袜带说了几句粗鲁的话，弗洛拉也只是做了一个简短但很尖锐的比喻，她把格斯说成历史上的犹大[①]。

① 《圣经》中背叛了耶稣的门徒。

译后语

就这篇文章简单说说语言的幽默：

这里是一个单身汉从第一人称视角讲故事，故事有五个人：单身汉、保姆和三个孩子。在进教堂参加婚礼时，单身汉看见保姆带着三个孩子面有愁色，便主动留下来帮忙；他不是以直白的语言而是以委婉的方式接近她，向她示好。进了教堂以后，他发现孩子们很淘气，但很可爱；他不是以平叙的方式而是以夸张的手法描述孩子们的表现。读者从文章里委婉和夸张的词句可以感受到一种幽默，幽默总是含蓄的。

(1) If a bachelor is worth his salt, he will make himself useful. I saw that nurse was in distress and anxious, so I stayed with her.

"我"(单身汉)看见保姆带孩子进教堂时有为难之感，便决定做点好事，帮她照管孩子，以示自己是个称职的单身汉，以期得到保姆的尊敬和好感。(委婉)

(2) And Gus said, "You wait a minute, my lady, till we get into church," after which awful speech I felt as if I was smoking in a powder magazine.

"我"听到格斯要报复弗洛拉，担心出事，好像正在弹药库里吸烟，会引起爆炸一样。(夸张)

(3) I broke out all over in a cold perspiration as I looked

at him.

"我"看见格斯在婚礼仪式上掏出喇叭要吹，出了一身冷汗。（夸张）

(4) She only gave one long, wild shriek, as from a lunatic in a padded cell at Bedlam...

这里使用了比喻，好像精神病院软壁病房里病患者的叫声。（夸张）

(5) This was the culminating point of my misfortunes.

把"我"和这些孩子在一起的经历说成"不幸遭遇"。（夸张）

(6) ... and Flora only drew a short, but trenchant, historical parallel between Gus and Judas Iscariot.

弗洛拉把格斯比喻成历史上的犹大。（夸张）

以上几个以委婉和夸张手法写出来的句子都渗透着一种幽默，善意的幽默，读来产生美感。

委婉和夸张的叙事方式为文章创造了幽默氛围，仔细阅读原文，细致体会其语言特色，翻译时选择恰当的词汇，组织相当的句子结构，考虑相应的行文语气，能够把原文的幽默氛围移植到译文里。

Leonard Courtney

伦纳德·考特尼(1832—1918),英国政治家、文人,曾做过律师、记者和政治经济学教师。后文选自他的 *Adresses* (1908—1909)。

Justice

Leonard Courtney

If we could get rid of injustice! How shall we labour to bring about that great result? How shall we get the rulers of nations to cease to aspire to obtain power over others; how shall we get the members of nations to be just to one another, so that they shall not even tolerate the thought of wrong doing? How shall we get amongst the nations what we have succeeded in obtaining within nations—a reference to law instead of to force, an appeal to the privileges and powers of society for enforcing justice, instead of a resort on one's own account to the force which one may command to compel justice? How, I say, can we hope to bring about this great result?

After all, the machinery of justice involves this fundamental notion, that when two persons are in disagreement there is a tribunal to which they can appeal. In a perfect form that tribunal is always in action, and each of the litigants can compel the other to come before it. Then you have established a law which does away with private violence, and if you got that among the nations you would have a law that did away with national violence.

正　义

伦纳德·考特尼

要是我们能摆脱不公正现象有多好啊！我们怎样努力才能实现这一美好的愿景呢？我们怎样才能让各国的统治者不再追求主宰别的国家？我们怎样才能让各国之间公正相处，这样，他们甚至连作恶的念头都不能容忍？我们怎样才能在国与国之间做到我们在国内已经做到的事情——诉诸法律而不是诉诸武力，呼吁运用公民的基本权利和社会力量来实施正义，而不是为了自身的利益而诉诸武力，强行实施正义？我说，我们怎样才能实现这一美好的愿景呢？

说到底，正义的机制包含这样一个基本的观念：当两个人有了纷争时，他们可以诉请法庭裁决。法庭总是以完善的形式运作，诉讼人可以迫使另一方出庭。那么，你就建立起一个排除个人之间发生暴力的法律，如果在国家之间也那样做，你就有了一个排除国家之间发生暴力的法律。

The first thing to which I would direct your attention is to use all your powers, all your opportunities to develop the strength, the scope, the purity of international law. Do as much as you can as individuals, influence your rulers as much as you can as citizens of free communities, to develop, strengthen, and purify international law—international law which rises above the separate nations, just as the municipal law of a community rises above its separate citizens.

The temptation to lust and rapine of unchecked human nature is under coercion in every society; and lovers of the larger civilization of the world must rejoice in the restraint of temptation which is found in compacts of international peace.

Without justice we can have no guarantee of permanent peace. With justice the peace of the world is unassailable.

我想提醒你们注意的第一件事是，运用你们所有的能力、所有的机会，来强化国际法的力量，扩大国际法的范围，并发展国际法的纯洁性。尽你们作为个人之所能，尽你们作为自由社会公民之所能，来影响你们的统治者，让他们发展、强化和纯洁国际法——超越各个国家的国际法，就像一个社会超越各个公民的国内法那样。

没有节制的人性对于欲望和掠夺的诱惑在每一个社会里都受到抑制，而热爱世界更广泛文明的人们一定会因为这一诱惑得到控制而感到欣慰，这一控制在国际和平的协议上体现出来。

没有正义，我们就不能保证有永久的和平。有了正义世界和平就牢不可破。

译后语

1. 排比句(parallelism)

这是一篇演说词,演说者为了把意思说清楚,取得好的效果,在这里使用了比较多的排比句(parallelism)。所谓排比句,就是句子中的各个成分,或整个句子、段落,或更大单位的平行安排,在意义上具有相同分量的成分,在结构上用相同的形式表现,也就是并列的概念以并列的结构来表现。例如:

He was possessed of a moral and physical courage which was equal to every emergency in which he was placed; **calm amidst excitement, patient under trials, never unduly elated by victory or depressed by defeat.**

这是谈美国南北战争中北军主帅尤里西斯·S.格兰特将军(Ulysses S. Grant,1822—1885,后成为美国第18届总统)在战争中的表现。这里,calm amidst excitement 和"patient under trials, never unduly elated by victory or depressed by defeat"就是句子中的并列成分。

在本文的第一个自然段里,以"How shall/can we"的相同结构开头的问句一连重复五次,形成了在句子层级上的排比句:

句(1) **How shall we** labour to bring about that great result?

句(2) **How shall we** get the rulers of nations to cease to aspire to obtain power over others;

句(3) **how shall we** get the members of nations to be just to one another...?

句(4) **How shall we** get amongst the nations what we have succeeded in obtaining within nations...?

句(5) **How**, I say, **can we** hope to bring about this great result?

句(5)与前四句在形式上略有区别,但基本结构一致。

下面的两句话是主从复合句,其中构成并列成分的是主句的宾语及其定语从句:

句(1) Then you have established a law which does away with private violence...

句(2) ... you would have a law that did away with national violence.

2. 对偶句(antithesis)

对偶也是常见的修辞手段,如《红楼梦》里刘姥姥说的"谋事在人,成事在天",霍克思译为"Man proposes, God disposes"。在这篇文章里,有一个很好的例子:

Without justice we can have no guarantee of permanent peace. **With justice** the peace of the world is unassailable.

其中,Without justice 和 With justice 构成对偶。演讲者为了取得他所期待的效果,运用排比和对偶的句式,以其特有的声音和节奏产生一种气势,给听众留下深刻印象。翻译这样的文章,一要让句子流畅,二要让句子有力,句子的流畅和力量带来美感。

James Whistler

詹姆斯·惠斯勒(1834—1903),美国画家。后文“Nature and Art”选自他的关于艺术的书信和评论集 *The Gentle Art of Making Enemies*。

Nature and Art

James Whistler

Nature contains the elements, in colour and form, of all pictures, as the keyboard contains the notes of all music.

But the artist is born to pick, and choose, and group with science, these elements, that the result may be beautiful—as the musician gathers his notes, and forms his chords, until he brings forth from chaos glorious harmony.

To say to the painter, that Nature is to be taken as she is, is to say to the player, that he may sit on the piano. ...

The dignity of the snow-capped mountain is lost in distinctness, but the joy of the tourist is to recognize the traveller on the top. The desire to see, for the sake of seeing, is, with the mass, alone the one to be gratified, hence the delight in detail.

And when the evening mist clothes the riverside with poetry, as with a veil, and the poor buildings lose themselves in the dim sky, and the tall chimneys become campanili, and the warehouses are palaces in the night, and the whole city hangs in the heavens, and fairy-land is before us—then the wayfarer hastens home; the working

自然与艺术

詹姆斯·惠斯勒

就色彩和形式而论，大自然包含所有图画的成分，就像琴的键盘包含所有乐曲的音符一样。

艺术家的天职是从这些成分中进行挑选，将它们科学地组合在一起，结果就可能是一幅美丽的画，就像音乐家用音符谱成和音，从无序的声音中创作出动听而和谐的乐曲一样。

如果对画家说他可以依照大自然本来的样子进行创作，就等于对演奏家说他可以一屁股坐在钢琴的琴键上。……

白雪覆盖的高山因为清晰可见而失去它的庄严，但旅游者却因能看见山顶上的人而喜形于色。大多数人只是为了看清而已，他们是要使自己的愿望得到满足，因此仅以能看清细节为快。

傍晚，富有诗意的迷雾像面纱一样笼罩着河边，破旧的建筑消失在朦胧的天空，高高的烟囱变成一座座钟楼，仓库恍如夜间的宫殿，整个城市悬在空中，宛若仙境展现在我们眼前，这时路上的人

man and the cultured one, the wise man and the one of pleasure, cease to understand, as they have ceased to see, and Nature, who, for once, has sung in tune, sings her exquisite song to the artist alone, her son and her master—her son in that he loves her, her master in that he knows her.

To him her secrets are unfolded, to him her lessons have become gradually clear. He looks at her flower, not with the enlarging lens, that he may gather facts for the botanist, but with the light of the one who sees in her choice selection of brilliant tones and delicate tints, suggestions of future harmonies.

He does not confine himself to purposeless copying, without thought, each blade of grass, as commended by the inconsequent, but, in the long curve of the narrow leaf, corrected by the straight tall stem, he learns how grace is wedded to dignity, how strength enhances sweetness, that elegance shall be the result.

In the citron wing of the pale butterfly, with its dainty spots of orange, he sees before him the stately halls of fair gold, with their slender saffron pillars, and is taught how the delicate drawing high upon the walls shall be traced in tender tones of orpiment, and repeated by the base in notes of graver hue.

In all that is dainty and lovable he finds hints for his own combinations, and *thus* is Nature ever his resource and always at his service, and to him is naught refused.

Through his brain, as through the last alembic, is distilled the refined essence of that thought which began with the Gods, and

们正匆匆赶路回家；劳动者和文化人，智者和寻乐者，因为他们再也看不见什么，他们也就再也不能理解，这时已经开始歌唱的大自然便把她美妙的歌只唱给艺术家——她的儿子和她的主人；说他是儿子是因为他爱她，说他是主人是因为他理解她。

只有对他，她才展现她的秘密；只有对他，她的含义才逐渐变得清晰。他观察着她的花朵，不是用为植物学家采集数据的放大镜，而是用一种光；他用这种光在她所选择的灿烂的色调和微妙的色彩中看见未来和谐的画面。

他不是像不谙此道的人们所赞扬的那样，不加思索地盲目描摹每一片草叶；他看到在又高又直的茎秆衬托下叶片的细长弧线，从中认识到优雅如何与庄严融为一体，力量如何增加甜美，随之而来的是高雅的艺术。

从淡色蝴蝶那带有鲜艳橘黄斑点的香橼色翅膀，他看见庄严的金色大厅以及里面又细又高的金黄顶柱，而且明白了怎样在墙面上方用轻柔的雌黄色、在下方用较暗的色调将精妙的图画绘制下来。

从所有娇巧和可爱的事物里，他都能得到如何搭配色调的启示，这样，大自然就成了供他汲取的资源，总是为他服务，从不拒绝提供任何东西。

通过他的大脑，如同通过最后一道蒸馏器，那始自诸神并由诸神委托他去实现的思想的精髓便

which they left him to carry out.

Set apart by them to complete their works, he produces that wondrous thing called the masterpiece, which surpasses in perfection all that they have contrived in what is called Nature; and the Gods stand by and marvel, and perceive how far away more beautiful is the Venus of Melos than was their own Eve.

提炼出来了。

由于受到诸神的青睐去完成他们的作品，他创作了被称之为杰作的绝妙之作，其完美程度超出诸神在大自然里所创造的一切；他们站在一旁，惊叹不已，并发现米洛斯岛上的维纳斯雕像比他们自己的夏娃要美丽得多。

译后语

这篇文章讲述自然、艺术与艺术家的关系，用三个比喻说明艺术和自然的关系；艺术家的创作基于自然，但艺术创作又不是照搬自然。第四、五、六段说艺术家与常人不同，艺术家能在白雪覆盖的山峦和夜幕降临的河边发现美。艺术家是自然的骄子，因为他热爱自然；也是自然的主人，因为他了解自然。第七、八、九、十段说自然是艺术创作的源泉，但它只有经过艺术家的创作才能成为艺术。最后一段说艺术家的杰作比自然界的东西更美。

文章里的修辞值得学习：

1. 比喻(simile，metaphor)

前三段是三个比喻：

(1) Nature contains the elements, in colour and form, of all pictures, as the keyboard contains the notes of all music.

(2) But the artist is born to pick, and choose, and group with science, these elements, that the result may be beautiful—as the musician gathers his notes, and forms his chords, until he brings forth from chaos glorious harmony.

(3) To say to the painter, that Nature is to be taken as it is, is to say to the player, that he may sit on the piano. ...

第五段里也有几个很好的比喻。

2. 省略句式(fragmentary elliptical sentences)

The desire to see, for the sake of seeing, is, with the mass, alone the one to be gratified, hence the delight in detail.

... and Nature, who, for once, has sung in tune, sings her exquisite song to the artist alone, her son and her master—her son in that he loves her, her master in that he knows her.

这种省略句式使句子简洁，节奏快，内涵丰富。

3. 排比句式(parallelism)

在第七、八、九三个段落里，作者有意重复一个相同的句式：

(1) ... but, in the long curve of the narrow leaf... he learns...

(2) In the citron wing of the pale butterfly... he sees...

(3) In all that is dainty and lovable, he finds...

这几个段落间的排比强调自然是艺术创作的源泉，艺术家在自然中发现美。

4. 拟人(personification)

文章里有几处使用了拟人修辞手法：

(1) Nature... sings her exquisite song to the artist alone...

(2) He looks at her flower...

5. 连词 and 的叠用(polysyndeton)

第五段开头有这样一句：

And when the evening mist clothes the riverside with poetry, as with a veil, and the poor buildings lose themselves in the dim sky, and the tall chimneys become campanili, and the warehouses are palaces in the night, and the whole city hangs in the heavens, and fairy-land is before us—

金岳霖在《论翻译》中说："有一位英国文学家说'And the Lord said'这几个字神妙到不可言状。"如果说这几个字真是如此"神妙"，那是和 And 的运用有关系。这里一连用了六个 and,不仅将六个从句紧密连接起来,产生环境描写的渐增效果(cumulative effect),而且为全句创造了十分优美平和的节奏和意境,朗读一下就会感觉到这句话的节奏美和意境美。

还有一个例子,美国作家 William Maxwell 在 *New Yorker* 杂志上写过一篇名为"Billie Dyer"的文章,其中有一句话是这样的:

Her father and mother ran away and were caught and returned, and General Smith put her father on the block and he was sold to someone in the South and never heard of again.

这两段文字在 and 的使用上异曲同工。

这篇文章对译者(或作家)有很好的启示,因为文学创作和文学翻译都属艺术范畴。如果说"Nature contains the elements, in color and form, of all pictures",我们可以说"A language contains the elements, in words and expressions, of all writings."。如果说"But the artist is born to pick, and choose, and group with science, these elements, that the result may be beautiful",我们可以说"But the writer or translator is born to pick, and choose, and group with science, these elements, that the result may be beautiful."。

Robert Falcon Scott

罗伯特·福尔肯·斯科特(1868—1912),英国探险家,1901年至1904年,领导第一次南极探险发现之旅(Discovery),未成功。1911年开始第二次南极探险之旅(*Terra Nova*),1912年1月到达目的地。因为瑞典人 Roald Amundsen 在他之前一个月已经到达那里,他成为第二个到达南极的人。由于疲劳、饥饿以及恶劣的天气,斯科特和他的队员死在回程的路上,但因他的勇敢,他在英国被视为英雄。本文来自 *The Voyages of Captain Scott: Retold from "The Voyages of the 'Discovery'" and "Scott's Last Expedition"*(by Charles Turley)。

The Death of Captain Oates

Robert Falcon Scott (retold by Charles Turley)

On this same day a blizzard met them after they had marched for half an hour, and Scott seeing that not one of them could face such weather, pitched camp and stayed there until the following morning. Then they struggled on again with the sky so overcast that they could see nothing and consequently lost the tracks. At the most they gained little more than six miles during the day, and this they knew was as much as they could hope to do if they got no help from wind or surfaces. "We have 7 days' food and should be about 55 miles from One Ton Camp to-night, $6 \times 7 = 42$, leaving us 13 miles short of our distance, even if things get no worse."

Oates too was, Scott felt, getting very near the end. "What we or he will do, God only knows. We discussed the matter after breakfast; he is a brave fine fellow and understands the situation, but he practically asked for advice. Nothing could be said but to urge him to march as long as he could. One satisfactory result to the discussion: I practically ordered Wilson to hand over the means of ending our troubles to us, so that any of us may know how to do

奥茨上校之死

罗伯特·福尔肯·斯科特

（由查尔斯·特雷重述）

在这同一天，他们行进了半个小时之后便遇上暴风雪，斯科特认为他们当中没有人能扛得住这样的天气，于是搭起帐篷，在里面一直待到转天早晨。然后，他们又挣扎前进，天上阴云密布，什么也看不见，结果他们迷失了方向。白天他们顶多走了六英里，他们很清楚，在风向和地面都不利的情况下，他们也就能走这么远。"我们还有 7 天的食物，从今天夜里算起，我们离'囤食补给站'应该还有大约 55 英里，6×7=42，即使情况不再恶化，我们还剩下 13 英里的路程。"

斯科特觉得，奥茨也快不行了。"我们怎么办，或者他怎么办，只有上帝知道。吃完早饭，我们讨论了这件事；他是一个很勇敢很优秀的人，理解处境的艰难，可是他还是征求了大家的意见。除了敦促他能走多远就走多远，没有什么可说的。讨论取得令人满意的结果：我实际上给威尔逊下了命令，让他把摆脱困境的方法交出来，这样我们大家就知

so. Wilson had no choice between doing so and our ransacking the medicine case."

Thus Scott wrote on the 11th, and the next days brought more and more misfortunes with them. A strong northerly wind stopped them altogether on the 13th, and although on the following morning they started with a favourable breeze, it soon shifted and blew through their wind-clothes and their mits. "Poor Wilson horribly cold, could not get off ski for some time. Bowers and I practically made camp, and when we got into the tent at last we were all deadly cold... We *must* go on, but now the making of every camp must be more difficult and dangerous. It must be near the end, but a pretty merciful end... I shudder to think what it will be like tomorrow."

Up to this time, incredible as it seems, Scott had only once spared himself the agony of writing in his journal, so nothing could be more pathetic and significant than the fact that at last he was unable any longer to keep a daily record of this magnificent journey.

"Friday, March 16 or Saturday 17. Lost track of dates, but think the last correct," his next entry begins, but then under the most unendurable conditions he went on to pay a last and imperishable tribute to his dead companion.

"Tragedy all along the line. At lunch, the day before yesterday, poor Titus Oates said he couldn't go on; he proposed we should leave him in his sleeping-bag. That we could not do, and we

道如何做了。威尔逊别无选择,或者照我的命令办,或者我们把他的药箱洗劫一空。”

斯科特在11日的日志上这样写道。接下来的几天给他们带来了更多的不幸。13日那天,一股强劲的北风让他们彻底停了下来,虽然第二天早晨他们出发时刮了顺风,但风向很快就变了,把他们的防风衣和手套都吹透了。“可怜的威尔逊冷得要命,一时脱不下滑雪板。实际上只有鲍尔斯和我干扎营的活儿,当我们进到帐篷里面时,都快冻死了。……我们*必须*继续走,可是,现在支帐篷肯定更困难更危险了。肯定接近末日了,但求是个仁慈的末日……一想起明天会怎样,我就不寒而栗。”

到这时为止,斯科特只有一次没有痛心地写日志,这似乎难以置信。因此当他最终无法继续逐日记录这次壮丽的旅程时,没有什么比这更可悲,更能说明问题了。

下一段日志的开头是:“星期五,3月16日,或星期六,17日。忘记日期了,可我想后者是对的。”然后,在极难忍受的情况下,他写下了对死去的伙伴最后的永恒的哀悼。

“到处弥漫着悲哀。前天吃午饭时,可怜的泰特斯·奥茨说他走不动了,他建议我们把他留在睡袋里。我们不能那样做,我们劝他下午行进时加把

induced him to come on, on the afternoon march. In spite of its awful nature for him he struggled on and we made a few miles. At night he was worse and we knew the end had come.

"Should this be found I want these facts recorded. Oates' last thoughts were of his Mother, but immediately before he took pride in thinking that his regiment would be pleased with the bold way in which he met his death. We can testify to his bravery. He has borne intense suffering for weeks without complaint, and to the very last was able and willing to discuss outside subjects. He did not—would not—give up hope till the very end. He was a brave soul. This was the end. He slept through the night before last, hoping not to wake; but he woke in the morning—yesterday. It was blowing a blizzard. He said, 'I am just going outside and may be some time.' He went out into the blizzard and we have not seen him since.

"I take this opportunity of saying that we have stuck to our sick companions to the last. In case of Edgar Evans, when absolutely out of food and he lay insensible, the safety of the remainder seemed to demand his abandonment, but Providence mercifully removed him at this critical moment. He died a natural death, and we did not leave him till two hours after his death.

"We knew that poor Oates was walking to his death, but though we tried to dissuade him, we knew it was the act of a brave man and an English gentleman. We all hope to meet the end with a similar spirit, and assuredly the end is not far."

劲。尽管对他来说这难以忍受，他还是挣扎着继续往前走，我们又前进了几英里。夜里，他的状况更糟了，我们知道末日已经来临。”

“假如这个情况将来能被发现，我希望这些事实被记入史册。”奥茨临终前想到他的母亲，可是，紧接着，他想到他的兵团会因为他勇敢面对死亡而感到欣慰，他便流露出自豪的神情。我们可以证实他的勇敢。几个星期以来，他忍受着极大的痛苦而不抱怨，直到最后，他还能够也愿意讨论外面的事情。至死他也没有——也不肯——放弃希望。他是个勇敢的人。最后的情况是这样的：前天夜里他睡了一夜，希望不再醒来，可是，昨天早晨他还是醒了。外面暴风雪肆虐。他说：‘我想出去一下，也许去一会儿。’于是，他走进了暴风雪，我们再也没见到他。

“我想利用这个机会说一说，我们一直陪伴着有病的伙伴，直到最后。比如埃德加·埃文斯，我们什么吃的都没有了，他也处于昏迷状态，为了其余人的安全，看来必须遗弃他，可是，就在这个关键时刻，上帝以仁慈的方式让他离开了。他安详地死去了，两个小时以后我们才离开。

“我们知道，可怜的奥茨自己出去是走向死亡，虽然我们尽力劝阻他，可我们知道那是一个勇敢者和英国绅士的行为。我们都希望以同样的精神迎接末日，肯定地讲，末日已经不远了。”

译后语

“The Death of Captain Oates”选自 *Scott's Last Expedition*，以日记形式描写英国南极探险队员在回程路上勇敢面对死亡的悲壮场景。

因为这篇文章主要内容是日记（当属应用文），其叙事的文字有其文体方面的特征：一是句子常有省略。

(1) One satisfactory result to the discussion:...

这里省略了 There was:“讨论取得令人满意的结果：……”

(2) Poor Wilson horribly cold, could not get off ski for some time.

这句话的前面部分省略了 was:“可怜的威尔逊冷得要命，一时脱不下滑雪板。”

(3) “Friday, March 16 or Saturday 17. Lost track of dates, but think the last correct,”

这个句子有两处省略了主语 I:“(I) Lost track of dates, but (I) think the last correct”(“星期五，3 月 16 日，或星期六，17 日。忘记日期了，可我想后者是对的”)。

(4) Tragedy all along the line.

这里或者省略了 There was，或者省略了 Tragedy 的谓语动词，如 prevailed 之类：“到处弥漫着悲哀”。

翻译时，有时汉语句子与英语省略的句式相似，如，例(2)省略了 was，其汉语译文“可怜的威尔逊冷得要命”也不需要“是”字。但汉语有时则需要将原文省略部分补上，如，例(1)的"取得"、例(3)的"我"和例(4)的"弥漫"等。

二是句子简洁，偶尔也使用简便形式。例如：

"We have 7 days' food and should be about 55 miles from One Ton Camp to night, 6×7=42, leaving us 13 miles short of our distance, even if things get no worse."

句子里的数字一律是阿拉伯数字，而且出现了乘法公式6×7=42。作为日记，译成汉语也未尝不可这样写(但一般情况下，汉语文章对于如何使用阿拉伯数字是有规定的)，于是：

> "我们还有7天的食物，从今天夜里算起，我们离'囤食补给站'应该还有大约55英里，6×7=42，即使情况不再恶化，我们还剩下13英里的路程。"

在寒冷饥饿的条件下写日记，文字简洁，句子简短，是很自然的。例如：

This was the end. He slept through the night before last, hoping not to wake; but he woke in the morning—yesterday. It was blowing a blizzard. He said, "I am just going outside and may be some time." He went out into the blizzard and we have not seen him since.

这小段里的句子很简洁，很简短，译文也应随原文尽量使句子简洁些，简短些：

> 最后的情况是这样的：前天夜里他睡了一夜，希望不再醒来；可是，昨天早晨他还是醒了。外面暴风雪肆虐。他说："我想出去一下，也许去一会儿。"于是，他走进了暴风雪，我们再也没见到他。

William Stanley Jevons

威廉·斯坦利·杰文斯(1835—1882),英国逻辑学家和经济学家。后文选自他的 *The Principles of Science*。

True Science

William Stanley Jevons

From science, modestly pursued, with a due consciousness of the extreme finitude of our intellectual powers, there can arise only nobler and wider notions of the purpose of Creation. Our philosophy will be an affirmative one, not the false and negative dogmas of Auguste Comte, which have usurped the name, and misrepresented the tendencies of a true *positive philosophy*. True science will not deny the existence of things because they cannot be weighed and measured. It will rather lead us to believe that the wonders and subtleties of possible existence surpass all that our mental powers allow us clearly to perceive. The study of logical and mathematical forms has convinced me that even space itself is no requisite condition of conceivable existence. Everything, we are told by materialists, must be here or there, nearer or further, before or after. I deny this—and point to logical relations as my proof.

真正的科学

威廉·斯坦利·杰文斯

从我们所适度从事的科学研究里(当然也认识到我们的智力有很大的局限性),可以产生关于天地万物意义的更崇高、更宽泛的概念。我们的哲学将是肯定的哲学,不是奥古斯特·孔德[①]的虚假和否定的教条,他的教条已经篡夺了真正实证哲学的名义,歪曲了真正实证哲学的趋势。真正的科学不因事物无法衡量而否认它们的存在。这倒使我们相信可能存在的事物的神奇和微妙超过了我们智力的认识能力。对于逻辑和数学形式的研究使我相信,甚至连空间本身也不是可以想象得到的事物的存在的必要条件。唯物论者告诉我们,世界上的一切事物一定是存在着的,或是在这里或是在那里,或是在近处或是在远处,或是在以前或是在以后。我否认这种说法——而且,我要指出逻辑关系作为我的证据。

---

① 孔德(1798—1857),法国哲学家,实证主义和社会学创始人。

... So far am I from accepting Kant's doctrine that space is a necessary form of thought, that I regard it as an accident, and an impediment to pure logical reasoning. Material existences must exist in space, no doubt, but intellectual existences may be neither in space nor out of space; they may have no relation to space at all, just as space itself has no relation to time. For all that I can see, then, there may be intellectual existences to which both time and space are nullities.

Now among the most unquestionable rules of scientific method is that first law that *whatever phenomenon is, is*. We must ignore no existence whatever; we may variously interpret or explain its meaning and origin, but, if a phenomenon does exist, it demands some kind of explanation. If then there is to be competition for scientific recognition, the world without us must yield to the undoubted existence of the spirit within. Our own hopes and wishes and determinations are the most undoubted phenomenon within the sphere of consciousness. If men do act, feel, and live as if they were not merely the brief products of a casual conjunction of atoms, but the instruments of a far-reaching purpose, are we to record all other phenomena and pass over these? We investigate the instincts of the ant and the bee and the beaver, and discover that they are led by an inscrutable agency to work towards a distant purpose. Let us be faithful to our scientific method, and investigate also those instincts of the human mind by which man is led to work as if the approval of a Higher Being were the aim of life.

我完全不能接受康德[①]的信条，即空间是思想的必要形式，我认为这是非本质属性，而且它妨碍了纯粹的逻辑推理。物质的东西一定存在于空间，这毫无疑问，可是，智力可能既不存在于空间之内，也不存在于空间之外；它也许和空间根本就没有关系，就像空间本身和时间没有关系一样。那么，就我所知，也许还存在着时间和空间对其都不起作用的智力。

在科学方法诸多最无可争议的规则里有一个首要的法则：不论是什么现象，现象就是存在。我们不能忽略任何的存在。我们可能用各种方式来阐明或解释它的意义和起源，可是，如果一个现象确实存在，它就要求某种解释。那么，如果为了得到科学的承认而出现了竞争，我们的外在世界就必须屈从于毫无疑问的内在精神的存在。我们自己的希望、愿望和决心是意识领域内最不可置疑的现象。假如人确实在行动，在感觉，在生活，似乎他们不只是由原子随意结合的短暂产物，而是为了实现某个长远目的的工具，难道我们要把所有其他现象都记录下来而偏偏绕过这些吗？我们观察研究蚂蚁、蜜蜂和海狸的本能，发现它们受一种难以捉摸的动因驱使，朝着一个遥远的目标而忙碌着。让我们忠实于我们的科学方法，也来观察研究人的头脑里的那些本能，人类凭借这些本能去工作，似乎把得到神灵的认可当作生活的目的。

---

① 康德(1724—1804)，德国哲学家，德国古典唯心主义哲学创始人。

译后语

这是一篇哲学论文，其语言有两个方面需要提出来略做说明，一是术语较多，二是句子较长。

1. 关于几个术语的翻译

翻译哲学文章，最好是读过一些哲学著作，具备一些哲学知识。而作为缺乏哲学专业知识的译者，翻译术语时主要是依据文本的上下文，参照词典，并结合日常积累的相关常识，力求将术语译得规范一些。如：

(1) Creation:《牛津高阶英汉双解词典》(*Oxford Advanced Learner's English-Chinese Dictionary*)解释为 the world and all the living things in it，即"世界"或"天地万物"。译文采用了后者，与上下文贴切。

(2) The purpose of Creation: purpose 可以作"目的"解，也可以作"意义"解，译文选择了"意义"，意思似乎更宽泛些。

(3) Positive philosophy:《英汉大词典》(陆谷孙主编)给的解释是"实证哲学"。

(4) Accident: 这是一个哲学或逻辑学词汇，《新牛津英语词典》(*The New Oxford Dictionary of English*)解释为"philosophy (in Aristotelian thought) a property of a thing which is not essential to its nature"，指事物的非本质属性。所以，译者将这个词所在的句子 that I regard it as an accident 译作"我认为这是非本质属性"。

尽管如此，术语的翻译仍难免有不符合规范的情况。

2. 关于几个长句的翻译

为了把句子所表达的概念说清楚，翻译时有时需要做些变通，如：

(1) From science, modestly pursued, with a due consciousness of the extreme finitude of our intellectual powers, there can arise only nobler and wider notions of the purpose of Creation.

这个句子比较长，主句之前有两个状语成分，为了把意思说清楚，句子也通顺，不妨将其主干"From science... there can arise..."部分突出，把句子的第二个状语 with a due consciousness of the extreme finitude of our intellectual powers 作为句子的主干部分的补偿成分放在括号内，这样可以使译文句子更紧凑。

如下所示：

从我们所适度从事的科学研究里（当然也认识到我们的智力有很大的局限性），可以产生关于天地万物意义的更崇高、更宽泛的概念。

(2) Our philosophy will be an affirmative one, not the false and negative dogmas of Auguste Comte, which have usurped the name, and misrepresented the tendencies of **a true *positive philosophy*.**

这个句子里有一个现象值得说一说，即 a true *positive philosophy* 作为定语既修饰 the name，也修饰 the tendencies，英语这样写是为了避免重复 a true *positive philosophy*，这是因为名词短语作定语时放在被修饰成分的后面，但在汉语里"真正实证哲学"作为定语需要重复，这是因为在汉语名词短语作定语是放在被修饰成分的前面。如下所示：

我们的哲学将是肯定的哲学，不是奥古斯特·孔德的虚假和否定的教条，他的教条已经篡夺了真正实证哲学的名义，歪曲了真正实证哲学的趋势。

(3) It will rather lead us to believe that the wonders and subtleties of possible existence surpass all that our mental powers allow us clearly to perceive.

这个句子也比较长，主要是“that”引起的宾语从句比较长，译文对其做了简化处理，如下所示：

这倒使我们相信可能存在的事物的神奇和微妙超过了我们智力的认识能力。

William Henry Hudson

威廉·亨利·哈德逊(1841—1922),英国作家、博物学者、鸟类学者。著述颇多,有*Green Mansions*(1904)、*Birds in Town and Village* (1920)和乌托邦小说*A Crystal Age* (1887)等。曾在作品中提出伊甸园乌托邦主题思想。后文"Pilgrims at the Land's End"选自*The Land's End*。文章通过对年迈旅行者的描述,表达暮年到来之时心境的苍凉和对世事的淡泊。另一篇"Birds and Death"则选自他的*Birds in Town and Village*。

Pilgrims at the Land's End

William Henry Hudson

There were days at the headland when I observed a goodish number of elderly men among the pilgrims, some very old, and this at first surprised me, but by-and-by it began to seem only natural. I was particularly impressed one day at noon in early spring in clear but cold weather with a biting north-east wind, when I found six or seven aged men sitting about on the rocks that lie scattered over the green slope behind the famous promontory. They were too old or too feeble to venture down on the rough headland: their companions had strayed away, some to the fishing cove, others along the higher cliffs, and left them there to rest. They were in great-coats with scarves and comforters round their necks, and hats or caps drawn well down; and they sat mostly in dejected attitudes, bending forward, their hands resting on the handles of their sticks, some with their chins on their hands, but all gazed in one direction over the

“陆地尽头”的朝圣者

威廉·亨利·哈德逊

在“陆地尽头”海岬[①]上，有几天我注意到来这里朝圣的人们当中有很多老年人，有的已经很老了。起初，我很惊讶，但渐渐觉得这不过是很正常的事情。给我印象特别深的是，早春的一天中午，天气晴朗，但是很冷，刮着刺骨的东北风。在那个著名的悬崖后面有一块绿草茵茵的斜坡，我看见六七个上了年纪的人坐在上面散落的岩石上。他们或因年纪太大或因身体太弱，不敢下到崎岖的海岬上：同行的人们都分头活动了，有的去了可捕鱼的小湾，有的爬到更高的悬崖上，留下他们在那里休息。他们都穿着厚厚的大衣，脖子上围着羊毛围巾，帽子拉得很低，坐在那里，大都情绪不高，身体向前佝偻着，手扶着拐杖握把，有的双手托着下巴，但全都把目光投向寒冷的灰蒙蒙的大海，凝视着同

① “陆地尽头”海岬（Land's End），又译为“兰兹角”，位于英格兰康沃尔郡最西端，因其悠久的历史而被视为圣地。

cold grey sea. Strangers to each other, unlike in life and character, coming from widely separated places, some probably from countries beyond the ocean, yet all here, silently gazing in one direction beyond that rocky foreland, with the same look of infinite weariness on their grey faces and in their dim sad eyes, as if one thought and feeling and motive had drawn them to this spot. Can it be that the sentiment or fancy which is sown in our minds in childhood and lies asleep and forgotten in us through most of our years, revives and acquires towards the end a new and strange significance when we have entered upon our second childhood? The period, I mean, when we recover our ancient mental possessions—the heirlooms which cannot be alienated or lost, which have descended to us from our remotest progenitors through centuries and thousands of years. These old men cannot see the objects which appear to younger eyes—the distant passing ships, and the land—that dim, broken line, as of a low cloud on the horizon, of the islands: their sight is altered from what it was, yet is, perhaps, now able to discern things invisible to us—other islands, uncharted, not the Cassiterides. What are they, these other islands, and what do we know of them? Nothing at all; indeed, nothing can be known to the generality; only these life-weary ancients, sitting on rocks and gazing at vacancy, might enlighten us if they would. Undoubtedly there are differ-

一个方向。他们互不相识，阅历不同，性格各异，又来自彼此相距遥远的地方，有的也许来自大洋彼岸的国度，然而，他们都到了这里，默默凝视着岩石嶙嶙的海岬外面同一个方向，灰暗苍老的脸上和黯淡悲凉的眼睛里都写着疲惫不堪的神情，似乎是同样的想法、同样的情感和动机把他们带到这个地方。也许是童年时播种于我们心中的情感或幻想，在沉睡并被忘记多年后，当我们进入第二童年[1]时又苏醒过来，在晚年获得了某种新奇的意义呢？我是指这一时期我们重新获得了远古的精神财富——那是远古的祖先历经千百年传给我们的传家宝，不能遗弃也不能失去。这些老人看不见出现在年轻人眼里的东西——远方航行的船只，还有陆地——群岛那模糊的不连贯的轮廓线，仿佛是低垂于地平线上的云：他们的视力已远不如从前，但他们现在也许能够看清我们看不见的东西——不是锡岛[2]，而是海图上未标明的别的岛屿。这些是什么岛屿呢，我们对它们了解多少呢？一点也不了解；的确，一般人是无法了解的；只有这些坐在岩石上茫然远望、对生活感到厌倦的老人，假如他们愿意的话，也许能启迪我们。毋庸置疑，他们所看到的景象是有

① 第二童年，指年长者认知能力下降，行为和判断力像儿童的时期。

② 锡岛(Cassiterides，源于希腊字 Κασσίτεροζ/Kassiteros)，位于西班牙西北方向的群岛，古代腓尼基人用物品交换锡的地方，故名锡岛。这个名称首次出现在古希腊历史学家希罗多德的著作里。

ences of sight among them which would make their descriptions vary, but they would probably all agree in affirming that the scene before them has no resemblance to the earlier vision. This grey-faced very old man with his chin on his hands, who looks as if he had not smiled these many years, would perhaps smile now if he were to recall that former vision, which came by teaching and served well enough during his hot youth and strenuous middle age. He does not see before him a beautiful blessed land bright with fadeless flowers, nor a great multitude of people in shining garments and garlands who will come down to the shore to welcome him with sounds of shouting and singing and playing on instruments of divers forms, and who will lead him in triumph to the gardens of everlasting delight and to mansions of crystal with emerald and amethyst colonnades and opal domes and turrets and pinnacles. Those glories and populous realms of joy have quite vanished: he sees now only what his heart desires—a silent land of rest. No person will greet him there; he will land and go up alone into that empty and solitary place, a still grey wilderness extending inland and upward hundreds of leagues, and immeasurable distance, into infinity, and rising to mountain ridges compared with which the Himalayas are but molehills. The sky in that still land is always pale grey-blue in colour, and the earth, too, is grey like the rocks, and the trees have a grey-green foliage—trees more ancient in appearance than the worn granite hills, with gnarled and buttressed trunks like vast towers and immense horizontal branches, casting a slight shade over many acres of ground . Onwards and upwards , with eyes downcast , he

差别的，因而他们的描述也各不相同。不过，他们大约都会承认，眼前的景象与他们早先之所见并无相同之处。这个双手托着下巴的神情忧郁的老者，看上去似乎多年不曾露过一丝笑容，假如他回想起往日的幻象——那来自别人教导的并在他激荡的青春时期和艰辛的中年岁月发挥过很好作用的幻象——他现在也许就微笑了。他再看不见眼前被永不凋谢的鲜花映得分外明媚的美丽的福地，也再看不见穿着华丽服饰戴着美丽花环的人群来到海滨，欢呼、唱歌、演奏各种各样的乐器来欢迎他，领他风风光光来到永乐花园和水晶宫里，那里环绕着镶有翡翠和紫水晶的柱廊，矗立着镶有猫眼石的圆顶，还有塔楼和尖顶。那些荣光和纷至沓来的喜悦已经消失：他现在看见的只是心之所盼——一块宁静的安息之地。在那里，不会有人去招呼他，他将独自走进那空旷寂寥的地方——那片静静的伸向内陆的灰暗的荒野，绵延逶迤，至千里之上，达无限之遥，然后耸起高高的山，与之相比，即使喜马拉雅山脉也变得不过小丘一般。在那块静寂的陆地上，天空总是淡淡的灰蓝色，土地也是石头一样的灰色，树木长着灰绿色的枝叶——那些树木看上去比风化的花岗岩小丘还要古老，长满节瘤的粗壮的树干有如硕大的塔，向外伸展的巨大树枝，将斑驳的阴影撒在数英亩的地面上。那老人眼睛看着地面，

will slowly take his devious way to the interior, feeling the earth with his staff, in search of a suitable last resting-place. And when he has travelled many, many leagues and has found it—a spot not too sunny nor too deeply shaded, where the old fallen dead leaves and dry moss have formed a thick soft couch to recline on and a grey exposed root winding over the earth offers a rest to his back—there at length he will settle himself. There he will remain motionless and contented for ever in that remote desert land where is no sound of singing bird nor of running water nor of rain or wind in the grey ancient trees: waking and sleeping he will rest there, dreaming little and thinking less, while year by year and age by age the memory of the world of passion and striving of which he was so unutterably tired grows fainter and fainter in his mind. And he will have neither joy nor sorrow, nor love nor hate, nor wish to know them any more; and when he remembers his fellow-men it will comfort him to think that his peace will never be broken by the sight of human face or the sound of human speech, since never by any chance will any wanderer from the world discover him in that illimitable wilderness.

继续向前走，向上爬，沿着曲折的小路向内陆慢慢走着，用手杖探路，寻找一个合适的最后安息之地。经过长途跋涉，他终于找到了——一个阳光柔和、树荫轻疏的地方，那里有陈年的落叶和干燥的苔藓，铺成厚厚的一片，像一张柔软的床，可以躺在上面安歇，裸露的灰色树根在地面上迂回蜿蜒，可供他倚着休息——他终于要在那里落脚了。他将一动不动、心满意足地永远留在那块遥远而荒芜的土地上；在那片古老的树林里，没有鸟儿啼鸣，没有流水潺潺，没有雨声，没有风声：不管是睡着还是醒着，他都将在那里休息，不做梦，更不思考，同时，年复一年，对于充满激情的世界的记忆，以及他为之而进行的奋斗（对此他已完全厌倦），在他心中已经变得越来越模糊。他将不再有喜悦，不再有悲伤，不再有爱，不再有恨，也不再想知道这一切；当他记起同伴时，想到他的宁静再也不会被人的面孔或声音所打破，他感到心安，因为世界上没有人会在那个无边无际的荒野上发现他。

（与卞建华合译）

译后语

这篇文章行文自然流畅，读来如行云流水，达到文学语言应有的美学境界。读者于不知不觉之中进入作者的思绪，融于文章的氛围，皆归功于其文笔之美。其行文特点有三：一是集中的主题和清晰的脉络，二是句子的衔接，三是长句的组织。

文章主题集中和脉络清晰是行文自然流畅的前提。“他”经过幻想的幼年时代、激荡的青春时期和艰辛的中年岁月，到了暮年，早先的激情和奋斗已经变得模糊；“他”现在很少做梦，想的更少，只想寻找一块宁静的安息之地，在那里，他只求不被人们打扰，便感到心安。这是作者对人生暮年的观察与理解。文章脉络清晰。先写“我”在海岬看到很多老年旅游者，“There were days at the headland when I observed **a goodish number of elderly men** among the pilgrims...”，这是作者最初看见的笼统的人数；其中有六七个上了年纪的人坐在散落的岩石上，“I was particularly impressed... when I found **six or seven aged men** sitting about on the rocks”，这给“我”留下特别深的印象；接着，作者对一个老者 **This grey-faced very old man** 做了细致具体的描写，写他忘记过去的荣光和喜悦、寻找安息之地的情形以及到达那里之后的心理。文章读来首尾贯通，一气呵成。

虽然文章衔接好，但句与句之间又没有过多使用连接成分，只有两处用了 and，如“**And** when he has travelled many, many leagues and has found it...”“**And** he will have neither joy nor sorrow...”，而

且都是出现在句首，这和在形式上起连接作用的 and 的用法略有不同，这里主要是在意义上起承上启下作用。同样出于衔接的考虑，文章多有句型的变化，除常用的陈述句之外，还有疑问句，如"Can it be that…?""What are they, these other islands, and what do we know of them?"还有句子开头形式的变化，如以独立主格形式开始的"Strangers to each other…"以副词开始的"Undoubtedly there are differences of sight…"和"There he will remain motionless and contented for ever…"，还有代词的使用等。这些句型的变化都有助于意义的连贯和行文的自然流畅。

此外，这篇文章有一个明显特点，长句子多，最长的近 80 个词。然而，由于英语严密的句法结构和作家灵活娴熟的文笔，句子读来并不觉生涩，文章也不觉冗长。翻译时，将很长的英语句子译成自然的汉语句子，除对文章行文特点要有宏观的了解，还需处理好句中的一些细节。

(1) I was particularly impressed one day at noon in early spring in clear but cold weather with a biting north-east wind, when I found six or seven aged men sitting about on the rocks that lie scattered over the green slope behind the famous promontory.

这句话的主句与它的状语从句间隔较大，由于主句带一个很长的时间状语"one day at noon in early spring in clear but cold weather with a biting north-east wind"，同时，从句也有一个很长的地点状语"on the rocks that lie scattered over the green slope behind the famous promontory"，这两个细节翻译时需处理好：

给我印象特别深的是，早春的一天中午，天气晴朗，但是很冷，刮着刺骨的东北风。在那个著名的悬崖后面有一块绿草茵茵的斜坡,我看见六七个上了年纪的人坐在上面散落的岩石上。

译文变换了句式,将原文的状语从句变为表语从句,将两个状语的位置做了调整,这样做是为了突出句子的核心意思,也使句子符合汉语的习惯,读来通顺自然。

(2) Can it be that the sentiment or fancy which is sown in our minds **in childhood** and lies asleep and forgotten in us **through most of our years**, revives and acquires **towards the end** a new and strange significance when we have entered upon our second childhood?

这句话以问句的形式谈到人生三个阶段的三种状态,童年时心中充满了情感或幻想,青壮年时期这些情感或幻想陷入沉睡并被忘记,老年时这些情感或幻想获得了某种新奇的意义。翻译时,首先能让"情感或幻想"这个概念贯穿人生三个时期,然后以问句的形式组织句子,主要是如何开头。这里做了如下处理:

也许是童年时播种于我们心中的情感或幻想,在沉睡并被忘记多年后,当我们进入第二个童年时又苏醒过来,在晚年获得了某种新奇的意义呢?

(3) **And** he will have neither joy nor sorrow, nor love nor hate, nor wish to know them any more; **and** when he remembers his fellow-men it will comfort him to think that his peace will never be broken by the sight of human face or the sound of human speech, since never by any chance will any wanderer from the world discover him in that illimitable wilderness.

这句话里有两个连接词 and,其作为连接词本身的意思并不重要,在这里主要是在意义上起承上启下作用,也使句子语气平和。它们没

有在译文里出现,但句子读起来仍然通顺自然。如:

> 他将不再有喜悦,不再有悲伤,不再有爱,不再有恨,也不再想知道这一切;当他记起同伴时,想到他的宁静再也不会被人的面孔或声音所打破,他感到心安,因为世界上没有人会在那个无边无际的荒野上发现他。

概括地说,这篇文章的句子虽然很长,但读来很自然很流畅:一是因为主题集中,脉络清晰;二是句子衔接好,主要是内在的因素起作用;三是长句的组织好。翻译时能处理好这几个方面及相关细节,译文就能够取得较好效果。

Birds and Death

William Henry Hudson

The bird, however hard the frost may be, flies briskly to his customary roosting-place, and, with beak tucked into his wing, falls asleep. He has no apprehensions; only the hot blood grows colder and colder, the pulse feebler as he sleeps, and at midnight, or in the early morning, he drops from his perch—dead.

Yesterday he lived and moved, responsive to a thousand external influences, reflecting earth and sky in his small brilliant brain as in a looking-glass; also he had a various language, the inherited knowledge of his race, and the faculty of flight, by means of which he could shoot, meteor-like, across the sky, and pass swiftly from place to place; and with it such perfect control over all his organs, such marvelous certitude in all his motions, as to be able to drop himself plumb down from the tallest tree-top, or out of the void air, on to a slender spray, and scarcely cause its leaves to tremble. Now, on this morning, he lies stiff and motionless; if you were to take him up and drop him from your hand, he would fall to the ground like a stone or a lump of clay—so easy and swift is the passage from life to death in wild nature! But he was never miserable.

鸟儿与死亡

威廉·亨利·哈德逊

不论霜有多么大，这只小鸟儿总是轻快地飞回它惯常栖息的地方，把嘴扎进翅膀里，就睡了。他无忧无虑；只是睡觉时身上的热血变得越来越冷，脉搏变得越来越弱，于是，半夜或拂晓时分，它从栖息的树枝上掉下来，死了。

昨天它还活着，还动着，对外界无数的影响反应敏锐，它那敏捷的小脑袋就像镜子一样反映着天地万物；而且，它的鸟语独特——这是该种鸟遗传下来的知识，而且它有飞行的天赋，能像流星一样划空而过，从一个地方迅速飞到另一个地方；借此天赋，它能完美地控制各个器官，在所有的动作中表现出令人惊奇的准确性，甚至能从高高的树梢上或天空中垂直而下，落在一棵纤细的花枝上，花枝上的叶子几乎一点也不颤动。现在，今天早晨，它却僵硬地一动不动地躺着。假如你把它拾起来，然后再放开手把它丢下去，它就像一块石头或一块土疙瘩一样掉在地上——自然界里从生到死的过程就是这样简单，这样迅速。可是它从未痛苦过。

译后语

这两段文字写小鸟，写小鸟的生与死，用了一些描写小鸟动作的词汇，如，“The bird… flies briskly”“with beak tucked into his wing”“he drops from his perch—dead”“he lived and moved”“he could shoot… across the sky, and pass swiftly from place to place”“he lies stiff and motionless”等。这些动词与小鸟动作的特点有关——轻、快、简单，同时，简单也符合小鸟从生到死的过程。

此文还有一个特点，用词简单，但句子较长，然而读起来并不觉得冗长臃肿，反而觉得意思清晰，行文轻松。译文似应再现这个效果。

Oliver Wendell Holmes

奥利弗·温德尔·霍姆斯(1809—1894),美国作家,同时代人认为他是美国 19 世纪最优秀作家之一,他也是哈佛大学医学院医学教授。他最初发表于 *The Atlantic Monthly* 上的系列随笔,后来收集在 *The Autocrat of Breakfast Table* (1858)一书中,后文"The Lost Sloop"即出自这本书。1882 年他从哈佛大学退休后,继续写作诗歌、小说和散文,直至 1894 年去世。

The Lost Sloop

Oliver Wendell Holmes

The firing of the great guns at the Navy-yard is easily heard at the place where I was born and lived. "There is a ship of war come in," they used to say, when they heard them. Of course, I supposed that such vessels came in unexpectedly, after indefinite years of absence,—suddenly as falling stones; and that the great guns roared in their astonishment and delight at the sight of the old war-ship splitting the bay with her cutwater. Now the sloop-of-war the Wasp, Captain Blakely, after gloriously capturing the Reindeer and the Avon, had disappeared from the face of the ocean, and was supposed to be lost. But there was no proof of it, and, of course, for a time, hopes were entertained that she might be heard from. Long after the last real chance had utterly vanished, I pleased myself with the fond illusion that somewhere on the waste of waters she was still floating, and there were years during which I never heard the sound of the great gun booming inland from the Navy-yard without saying to myself, "The Wasp has come!" and almost thinking I could see her, as she rolled in, crumpling the water before her,

失踪的战舰

奥利弗·温德尔·霍姆斯

我出生和居住的地方很容易听见海军船坞打炮的声音。“有战舰进港了。”人们听见炮声时常常这样说。当然啦，我想，这些船只一走多少年，突然像石头落地一样回来，人们会感到意外；当他们看见战舰的船头划开水面驶进港口，听见炮声轰隆隆响起时，真是又惊又喜。现在，黄蜂号战舰，在舰长布莱克利光荣地俘获“驯鹿”号和埃文号战舰以后，便从大洋上消失了，人们认为她失踪了。可是，这并没有得到证实，而且，当然，人们一时还抱有希望，希望还能听到她的消息。最后一个真正的机会彻底消失了，在那以后很久，我还在痴迷地幻想，认为她仍然漂流在人迹罕至的大洋上的什么地方，这样来哄自己高兴，而且，很多年来，我每每听见从海军船坞朝内地传来的炮声，总是自言自语道：“黄蜂号回来了！”我几乎想，当她风尘仆仆、乘风破浪回来时，船身附着甲壳动物，桅杆被折断，

weather-beaten, barnacled, with shattered spars and threadbare canvas, welcomed by the shouts and tears of thousands. This was one of those dreams that I nursed and never told. —Let me make a clean breast of it now and say, that, so late as to have outgrown childhood, perhaps to have got far on toward manhood, when the roar of the cannon has struck suddenly on my ear, I have started with a thrill of vague expectation and tremulous delight, and the long unspoken words have articulated themselves in the mind's dumb whisper, *The Wasp has come*!

船帆破得露出线来，我能看见成千上万的人们眼含泪水大声欢呼着迎接她返航。这是我心中的一个梦想，从未对人讲过，现在让我都说出来吧，及至后来走出孩童时代，也许快到成年的时候，每当轰轰的炮声突然在我的耳际响起，我就一惊，心中隐约的期待和令我全身颤抖的愉悦让我激动不已，我便在心中不由自主地小声说出长期未曾说过的话——黄蜂号回来啦！

译后语

关于英语被动语态

在英语里被动语态使用频率比汉语高，在较多情况下译成汉语时需将其变成主动语态。下面三个句子的行为实施者没有在句子里出现，出现的只是行为的被实施者。如：

(1) The firing of the great guns at the Navy-yard is easily heard at the place where I was born and lived.

我出生和居住的地方很容易听见海军船坞打炮的声音。

(2) Now the sloop-of-war the Wasp... had disappeared from the face of the ocean, and was supposed to be lost.

现在，黄蜂号战舰……便从大洋上消失了，人们认为她失踪了。

(3) But there was no proof of it, and, of course, for a time, hopes were entertained that she might be heard from.

可是，这并没有得到证实，而且，当然，人们一时还抱有希望，希望还能听到她的消息。

Archibald Philip Primrose

阿奇博尔德·菲利普·普里姆罗斯(1847—1929),第五代罗斯伯里伯爵(Earl of Rosebery),英国自由党政治家。1855年,加入首相格拉德斯通(William Ewart Gladstone)内阁,历任外交部部长等职。1894年,格拉德斯通辞职,普里姆罗斯接任英国首相,任期很短。"The Elder and the Younger Pitts"一文选自 *Pitt*。

The Elder and the Younger Pitts

Archibald Philip Primrose

It is perhaps unnecessary to say more of the circumstances and surroundings of Pitt. But it is impossible to complete any sketch of his career, or indeed to form an adequate estimate of his character, without setting him, if only for a moment, by the side of Chatham. Not merely are they father and son; not merely are they the most conspicuous English Ministers of the eighteenth century; but their characters illustrate each other and yet it is impossible for men to be more different. Pitt was endowed with mental powers of the first order; his readiness, his apprehension, his resource were extraordinary; the daily parliamentary demand on his brain and nerve power he met with serene and inexhaustible affluence; his industry, administrative activity, and public spirit were unrivalled, it was perhaps impossible to carry the force of sheer ability further; he was a portent. Chatham in most of these respects was inferior to his son.

老少皮特

阿奇博尔德·菲利普·普里姆罗斯

也许，关于皮特[①]的情况和环境不必多说了。可是，如果不把他和查塔姆一世伯爵[②]做一下对比，哪怕只是瞬间的对比，要想全面描述他的生涯，或者充分评价他的性格，那是不可能的。不只是因为他们是父子，不只是因为他们是18世纪英国最显赫的大臣，而是因为他们的性格相互反衬；而且，不会有人比他们在性格方面的差异更大。皮特天生具有一流的智力，他的敏捷，他的颖悟，他的谋略，都是出类拔萃的；议会日常工作对他的智力和魄力的挑战他都能泰然处之，游刃有余；他的勤奋，他的行政活动，以及他的公益精神，无人能与之相比，也许，要使才能发挥更大的威力已不再可能，他是奇才。查塔姆一世伯爵在这些方面多不及他的儿子。

① 此处指小威廉·皮特(William Pitt the Younger，1759—1806)，英国历史上最著名的首相(1783—1801，1804—1806)。

② 指老威廉·皮特(William Pitt the Elder，1708—1778)，18世纪英国最伟大的政治家，曾任首相等职，是小威廉·皮特的父亲。

He was a political mystic; sometimes sublime, sometimes impossible, and sometimes insane. But he had genius. It was that fitful and undefinable inspiration that gave to his eloquence a piercing and terrible note which no other English eloquence has touched; that made him the idol of his countrymen, though they could scarcely be said to have seen his face or heard his voice or read his speeches; that made him a watchword among those distant insurgents whose wish for independence he yet ardently opposed; that made each remotest soldier and bluejacket feel when he was in office that there was a man in Downing Street, and a man whose eye penetrated everywhere; that made his name at once an inspiration and a dread; that cowed the tumultuous Commons at his frown. Each Pitt possessed in an eminent degree the qualities which the other most lacked: one was formed by nature for peace, the other for war. Chatham could not have filled Pitt's place in the ten years which followed 1783: but, from the time that war was declared, the guidance of Chatham would have been worth an army. No country could have too many Pitts: the more she has the greater will she be. But no country could afford the costly and splendid luxury of many Chathams.

他在政治上是不可捉摸的；有时令人崇敬，有时让人难以忍受，有时又十分荒唐。但是，他有天赋。是时而出现的、难以确切表述的灵感赋予他流利的口才一种尖锐的、令人生畏的特征，使英国其他的雄辩术望尘莫及；这使他成为他的同胞崇拜的偶像，虽然他们几乎没见过他的面孔，或没听过他的声音，或没读过他的讲演；这使他在远方叛乱者当中变成一个口号，然而，他对他们要求独立的愿望是强烈反对的；他在任的时候，让远方每一个士兵和水兵都感觉到在唐宁街有一个人，一个目光犀利洞察一切的人；这使他的名字既能让人受到鼓舞，也能让人感到恐惧；这让群情激昂的英国下议院议员们一看见他皱起眉头便感到害怕。一个皮特往往具有另一个皮特不怎么具备的十分鲜明的品质：一个生来是为了和平，另一个是为了战争。在 1783 年以后的十年里，查塔姆一世伯爵即使在世也填补不了皮特的位置；可是，从宣战[①]的时候起，若有查塔姆一世伯爵执导，能顶得上一个兵团的威力。没有一个国家会嫌拥有的皮特式人物太多——拥有的越多国家就越伟大。可是，也没有一个国家消受得起拥有很多查塔姆一世伯爵式人物——那是昂贵而豪华的奢侈。

---

① 宣战，指 1793 年 2 月 1 日法国对英国宣战。

译后语

1. 关于人物描写的词汇

这篇短文谈人的性格和品质，使用了一些相关的词汇，如：mental powers（智力）、readiness（敏捷）、apprehension（颖悟）、resource（谋略）、industry（勤奋）、public spirit（公益精神）等。描写人物时，各种语言都有一套常用的、约定俗成的词汇，读书时注意积累，对学习英语写作和做汉英翻译都有帮助。

2. 关于名词与形容词搭配

文章里还有较多的名词和形容词搭配，值得借鉴，如：

（1） ...the most **conspicuous** English Ministers of the eighteenth century...

这里的 conspicuous 与汉语“显赫的”意思相当，也可以说 conspicuous statesmen（显赫的政治家）等。

（2） ... the daily parliamentary demand on his brain and nerve power...

议会日常工作对……提出的挑战（或要求），也可以说“administrative demand on... ”（行政工作对……提出的要求或挑战）等。

（3） ... fitful... inspiration...

fitful 意为“happening for short periods; not continuous or regular”，根据这个意思，此例可以译为“时而出现的……灵感”；因而，也可以说“a fitful night's sleep”（夜间时睡时醒）（《牛津高阶英汉双解词典》）、“fitful conversation(s)”（断断续续的谈话）（《英汉大词

典》,第二版)等。

(4) ... the tumultuous Commons...

这里是形容议员在议会里大声喧哗的情景,也作热情解,如"a tumultuous reception/welcome"(热情的招待/欢迎)(《英汉大词典》,第二版)之说。

除名词与形容词的搭配,英语里还有围绕动词形式和其他形式的搭配,有固定搭配的,也有灵活搭配的,多得很。在写作和翻译中对英语做恰当搭配是一个重要环节。多听多读,通过听与读培养对英语的语感(sense of language),是学好英语的有效途径。

3. 解释几个译句

(1) ... but their characters **illustrate** each other...

illustrate 可以根据字典的一个解释来翻译,即 to make the meaning of sth clearer。结合上下文,这句话是说父子的性格各异,两相对照,一个人的性格使另一个人的性格更清楚,更鲜明。这里将其译作"而是因为他们的性格相互反衬",符合原意。

(2) ... the daily parliamentary **demand** on his brain and nerve power he met with serene and inexhaustible **affluence**...

这句话里有两处需要解释,一是 demand,二是 affluence。demand 在多数情况下译为"要求",此句话可以译为"议会日常工作对他的智力和魄力的要求",但从意思上和语气上看,"要求"显得平淡,因而将其译成"挑战",意思和语气更强些,也与后面的"泰然处之,游刃有余"相匹配。关于 affluence,《新牛津英语词典》(*The New Oxford Dictionary of English*)说,affluent 和 affluence 除作"富有"讲之外,在中古英语里还可以解释为"(of water) flowing freely or in great quantity",意为"水的流畅或水的大量流动"。此处译文取“流畅”解，故译作“泰然处之，游刃有余”，比较接近原文意思。

（3）... the **guidance** of Chatham

在这里，guidance 是“指导”或“领导”的意思，不一定是亲临前线“指挥”打仗。

（4）But no country could afford the costly and splendid luxury of many Chathams.

这句话是说，一个国家有一个 Chatham 就很难得了，有很多 Chathams 就是奢侈了。由于汉英两种语言有时在语义结构上的差异很大，这句话照原文句式翻译比较困难，需根据原文意思，汉语怎么通顺就怎么说。此处译为：“可是，也没有一个国家消受得起拥有很多查塔姆一世伯爵式人物——那是昂贵而豪华的奢侈。”这样译也许仍有改进之处。

Richard Jefferies

理查德·杰弗里斯(1848—1887),英国自然文学作家,以描写乡村生活和自然历史闻名。作品有儿童读物 *Bevis*(1882)、科幻小说 *After London*(1885),此外还有描写自然与人的小说 *The Amateur Poacher*(1879)和散文集 *Round about a Great Estate*(1880)。后文"The Wheat"选自杰弗里斯最后的散文集 *Field and Hedgerow*,此书是在他去世后由他的遗孀结集出版的。

这篇文章说麦子关系到国家存亡,一百多年前的英国作家能提出如此卓越的见解,非常了不起。当今世界上粮价不稳,时而引发危机。我们国家也有过教训,现在非常重视粮食生产,我们的领导人曾说过,"手里有粮,心里不慌"。可以说,粮食之于人民的生活和国家的稳定是头等重要的事情。但我们重视粮食完全是为了国计民生,在国际交往中从不以粮食做筹码,更不以粮食为本钱去图谋什么。

The Wheat

Richard Jefferies

If you will look at a grain of wheat you will see that it seems folded up: it has crossed its arms and rolled itself up in a cloak, a fold of which forms a groove, and so gone to sleep. If you look at it some time, as people in the old enchanted days used to look into a mirror, or the magic ink, until they saw living figures therein, you can almost trace a miniature human being in the oval of the grain. It is narrow at the top, where the head would be, and broad across the shoulders, and narrow again down towards the feet; a tiny man or woman has wrapped itself round about with a garment and settled to slumber. Up in the far north, where the dead ice reigns, our arctic explorers used to roll themselves in a sleeping-bag like this, to keep the warmth in their bodies against the chilliness of the night. Down in the south, where the heated sands of Egypt never cool, there in the rock-hewn tombs lie the mummies wrapped and lapped and wound about with a hundred yards of linen, in the hope, it may be, that spices and balm might retain within the sarcophagus some small fragment of human organism through endless ages, till

麦　子

理查德·杰弗里斯

如果你看看一颗麦粒，你会发现它好像是被包裹着的：它抱起双臂，把自己裹在斗篷里，合缝的地方形成一个沟，就这样进入了梦乡。如果你看上一会儿，就像从前人们在施了魔法的日子里照镜子或察看神奇墨水那样，直到在里面看见活的人影，你几乎总能在麦粒的椭圆里发现一个小人儿。小人儿的上面窄，那是头的位置，肩部宽，下面靠近脚的地方又窄下来；一个小人儿，或男或女，用一件外衣把自己从上到下裹起来，然后睡着了。远在冰封的北极，我们的探险家们为抵御黑夜的严寒保持体温，就像这样钻进睡袋里。在南方，埃及的炎热的沙漠永远也不会变凉，在那里的岩石凿成的墓穴里，躺着许多用上百码亚麻布绕着身体缠了又缠裹了又裹的木乃伊，可能是希望，在石棺里用香料和香膏保存一点人体组织，经过千秋万代，

at last the gift of life revisited it. Like a grain of wheat the mummy is folded in its cloth. And I do not know really whether I might not say that these little grains of English corn do not hold within them the actual flesh and blood of man. Transubstantiation is a fact there.

Sometimes the grains are dry and shrivelled and hard as shot, sometimes they are large and full and have a juiciness about them, sometimes they are a little bit red, others are golden, many white. The sack stands open in the market—you can thrust your arm in it a foot deep, or take up a handful and let it run back like a liquid stream, or hold it in your palm and balance it, feeling the weight. They are not very heavy as they lie in the palm, yet these little grains are a ponderous weight that rules man's world. Wherever they are there is empire. Could imperial Rome have only grown sufficient wheat in Italy to have fed her legions Caesar would still be master of three-fourths of the earth. Rome thought more in her latter days of grapes and oysters and mullets, that change colour as they die, and singing girls and flute-playing, and cynic verse of Horace—anything rather than corn. Rome is no more, and the lords of the world are they who have mastership of wheat. We have the mastership at this hour by dint of our gold and our hundred-ton guns, but they are telling our farmers to cast aside their corn, and to grow tobacco and fruit and anything else that can be thought of in preference. The gold is slipping away. These sacks in the market open to all to thrust their hands in are not sacks of corn but of

也许生命最终会重回它的身上。木乃伊被裹在布里,像麦粒一样。我真的不知道我是否可以说,这些英格兰麦子的小小麦粒包含人的血和肉。在这里,"实体转换"是事实。

有时候,麦粒干燥、枯萎,如子弹般坚硬;有时候,麦粒硕大、丰满,似含汁液;有时候,它们有点发红,其他的大都金黄色,很多是白色。盛麦子的麻袋敞着口立在市场上——你可以把胳膊插进去一英尺深,或者抓上一把麦粒,然后让它像液体一样流回去,或者把它托在你的手掌上,保持平衡,掂掂它的分量。它们在手掌上并不感觉很重,然而,这些小小的麦粒却具有统治人类世界的举足轻重的分量。哪里有麦子哪里就有帝国。罗马帝国只要能在意大利种植足够的麦子养活其军团,恺撒就仍会主宰地球上四分之三的地方。在后期,罗马帝国更重视葡萄、牡蛎和死后就变颜色的鲱鲤,更重视歌女和笛子演奏,以及贺拉斯那些愤世嫉俗的诗——什么都重视,就是不重视麦子。罗马帝国已不复存在,掌握麦子的人是世界的主人。眼下,我们凭借黄金和上百吨重的大炮进行统治,可是他们却告诉我们的农民撇开麦子去种植烟草和水果,以及可以优先考虑的任何别的东西。黄金正在悄悄流失。市场上那些敞着口让人们伸进手去的麻袋里面盛的不是小麦籽,而是

golden sovereigns, half-sovereigns, new George and the dragon, old George and the dragon, Sydney mint sovereigns, Napoleons, half-Napoleons, Belgian gold, German gold, Italian gold; gold scraped and scratched and gathered together like old rags from door to door. Sacks full of gold...

英国金镑、半镑金币、新的圣乔治和蛟龙硬币[①]、老的圣乔治和蛟龙硬币、悉尼造币厂造的英国金镑、拿破仑金币、半值拿破仑金币、比利时金币、德意志金币、意大利金币；挨家挨户敛来的像破布片似的已被刮损的、带划痕的金币。一个个装满金币的麻袋……

① 带有圣乔治头像和蛟龙的英国硬币。圣乔治为公元3世纪英格兰基督教殉教者，传说曾杀蛟龙救少女。

译后语

文章分两个段落，第一段写麦粒的外形。一颗麦粒本是一个普通的无生命的物体，作者运用拟人手法赋予它人的形象与生命，使它由静态变为动态，在我们眼前全然成了一个机体完整、机能健全的小生命，读来趣味盎然。麦子是常见的东西，但我们很少有人琢磨过麦粒像什么。经过作者的一番描写，我们真想找来一颗仔细端详，这可能是文学语言的一个艺术功能。

作者由麦粒想到北极探险家在寒冷的夜里钻进睡袋取暖的姿态，又想到在埃及用亚麻布裹着身体的木乃伊。

为了把无生命的麦粒描绘成一个有生命的人的形象，作者使用了一些具体的词汇，来表现人的形体和动作特征。虽然这些多是常用词，本身并不复杂，但在构成词组或组成句子时，很讲究搭配得当，使其符合英语习惯，这是特别值得我们学习英语的人借鉴的，也是翻译时需要特别给予注意的。来看几个例句：

(1) ... it seems folded up: it has crossed its arms and rolled itself up in a cloak...

……它好像是被包裹着的：它抱起双臂，把自己裹在斗篷里……

(2) It is narrow at the top ... and broad across the shoulders, and narrow again down towards the feet...

小人儿的上面窄……肩部宽，下面靠近脚的地方又窄下来……

(3) ... a tiny man or woman has wrapped itself round about with a garment and settled to slumber.

一个小人儿,或男或女,用一件外衣把自己从上到下裹起来,然后睡着了。

(4) ... our arctic explorers used to roll themselves in a sleeping-bag like this...

……我们的探险家们就像这样钻进睡袋里……

(5) ...there in the rock-hewn tombs lie the mummies wrapped and lapped and wound about with a hundred yards of linen...

……在那里的岩石凿成的墓穴里,躺着许多用上百码亚麻布绕着身体缠了又缠裹了又裹的木乃伊……

翻译这样的句子,尽量在汉语里找到相应的词汇,使译文句子像原文那样简单通俗。

Robert Louis Stevenson

罗伯特·路易斯·史蒂文森(1850—1894),苏格兰小说家、散文家、诗人,写过好几部经典儿童文学作品,其中 *Treasure Island* (1883)为其最成功的作品之一,自问世一百多年以来,深受世界读者喜爱。后文"Night among the Pines"选自 *Travels with a Donkey in the Cevennes* (1879),是一部描写作者在法国南部山区徒步旅行的书。

Night among the Pines

Robert Louis Stevenson

A faint wind, more like a moving coolness than a stream of air, passed down the glade from time to time; so that even in my great chamber the air was being renewed all night long. I thought with horror of the inn at Chasserades and the congregated nightcaps; with horror of the nocturnal prowesses of clerks and students, of hot theatres and pass-keys and close rooms. I have not often enjoyed a more serene possession of myself, nor felt more independent of material aids. The outer world, from which we cower into our houses, seemed after all a gentle habitable place; and night after night a man's bed, it seemed, was laid and waiting for him in the fields, where God keeps an open house. I thought I had rediscovered one of those truths which are revealed to savages and hid from political economists: at the least, I had discovered a new pleasure for myself. And yet even while I was exulting in my solitude I became aware of a strange lack. I wished a companion to lie near me in the starlight, silent and not moving, but ever within touch. For

松林之夜

罗伯特·路易斯·史蒂文森

一阵微风时而从林中空地掠过，与其说是一股气流，不如说更像一股流动的凉意；所以，甚至在我的大寝室里，空气整夜都是新鲜的。我怀着嫌恶的心情想起沙瑟拉代镇那家小客店和旅客们夜间聚集在一起饮酒的情景，想起那些夜间活跃的职员和学生们的举动，想起热气腾腾的剧院、万能钥匙以及闷热的房间。我很少像现在这样享受宁静，也没有像现在这样感到无需依赖世俗的帮助。外面的世界（我们从那里退缩到房子里）看来毕竟是个可居住的温馨场所；夜复一夜，一张男人的床好像已经安置在田地里（上帝在那里敞开了大门），等着他来。我想，我又发现了一个真理，那是示于野蛮人而隐于政治经济学家的真理之一：至少，我为自己发现了一种新的愉悦。然而，即使在我因独处而感到欢欣的时候，我仍然意识到一种异样的缺失。我希望有一个伙伴在星光下躺在我的近旁，静静地，一动不动，但总是在伸手可及的地方。因为

there is a fellowship more quiet even than solitude, and which, rightly understood, is solitude made perfect. And to live out of doors with the woman a man loves is of all lives the most complete and free.

As I thus lay, between content and longing, a faint noise stole towards me through the pines. I thought, at first, it was the crowing of cocks or the barking of dogs at some very distant farm; but steadily and gradually it took articulate shape in my ears, until I became aware that a passenger was going by upon the high road in the valley, and singing loudly as he went. There was more of goodwill than grace in his performance; but he trolled with ample lungs; and the sound of his voice took hold upon the hillside and set the air shaking in the leafy glens. I have heard people passing by night in sleeping cities; some of them sang; one, I remember, played loudly on the bagpipes. I have heard the rattle of a cart or carriage spring up suddenly after hours of stillness, and pass, for some minutes, within the range of my hearing as I lay abed. There is a romance about all who are abroad in the black hours, and with something of a thrill we try to guess their business. But here the romance was double: first, this glad passenger, lit internally with wine, who sent up his voice in music through the night; and then I, on the other hand, buckled into my sack, and smoking alone in the pinewoods between four and five thousand feet towards the stars.

个中有一种伙伴关系比独处更安静,如能正确体悟其中奥秘,那是达到极致的独处。一个男人和他所爱恋的女人一起生活在户外是所有生活中最完美、最自由的。

我躺着,一面感到满足,一面心怀渴望,就在这时,一个微弱的声音穿过松林悄然而至。开始,我以为是远处农场的雄鸡的啼声或是狗的叫声,可是这声音一直没断,渐渐变得很清晰,后来我意识到是一个旅行者正从山谷里的路上经过,一边走一边大声唱。在他的歌唱里真情多于优雅;他可着嗓门大声唱,他的歌声冲到山坡上,震荡着树木茂密的山谷里的空气。我听见过夜间从沉睡的城市里经过的人们,有的唱着歌,有一个人,我记得,大声吹着风笛。我曾听见,几个小时的寂静之后,突然响起二轮马车或四轮马车的声音,我躺在床上一连几分钟听着马车走过。所有黑夜里来到户外的人都有一种浪漫情怀,我们怀着激动的心情努力猜测他们在做什么。但在这里浪漫情怀是双重的:首先是这个兴高采烈的旅行者,醉意尚浓,放声歌唱,歌声穿过夜空;然后是我,钻进睡袋,扣上锁扣,在离群星四五千英尺的松林里独自吸烟。

译后语

关于英语的插入成分。英语句子里常有插入成分，对前面的信息加以补充或说明，使意思更确切、更清晰，也使句子语气和节奏产生起伏顿挫的效果。插入成分有单词、短语或句子等，常出现在主语和谓语之间，有时出现在动词和与其搭配的介词之间，有时作为定语或状语出现在句子适当的位置上。

(1) A faint wind, more like a moving coolness than a stream of air, passed down the glade from time to time…（介词短语：位于主语和谓语之间）

(2) I thought with horror of the inn at Chasserades and the congregated nightcaps…（介词短语：位于动词和与其搭配的介词之间）

(3) The outer world, from which we cower into our houses, seemed after all a gentle habitable place…（非限定性定语从句：位于主语和谓语之间）

(4) … one, I remember, played loudly on the bagpipes.（短句：位于主语和谓语之间）

(5) … and pass, for some minutes, within the range of my hearing as I lay abed.（介词短语作状语：位于谓语动词之后）

(6) … first, this glad passenger, lit internally with wine, who sent up his voice in music through the night…（分词短语作状语：位于主语之后）

翻译带有插入成分的英语句子有时可以直译(即不变动插入成分的位置),意思不受损失,也符合汉语习惯。如例(4):

> ……有一个人,我记得,大声吹着风笛。

如例(6):

> ……首先是这个兴高采烈的旅行者,醉意尚浓,放声歌唱,歌声穿过夜空;

但常常需要变通(即按照汉语习惯改变插入成分的位置)。如例(1):

> 一阵微风时而从林中空地掠过,与其说是一股气流,不如说更像一股流动的凉意;

如例(2):

> 我怀着嫌恶的心情想起沙瑟拉代镇那家小客店和旅客们夜间聚集在一起饮酒的情景……

有时也需要改变插入成分的形式。如例(3):

> 外面的世界(我们从那里退缩到房子里)看来毕竟是个可居住的温馨场所……

这个句子里的非限定性定语从句 from which we cower into our houses,处理起来比较困难,故将其放在括号(也是插入语的一种形式)里。

George Gissing

乔治·吉辛(1857—1903),英国小说家,著有20多部小说,比较成功的有*Workers in the Dawn*(1880)、*New Grub Street*(1891)、*Charles Dickens: A Critical Study*(1898)、*The Private Papers of Henry Ryecroft*(1903)等。*The Private Papers of Henry Ryecroft*是一部半自传体散文集,作者在书中吐露了对古今一系列问题的见解——个人的困顿、伦敦贫民窟生活、罗马文化、当代伦理,多处谈及自己的读书生活,以及对于书籍的痴爱之情。后文即选自该书。全书分四章:"春""夏""秋""冬"。李霁野曾有译文,书名为《四季随笔》。

Shakespeare's Island

George Gissing

Today I have read *The Tempest* ... Among the many reasons which make me glad to have been born in England, one of the first is that I read Shakespeare in my mother tongue. If I try to imagine myself as one who cannot know him face to face, who hears him only speaking from afar, and that in accents which only through the labouring intelligence can touch the living soul, there comes upon me a sense of chill discouragement, of dreary deprivation. I am wont to think that I can read Homer, and, assuredly, if any man enjoys him, it is I; but can I for a moment dream that Homer yields me all his music, that his word is to me as to him who walked by the Hellenic shore when Hellas lived? I know that there reaches me across the vast of time no more than a faint and broken echo; I know that it would be fainter still, but for its blending with those memories of youth which are as a glimmer of the world's primeval glory. Let every land have joy of its poet; for the poet is the land itself, all its greatness and its sweetness, all that incommunicable heritage for which men live and die.

莎士比亚之岛

乔治·吉辛

今天我读了《暴风雨》……我很庆幸自己出生在英格兰，理由很多，一个重要理由是，我能用我的母语阅读莎士比亚。假如我想象自己不能面对面去认识他，只能听他从遥远的地方讲话，而且是使用一种令人费解的口音，我会感到心灰意冷，也会因为被剥夺了一种权利而感到沮丧。我常这样想，我可以读懂荷马，而且可以肯定地说，假如有谁欣赏荷马的作品，那就是我；可是，我能梦想完全领悟他的音乐吗？我能像当初在古希腊海滩上漫步的古希腊人那样领会他诗篇里的用字吗？我知道，越过广袤的时空传到我耳边的只不过是一个微弱的、断断续续的回声；我也知道，若不是这回声融汇着作为世界远古时代荣光火花的富有青春活力的记忆的话，这微弱的回声还会更加微弱。让每个国度都为它的诗人而感到欣慰吧；因为诗人就是这国度本身，就是它的伟大和温馨所在，就是人们置生死于不顾而要继承的遗产——只能意会不能言传的遗产。

As I close the book, love and reverence possess me. Whether does my full heart turn to the great Enchanter, or to the Island upon which he has laid his spell? I know not. I cannot think of them apart. In the love and reverence awakened by that voice of voices, Shakespeare and England are but one.

当我合上这本书时，心中充满了爱和崇敬。我的心是转向这位伟大的魔法师，还是转向他施过魔法的岛屿？我不知道。我不能将他们分开。那伟大的声音在我心中所唤起的“爱”和“崇敬”，已将莎士比亚和英格兰融为一体。

译后语

当我们阅读一个伟大作家的作品之后，心中会油然生出对作家的无限崇敬和对产生伟大作家的祖国的无限热爱，这是一种崇高的感情。用语言把这种感情表达出来，句子结构难免有些复杂，需要语言技巧。吉辛成功地表达了自己真挚的情感。

(1) Among the many reasons which make me glad to have been born in England, one of the first is that I read Shakespeare in my mother tongue.

这样的句式很好，既有用，又好学，翻译起来也不困难。世界上各国都有让自己的人民感到骄傲的事情，我们中国有说不完的让我们感到自豪的事情，比如，英国有莎士比亚，中国有《红楼梦》。我们不妨仿造这个句式说：

> Among the many reasons which make me glad to have been born in China, one of the first is that I read *Hong Lou Meng* in my mother tongue.

(2) If I try to imagine myself as one who cannot know him face to face, who hears him only speaking from afar, and that in accents which only through the labouring intelligence can touch the living soul, there comes upon me a sense of chill discouragement, of dreary deprivation.

这个句子可谓长而复杂，主句部分 there comes upon me a sense of chill discouragement, of dreary deprivation，意思清晰，但它

的条件从句却套着三个定语从句:“who...”“who...”“which...”。翻译时弄清楚句子的结构关系,意思也不难掌握。

其余的几个句子同样值得推敲体味,会有收益。

另附王宏印教授的点评:

一个人文主义者,在他读到一篇文学名篇的时候,他所产生的激动和感受,往往是难以用语言来形容的。而当他发觉自己原来能够用母语来读自己喜欢的作家时,他对于祖国语言的自豪感就会同他对于祖国的热爱融为一体。而当他总是意识到他是通过翻译阅读一篇文学名篇时,他心理上的不安全感、语言上的隔膜感以及文化上的夹生感,就会使他产生一种莫名其妙的惆怅和难以满足的向往。然而,由于对人性和人类文化的深刻洞察力,这种向往使他坚信,每一个民族都有自己的诗人,作为文化的制高点和体现,作为本民族和全人类可以引以为豪的先进代表,来和我们交流。于是,我被感染了,我被扩大了。这就是读者面前这篇短文的作者要告诉我们的,不,准确地说,是通过译者的忠实翻译已经传达给我们的。

当我们阅读一篇优秀的译文而为它本身的魅力所打动、所激动时,我们是否想过,尽管作者声称有某种“只能意会不能言传的遗产”,而译者却坚信他的译笔有一种几近于原作的魅力,使我们读他的译作一如读原作一样。这一在翻译理论上很难说得清的可译性问题,或者说翻译之所以存在的根据问题,会轻而易举地为一篇译文的阅读效果所证实。明乎此,那么,我的解说和例证便是多余的。还是让我们重读一遍这篇颇有趣味的散文吧。

Arthur Clutton-Brock

亚瑟·克拉顿-布罗克(1868—1924),英国散文家、文艺批评家。后文选自他的*Modern Essays*。

The Cardinal Virtue of Prose

Arthur Clutton-Brock

Prose of its very nature is longer than verse, and the virtues peculiar to it manifest themselves gradually. If the cardinal virtue of poetry is love, the cardinal virtue of prose is justice; and, whereas love makes you act and speak on the spur of the moment, justice needs inquiry, patience, and a control even of the noblest passions... By justice here I do not mean justice only to particular people or ideas, but a habit of justice in all the processes of thought, a style tranquillized and a form moulded by that habit. The master of prose is not cold, but he will not let any word or image inflame him with a heat irrelevant to his purpose. Unhasting, unresting, he pursues it, subduing all the riches of his mind to it, rejecting all beauties that are not germane to it; making his own beauty out of the very accomplishment of it, out of the whole work and its proportions, so that you must read to the end before you know that it is beautiful. But he has his reward, for he is trusted and convinces, as those who are at the mercy of their own eloquence do not;

散文最重要的品质

亚瑟·克拉顿-布罗克

就其本质而言，散文比韵文篇幅长，因而其特有的品质是逐渐表现出来的。如果说诗歌最重要的品质是爱，散文最重要的品质就是公正；爱使你因一时冲动而采取行动、表达自己，但要做到公正则需要调查，需要耐心，需要控制激情，即使这种激情是最崇高的。说起公正，我不是针对具体的人或具体的想法，而是指在思想的全过程中的一种公正的习惯，一种由此习惯所形成的沉静的文风和由此习惯所造就的形式。散文大师并不冷漠，但他也不允许那些含有激情但又与他的初衷毫不相干的字词或形象来激发他的感情。他不慌不忙又永不停止地追求着，克制着他丰富的主观色彩，抛弃所有无关的藻饰，他从完成的作品里，从作品的整体和各部分之间恰当的比例里，创造着他自己的美，所以，你要想知道作品是美的，就必须把它读完。然而，他也得到应有的奖赏，因为人们信任他，他令人信服，正像那些依靠言辞雄辩的人不能令人信服一样，

and he gives a pleasure all the greater for being hardly noticed. In the best prose, whether narrative or argument, we are so led on as we read, that we do not stop to applaud the writer, nor do we stop to question him.

而且,正因为他不显声露色而能给人更大的愉悦。在阅读最好的散文时,无论是叙事的还是说理的,我们会一直读下去,不会停下来为作者欢呼,也不会停下来向作者发问。

译后语

一篇关于散文的散文

“The Cardinal Virtue of Prose”是一篇关于散文的短论，文章从散文本身、作者、读者三个角度论述散文。前三句讲散文本身，中间三句讲作者，最后一句讲读者。讲散文时由 Prose 起始，讲作者时由 The master of prose 起始，讲读者时由“In the best prose...we... ”起始。从形式到内容，这三部分的衔接与连贯都是内在的，在它们之间没有使用连接词。主题集中，思路清晰，发展自然。

在第一部分，作者从三个方面论述散文的性质：首先说“the cardinal virtue of prose is justice”，所谓 justice，是指“真实”“公正”地反映思想、感情和事物；接着说“justice needs inquiry, patience, and a control even of the noblest passions...”，是指这种“真实”和“公正”需要“调查”“耐心”和“控制激情”；最后，作者进一步明确为“but a habit of justice in all the processes of thought, a style tranquillized and a form moulded by that habit”，所谓 justice，是指思想过程中“真实”和“公正”的习惯，以及由此习惯所形成的沉静的文风和由此习惯所造就的形式。这部分是文章的核心。

这篇文章很短，只有一个段落，七句话，244 个词，但论述的题目很大。

此外，作为论说文，它还有以下特征：

1. 多用具有确定意义的动词和句式，仅 is 就出现六次，are 出现三次，还有“love makes you act and speak...”“By justice here I do not mean... but...”“he pursues it...”等。

2. 多用具有实义的名词，而少用内容伸缩性较大的形容词和副词，如 habit、style、form、beauty、accomplishment、reward 等。

3. 为使行文简洁，作者使用了：(1)介词短语，如 of its very nature、By justice、out of the whole work and its proportions；(2)起修饰作用的形容词短语，如 and the virtues peculiar to it、with a heat irrelevant to his purpose、a pleasure all the greater for being hardly noticed；(3)起限定作用的过去分词短语，如 a style tranquillized and a form moulded by that habit；(4)作状语的现在分词短语，如 subduing all the riches 和 rejecting all beauties 等。

4. 为增强文章的说服力，作者使用了一些带对偶性质的句子，如：“If the cardinal virtue of poetry is love, the cardinal virtue of prose is justice”和“... we do not stop to applaud the writer, nor do we stop to question him.”。

5. 为说理周密透彻，句式较长、较复杂，最长的 57 个词，最短的也有 18 个词之多，平均每句话 35 个词；多是主从句和复合句，没有简单句。

作者在解释 justice 时说：“justice needs inquiry, patience, and a control even of the noblest passions”。关于散文的写法，美国散文家 E. B. White 也有类似的见解，他说：“Write in a way that draws the reader's attention to the sense and substance of the writing, rather than to the mood and temper of the author.”(*The Elements of Style*, 1979)他们的主张是一致的。

关于诗歌与散文的区别，Sir Arthur Quiller-Couch 说：“I

should prefer ‘a high compelling emotion’ to Mr. Clutton-Brock’s ‘Love’, however widely interpreted, as the virtue of Poetry; and Persuasion rather than Justice as the first virtue of Prose, whether in narrative or in argument.”(*The Oxford Book of English Prose*, 1925)

朱光潜认为:“就形式说,散文的音节是直率的,无规律的;诗的音节是循环的,有规律的。就实质说,散文宜于叙事说理,诗宜于抒情遣兴。”(《艺文杂谈》,1981)

这些论述对于理解散文的本质都很有帮助。

学习散文英译者宜多读英文散文,以学会用英语描写、叙述和论辩,从而提高翻译的能力。

Charles Edward Montague

查尔斯·爱德华·蒙塔古(1867—1928),英国戏剧评论家、小说家,主要作品有小说 *A Hind Let Loose* (1910)、*The Morning's War* (1913)、*Rough Justice* (1926)、戏剧评论 *Dramatic Values* (1911)和散文集 *Disenchantment* (1922)。"The Faculty of Delight"一文即出自 *Disenchantment*。在这篇短文里,作者讨论了关于人的天性的一个方面,也以一个教育家的眼光指出,正确的教育可以将这种天赋引导到"知识""智慧"和"高尚的情操"的发展方向。作者只用很短的篇幅,讨论了"人"和"培养人"的大题目,可见其见解之深邃,语言修养之深厚。

The Faculty of Delight

Charles Edward Montague

Among the mind's powers is one that comes of itself to many children and artists. It need not be lost, to the end of his days, by any one who has ever had it. This is the power of taking delight in a thing, or rather in anything, everything, not as a means to some other end, but just because it is what it is, as the lover dotes on whatever may be the traits of the beloved object. A child in the full health of his mind will put his hand flat on the summer turf, feel it, and give a little shiver of private glee at the elastic firmness of the globe. He is not thinking how well it will do for some game or to feed sheep upon. That would be the way of the wooer whose mind runs on his mistress's money. The child's is sheer affection, the true ecstatic sense of the thing's inherent characteristics. No matter what the things may be, no matter what they are good or no good for, there they are, each with a thrilling unique look and feel of its own, like a face; the iron astringently cool under its paint, the painted wood familiarly warmer, the clod

感知快乐的天赋

查尔斯·爱德华·蒙塔古

在人的心理能力中，有一种是很多孩子和艺术家自然就有的。不论是谁，一旦有了这种能力，直到他生命的最后一天也不一定会丧失。这就是从某一事物，或任一事物，每一事物，都能感受快乐的能力，不是为了某一目的，只是因为它就是这样，这好比一个人喜爱一样东西，不论它有什么特征他都喜爱。一个心理健全的孩子会把他的手掌平放在夏天的草皮上，抚摩它，在他感觉到具有弹性又很坚实的地球表面时，他心里便产生一种快乐的冲动。他不是在想，要是在上面做游戏或放羊什么的该有多好哇。那岂不是就像求婚者一心只想着女友的钱财一样吗？而孩子则完全是因为喜爱，是事物内在的特质真正让他有一种欣喜若狂的感觉。不论是什么事物，也不论它们有没有用途，它们就在那里，每一样东西都有其使人激动的独特外观和感觉，就像人的面孔；上过油漆的铁器使人感觉冷峻，而上过油漆的木器则让人感觉温和而亲切，当土块

crumbling enchantingly down in the hands, with its little dry smell of the sun and of hot nettles; each common thing a personality marked by delicious differences.

The joy of an Adam new to the garden and just looking round is brought by the normal child to the things that he does as well as those that he sees. To be suffered to do some plain work with the real spade used by mankind can give him a mystical exaltation: to come home with his legs, as the French say, re-entering his body from the fatigue of helping the gardener to weed beds sends him to sleep in the glow of a beatitude that is an end in itself...

The right education, if we could find it, would work up this creative faculty of delight into all its branching possibilities of knowledge, wisdom, and nobility. Of all three it is the beginning, condition, or raw material.

在手里松动而散发出阳光和热荨麻的微干的气味时，简直让人陶醉；每一样普通的东西都有它自己的“性格”，而这“性格”都有其不同的宜人的特征。

亚当初来伊甸园举目四望时所感到的那种快乐，一个正常孩子在其所做及所见的事物里都可以感觉到。在他被允许使用人类常用的铁锹去做一些简单的体力劳动时，他会感到一种神奇的兴奋：他拖着双腿回到家（就像法国人常说的那样），由于他已从帮助园丁在花坛里锄草而产生的疲劳中恢复过来，在一种幸福感的光辉里进入梦乡，这本身就是目的……

正确的教育，如果我们能够发现它，可以调动这一带有创造性的感知快乐的天赋，使其进入所有可能的方面——知识、智慧和高尚的情操。对于这三者，这种感知快乐的心理能力是开始，是条件，或是原始材料。

译后语

从本文的写作与翻译看，有以下几个地方值得提出：

1. 叙事视角的变化。

阅读这篇文章时如能注意到其叙事视角的变化，对翻译是有帮助的。

因为是讲人的"感知快乐的天赋"，文章一开始便以"one (of the mind's powers)"为出发点，解释这种天赋的本质特征；接着转向 a child，讲具有这种天赋的孩子的表现，他不是受某种功利的驱使，而完全是出于喜爱(sheer affection)，是事物内在的特质真正让他有一种欣喜若狂的感觉(the true ecstatic sense of the thing's inherent characteristics)；然后转向事物(the things)，每一样东西都有使人激动的独特外观和感觉(a thrilling unique look and feel)，比如 the iron、the painted wood、the clod 等；然后讲 the joy，人与物相接触以后，便产生一种快乐，一个正常孩子在其所做及所见的事物里所感觉到的快乐和亚当初来伊甸园时所感受到的快乐一样；最后落到教育之于这种天赋的启迪作用，"The right education... would work up this creative faculty..."。而这几个不同的视角都是指向这个"心理能力"的，使文章围绕着一个焦点搭建起来。我们阅读时会感觉到文章之美，文章的力量。这和它语言本身的魅力及其严密的结构有直接的关系。

特别是文章的第一句"Among the mind's powers is one that comes of itself to many children and artists."以介词开始，最后一句"Of all three it is the beginning, condition, or raw material."也以介

词开始，这是为了强调、突出句子中的主语，而这两句话的主语的所指又是相同的。这种形式上的首尾照应和意义上的前后一致与深化，使文章形成一个文气贯通的整体。

2. 句子开始方式(opening)的变化。

这篇文章共有12个句子，其中以普通名词开始的有4句，以人称代词开始的有2句，以指示代词开始的有2句，以介词短语开始的有2句，以不定式开始的有1句，以状语从句开始的有1句。在一篇如此短的文章里，有如此多的句子开始方式，再加上字词和短语的巧妙运用，使文章读起来生动活泼，韵味十足。翻译时也要根据原文考虑句子开始方式的变化。

3. 被动语态的翻译。

有时英语的某些被动句式翻译成汉语时需变成主动句式，如第一段的第二句"It need not be lost, to the end of his days, by any one who has ever had it."，和第二段的第一句"The joy of an Adam new to the garden and just looking round is brought by the normal child to the things that he does as well as those that he sees."，都是被动句式的例子。我们操汉语的人若用英语来写或译这样的意思时，可能不是采用这样的句式。这是因为汉语的思维方式和表达方式与英语之间存在差异，有时是和叙事视角有关。在汉语，多以行为的主体为主语；在英语，常有以行为客体为主语的情况。对于这种情况，英语的作者或读者都不会有异样感觉；但在汉语，这句话的意思习惯上是用主动句式表达的。所以，翻译这种句子，需注意两个方面：一要语句通顺，通常要照顾汉语的表达习惯（有些翻译特意要保留源语的语义特征，那属于另外一种译法）；二要关照上下文，使其衔接自然，所译句子要有承上启下的作用。

Harold Fielding Hall

哈罗德·菲尔丁·霍尔(1859—1917),英国作家,1887 年至 1891 年间曾在缅甸任高级官员。主要著作有:*The Soul of a People* (1898)、*The Inward Light* (1908)、*One Immortality* (1909)、*The World Soul* (1913)等。后文选自 *The Inward Light*。

A Burmese on the English

Harold Fielding Hall

It is not only that when you get an order you obey it, though it come from so very far away—that is wonderful enough to us—but you obey it willingly. You act as if it was something you wanted to do yourself, something you thought of in yourself for your own advantage. You understand not only what the order says but what it means, almost as if you yourself had said it. You are not servants who obey orders, you are as the hand or foot that acts as the brain designs. You live here widely separated, many thousand miles from your small island, but yet you are not divided from it. You are all held together by nerves in the invisible air that make you one. Therefore your Government is you, not your master, your teacher, your commander, but yourself. You feel as we do about our family and our village, that it is ourselves. That is what we notice and wonder at in you. When we see two or three Englishmen alone governing a great district, you appear to us not individuals but tiny

一个缅甸人谈英国人

哈罗德·菲尔丁·霍尔

你们不仅仅是接到命令就服从，哪怕命令来自遥远的地方——这已经让我们感到够惊奇的了——而且你们还是心甘情愿地服从。你们执行命令时好像那是你们自己要做的事情，是你们内心所想的对于你们自己有利的事情。你们不仅明白命令的内容，而且理解它的意义，几乎就像你们自己起草的一样。你们不是服从命令的仆人，你们就像按照大脑的设计而行动的手或脚。你们远隔重洋住在这里，与你们的小岛相距几千英里，然而你们并没有被阻隔。你们被分布在看不见的空气里的神经系统联系在一起。因此，你们的政府就是你们，不是你们的主人、你们的老师、你们的司令，而是你们自己。你们的感觉就如同我们对家庭和家乡的感觉，那其实就是对我们自己的感觉。这就是我们在你们身上所见并为之感到惊奇的东西。当我们看到只有两三个英国人统辖一个很大的地区时，在我们看来，你们不是单个的个人，而是一个巨大的生命体的微小的指尖，

finger-tips of a great living thing whose heart and brain are far away. Yet if the finger-tip be touched the whole responds. And what one of you does, that is the act of the whole.

这个生命体的心脏和大脑却在遥远的地方。然而,如果指尖被触动,整体就做出反应。而你们一个人所做的事,其实就是整体的行动。

译后语

19 世纪，英国殖民者以其占领的印度为基地，对缅甸进行扩张，共发动三次战争，分别在 1824 年、1852 年和 1885 年。1885 年的第三次英缅战争之后，缅甸完全被英国占领。

作为被殖民的缅甸人颂扬殖民者的统治，这是一个复杂现象。从今天我们读者的角度看，这里当然有写书者的立场，也有文章叙事者缅甸人关于殖民者与被殖民者意识的缺失，但也有可以理解的一面，那就是，当他亲眼看到英国人在实施殖民统治的过程中，表现出上下的一致、组织的严密、管理的高效，难免要表示由衷的赞叹。

本文译者选择这篇文章，主要是看中了它优美的文字。这是一百年前(1908 年)写的东西，其文字简单得几乎和今天的英语没有区别，具有英语专业本科程度的读者读起来不会遇到文字困难。这样的东西读起来懂虽好懂，但写起来却很难。难在用如此简单的文字表达如此复杂的内容，而且清清楚楚，耐人寻味。比如“You act as if it was something you wanted to do yourself...”和“You understand not only what the order says but what it means, almost as if you yourself had said it.”所用的字词再普通不过。这是语言的修养，是我们努力的方向。再有，文章里使用了微妙、恰当而又独具特色的比喻：“You are all held together by nerves in the invisible air that make you one.”只用了十几个词，却表达了这么复杂的事情，完全是比喻的功能，比喻的力量。人们说话写文章常常使用比喻，但多是用来用去的同样的比喻，没有味道。恰当而独特的比喻能增加文章的审美内涵,能取得直言陈述难以取得的效果,读来使人心情愉悦。

关于这篇文章的翻译,也有几个地方值得说一说。

(1) A Burmese **on** the English

这是文章的标题,像论文的题目,一般英语论文中的 on 多用"论"来翻译,不过这只是从 *The Inward Light* 中节选的一个章节,从内容看,用"谈"比较合适。

(2) **You act** as if it was something you wanted to do yourself...

这里的 You act 就是指执行命令,宜结合上下文做具体翻译,不宜泛译。

(3) You understand not only **what the order says but what it means**, almost as if you yourself had said it.

关于 what the order says but what it means 的翻译,可以做不同的处理,可以将这句话翻译成"你们不仅明白命令说的什么,而且理解它意味着什么",也不妨将其翻译成"你们不仅明白命令的内容,而且理解它的意义",如译文所示,这样简洁些,有力些。

(4) When we see two or three Englishmen **alone** governing a great district, you appear to us not individuals but tiny finger-tips of a great living thing **whose heart and brain are far away**.

这句话里有两个地方如何翻译值得斟酌,一是 alone,二是 a great living thing 的从句 whose heart and brain are far away。前者可以译成"单独",即"两三个英国人单独……",或者译成"只有",即"只有两三个英国人……",两种译法看来都可以,参考译文里采取了第二个译法;后者是一个定语从句,修饰 a great living thing,按照汉语习惯,将定语从句放在所修饰成分的前面,译文可能会很别扭,不自然,因此将这个定语从句放在其所修饰成分的后面单独翻译出

来,这样意思清楚,读起来也自然。整句译文如下:

当我们看到只有两三个英国人统辖一个很大的地区时,在我们看来,你们不是单个的个人,而是一个巨大的生命体的微小的指尖,这个生命体的心脏和大脑却在遥远的地方。

George Moore

乔治·穆尔(1852—1933),英国作家。青年时期居住在巴黎,曾就学于多个艺术学校。因受左拉、福楼拜、屠格涅夫和19世纪现实主义作家的影响,穆尔转向写作,于1883年发表第一部小说*A Modern Lover*,1894年发表他最著名的小说*Esther Waters*,后文是其中的一个片段。

Esther's Son

George Moore

At twelve o'clock Esther and Mrs. Barfield walked out on the lawn. A loud wind came up from the sea, and it shook the evergreens as if it were angry with them. A rook carried a stick to the tops of the tall trees, and the women drew their cloaks about them. The train passed across the vista, and the women wondered how long it would take Jack to walk from the station. Then another rook stooped to the edge of the plantation, gathered a twig, and carried it away. The wind was rough; it caught the evergreens underneath and blew them out like umbrellas; the grass had not yet begun to grow, and the grey sea harmonized with the grey-green land. The women waited on the windy lawn, their skirts blown against their legs, keeping their hats on with difficulty. It was too cold for standing still. They turned and walked a few steps towards the house, and then looked round.

A tall soldier came through the gate. He wore a long red cloak, and a small cap jauntily set on the side of his close-clipped head. Esther uttered a little exclamation, and ran to meet him.

埃斯特的儿子

乔治·穆尔

12 点的时候，埃斯特和巴菲尔德夫人出来走到草坪上。海风呼呼作响，吹得常青树摆来摆去，好像风在和它们生气。一只秃鼻乌鸦叼着一根树枝飞到高高的树梢上，两个妇人紧紧地抓着斗篷裹住身子。火车从视野远处经过，妇人们心想，杰克从火车站走过来得需要多长时间呢。然后，又一只秃鼻乌鸦俯冲下来飞到农场边上，叼起一根短枝，飞走了。风很大，横扫下面的常青树，吹得树冠张开来就像雨伞一样；草还没有开始长起来，灰蒙蒙的海水和灰绿色的大地浑然一体。她们站在临风的草坪上，吃力地捂住头上的帽子，风把她们的裙子吹得紧贴在腿上。一动不动地站在那里太冷了，她们转过身来，朝房子那边走了几步，然后，左右张望着。

一个身材高大的士兵从院门走进来。他身穿一件长长的红色斗篷，头发剪得很短，头上侧戴着一顶小帽，很神气。埃斯特发出轻轻的惊叹声，跑

He took his mother in his arms, kissed her, and they walked towards Mrs. Barfield together. All was forgotten in the happiness of the moment—the long fight for his life, and the possibility that any moment might declare him to be mere food for powder and shot. She was only conscious that she had accomplished her woman's work—she had brought him up to man's estate; and that was her sufficient reward. What a fine fellow he was! She did not know he was so handsome, and blushing with pleasure and pride she glanced shyly at him out of the corners of her eyes as she introduced him to her mistress.

"This is my son, ma'am."

Mrs. Barfield held out her hand to the young soldier.

"I have heard a great deal about you from your mother."

"And I of you, ma'am. You've been very kind to my mother. I don't know how to thank you."

And in silence they walked towards the house.

过去迎接他。他将母亲抱在怀里，吻了她，便一起朝巴菲尔德夫人走过来。在那幸福的瞬间，她把一切都忘记了，忘记了为养活他所经历的漫长的艰难岁月，忘记了在战场上他随时都有可能成为火药和子弹的牺牲品。她只是意识到，她完成了作为女人应做的事情——她已经把他抚养成人；这对她已是足够的奖赏。他是多么好的小伙子呀！她竟然不知道他是如此的英俊，在向她的女主人介绍他时，她羞涩地从眼角看了他一眼，喜悦的心情和自豪感使她脸上泛起了红晕。

“这是我的儿子，夫人。”

巴菲尔德夫人把手朝年轻的士兵伸过去。

“我从你母亲那里听到很多关于你的事情。”

“我也从母亲那里听到了很多关于您的事情，夫人。您对我母亲一直都非常好。我真不知道怎么感谢您。”

然后，他们没再说什么，一起朝房子走去。

译后语

虽然本文节选自 *Esther Waters*，却是一个可以独立成篇的完整故事：有时间，有地点，有环境，有人物，有情节，情节有开始，有结尾。故事的焦点是母亲迎接从前线归来的儿子，她的女主人巴菲尔德夫人陪着她，站在风里等。

文章描写天气，是为了陪衬母亲想念儿子的心情；描写乌鸦衔枝筑巢，是暗示母亲为了抚育儿女的艰辛以及母子间的亲情，都与故事主题相关。

作家写天气，写乌鸦，写大海，写大地，都只是寥寥几笔，描绘出鲜明的画面，使读者身临其境。写人物时，也只是写了他们穿着什么，做着什么，没有说一句直抒感情的话。但通过儿子归来时他们之间的简短对话，能体会出他们各自的心情和他们之间的关系。母亲说："这是我的儿子，夫人。"她的喜悦，她的自豪感，都在其中；巴菲尔德夫人说："我从你母亲那里听到很多关于你的事情。"这是对杰克含蓄的赞赏；杰克的回答则表达了他对女主人的敬意和感激，以及对母亲的爱。

我们读罢这篇文字，感受到很多东西：母亲一生的勤劳、艰辛，对儿子的爱心和自豪感，对女主人的谦恭和尽职；女主人的善良、文化和修养；儿子杰克的勇敢和礼貌；等等。此外，他们都善于含蓄地表达自己的感情。作家在不言之中让我们体会到很多美好的东西，这是艺术的功能。作家是艺术家。

翻译时体会其简洁含蓄的文字风格及作家生动描写自然景物、

准确塑造人物形象的技巧,可以帮助我们再现译文的行文风格。

我们说到原文的"简洁含蓄的文字风格",这种文字翻译起来有时更是困难,特别是当这种文字是经过作者的有意提炼,为了含蓄地表现人物的情感时,翻译时就更觉困难,因为译文也要简洁,也要含蓄,而且更要自然。往往在原文是很自然的文字,在译文里偏偏不太自然。因此,要满足这几个方面的要求,需要对文章进行反复斟酌,反复推敲。我们一起研究下面的几个例子。

(1) At twelve o'clock Esther and Mrs. Barfield walked out on the lawn.

12点的时候,埃斯特和巴菲尔德夫人出来走到草坪上。

(2) ... and the women drew their cloaks about them.

……两个妇人紧紧地抓着斗篷裹住身子。

(3) The train passed across the vista...

火车从视野远处经过……

(4) The women waited on the windy lawn, their skirts blown against their legs, keeping their hats on with difficulty.

她们站在临风的草坪上,吃力地捂住头上的帽子,风把她们的裙子吹得紧贴在腿上。

(5) Esther uttered a little exclamation, and ran to meet him.

埃斯特发出轻轻的惊叹声,跑过去迎接他。

(6) ... the long fight for his life...

……为养活他所经历的漫长的艰难岁月……

(7) ... and that was her sufficient reward.

……这对她已是足够的奖赏。

(8) ... and blushing with pleasure and pride she glanced shyly at him out of the corners of her eyes as she introduced him to her mistress.

……在向她的女主人介绍他时，她羞涩地从眼角看了他一眼，喜悦的心情和自豪感使她脸上泛起了红晕。

Olive Schreiner

奥利夫·施赖纳(1859—1920),南非作家,关注种族问题和妇女命运。她的长篇小说 *The Story of an African Farm* (1883)自出版之日起便受到好评,至今享有很高声誉。后文是这篇小说最后一章"Waldo Goes Out to Sit in the Sunshine"结尾的一段文字。

Waldo

Olive Schreiner

Sitting there with his arms folded on his knees, and his hat slouched down over his face, Waldo looked out into the yellow sunshine that tinted even the very air with the colour of ripe corn, and was happy.

He was an uncouth creature with small learning, and no prospect in the future but that of making endless tables and stone walls, yet it seemed to him as he sat there that life was a rare and very rich thing. He rubbed his hands in the sunshine. Ah, to live on so, year after year, how well! Always in the present; letting each day glide, bringing its own labour, and its own beauty; the gradual lighting up of the hills, night and the stars, firelight and the coals! To live on so, calmly, far from the paths of men; and to look at the lives of clouds and insects; to look deep into the heart of flowers, and see how lovely the pistil and the stamens nestle there together; and to see in the thorn-pods how the little seeds suck their life through the delicate curled-up string, and how the little embryo sleeps inside! Well, how well, to sit so on one side, taking no part

沃尔多

奥利夫·施赖纳

沃尔多手臂抱着双膝坐在那里，帽檐耷拉下来遮着前额，看着远处金黄色的阳光，阳光甚至将空气都染上了一层熟透的小麦的颜色，他感到幸福。

他是个粗人，没有多少文化，只会没完没了地做桌子，垒石墙，没有什么前程，但是，他坐在那里的时候，却觉得生活是那样的不同寻常，那样的丰富多彩。他在阳光下搓着双手。啊，就这样生活着，年复一年地，多好啊！总像现在这样，让每一天悄然而逝，带来它自己的成果，带来它自己的美丽；慢慢亮起来的小山、夜色和星辰，还有壁炉的火光和煤炭。就这样生沽着，安安静静地，远离人间踪迹；看着那缓缓飘动的白云和盈盈飞舞的昆虫；仔细观察花儿的内心，看着雌蕊和雄蕊是多么亲热地依偎在一起；看着那刺荚里小小的种子是如何通过细微的卷曲的荚筋吸吮生命的汁液，以及那小小的胚胎是如何卧在里面睡眠。好哇，就这样坐在一旁，

in the world's life; but when great men blossom into books looking into those flowers also, to see how the world of men too opens beautifully, leaf after leaf. Ah! Life is delicious; well to live long, and see the darkness breaking, and the day coming. The day when soul shall not thrust back soul that would come to it; when men shall not be driven to seek solitude, because of the crying out of their hearts for love and sympathy. Well to live long; life is sweet, sweet, sweet! In his breast pocket, where of old the broken slate used to be, there was now a little dancing shoe of his friend who was sleeping. He could feel it when he folded his arm tight against his breast; and that was well also. He drew his hat lower over his eyes, and sat so motionless that the chickens thought he was asleep, and gathered closer around him. One even ventured to peck at his boot; but he ran away quickly. Tiny, yellow fellow that he was, he knew that men were dangerous; even sleeping they might awake. But Waldo did not sleep, and coming back from his sunshiny dream, stretched out his hand for the tiny thing to mount. But the chicken eyed the hand askance, and then ran off to hide under its mother's wing, and from beneath it it sometimes put out its round head to peep at the great figure sitting there. Presently its brothers ran off after a little white moth, and it ran out to join them; and when the moth fluttered away over their heads they stood looking up disappointed, and then ran back to their mother.

Waldo through his half-closed eyes looked at them. Thinking, fearing, craving, those tiny sparks of brother life , what were they,

不涉世事，多么好哇；然而，当伟人们如花绽放在书籍中时，他也仔细观察那些“花儿”，看见人间世界也在一页一页地以美丽的姿态展示着自己。啊！生活多美好。长久地活着多好啊，看着黑暗消逝，看着那一天到来。那一天，试图亲近灵魂的灵魂不再遭排斥；那一天，人们因为心灵呼唤着爱和同情而不再被迫寻求孤寂。长久地活着多好啊，生活是甜蜜的，甜蜜的，甜蜜的！在他上胸的口袋里，往日那里有破碎的石片，现在装着他长眠的朋友的一只小舞鞋。当他弯着一只胳膊紧紧地捂在胸上时，他能摸到它；那也让他感觉很好。他把帽檐拉下来遮住眼睛，一动不动地坐着，小鸡以为他在睡觉，便围了上来。有一只竟然过来啄他的靴子，但又赶紧跑了。这虽是一只很小的小黄鸡，但它知道人是危险的，即使睡着了也可能醒来。可是沃尔多并没有睡着，他从阳光灿烂的梦中醒来，伸出手引小家伙爬上来。小鸡怀疑地看着他的手，然后跑了，躲进妈妈的翅膀下，偶尔也探出圆圆的脑袋偷看坐在那里的巨人。一会儿，它的几个兄弟跑着去追逐一只小白蛾，它也跟着一起追；蛾子在它们的头上扑打着翅膀飞走了，它们就失望地站在那里仰头看，然后又跑回妈妈那里。

沃尔多虚睁着眼睛看着它们。他在想着，怕着，渴望着，那些兄弟间友爱生活的小火花，真真切

so real there in that old yard on that sunshiny afternoon? A few years—where would they be? Strange little brother spirit! He stretched his hand towards them, for his heart went out to them; but not one of the little creatures came nearer him and he watched them gravely for a time; then he smiled, and began muttering to himself after his old fashion. Afterwards he folded his arms upon his knees, and rested his forehead on them. And so he sat there in the yellow sunshine, muttering, muttering, muttering to himself.

It was not very long after when Em came out at the back-door with a towel thrown across her head, and in her hand a cup of milk.

"Ah," she said, coming close to him, "he is sleeping now. He will find it when he wakes, and be glad of it."

She put it down upon the ground beside him. The mother-hen was at work still among the stones, but the chickens had climbed about him, and were perching on him. One stood upon his shoulder, and rubbed its little head softly against his black curls; another tried to balance itself on the very edge of the old felt hat. One tiny yellow stood upon his hand, and tried to crow; another had nestled itself down comfortably on the old coat-sleeve, and gone to sleep there.

Em did not drive them away; but she covered the glass softly at his side. "He will wake soon," she said, "and be glad of it."

But the chickens were wiser.

切地，就在那古老的院落里，就在那阳光明媚的午后，它们是什么呢？几年以后，它们又会在哪里呢？奇怪而又可爱的兄弟间的情谊！他把手朝它们伸过去，因为他的心向着它们；可是这些小家伙没有一个肯过来，他表情严肃地看着它们，一会儿，他笑了，又开始自言自语地嘟哝起来，还是老样子。后来他双臂抱膝，把头靠在臂上。就这样，他在金黄色的阳光下坐着，一直在跟自己嘟哝着。

不久，艾姆从后门出来，头上蒙着一条毛巾，手里端着一杯牛奶。

“啊，”她边说边走上前来，“他睡了。他醒来会看见的，他会高兴的。”

她把牛奶放在他身边的地上。母鸡仍在碎石中间觅食，可是小鸡们已经爬到他身上，在那里栖息了。一只站在他肩上，在他黑色的卷发上轻轻地蹭着它的小脑袋；另一只正晃晃悠悠地站在他那顶破旧的毡帽檐上。一只小黄鸡站在他的手上，正要叫；还有一只舒舒服服地卧在他那件旧外套的袖子上，已经睡着了。

艾姆没有赶它们，但是她把他身边的杯子轻轻地盖上了。“他一会儿就会醒的，”她说，“他会高兴的。”

可是，小鸡更聪明。

译后语

在这段文字里，沃尔多虽然没有一句台词，但通过作者对他内心感受和身体动作的描写，读者被融入了他的感觉、他的感情和他的思想。沃尔多没有多少文化，会做木工，也会做瓦工，但他对生活、对大自然和身边事物的感觉非常细腻。他感觉生活是美好的，不同寻常，丰富多彩。当他“看着远处金黄色的阳光，阳光甚至将空气都染上了一层熟透的小麦的颜色，他感到幸福。”他与人世无争，与自然和谐相处，他很满足，希望生活“总像现在这样”。

沃尔多的感情生活丰富。他“仔细观察花儿的内心，看着雌蕊和雄蕊是多么亲热地依偎在一起；看着那刺荚里小小的种子是如何通过细微的卷曲的荚筋吸吮生命的汁液，以及那小小的胚胎是如何卧在里面睡眠。”他将自己的情感延伸到大自然，自然界的一切都是有感情、有生命的。

在沃尔多的心中，小鸡是可爱的，“他的心向着它们”。当小鸡害怕时，就“躲进妈妈的翅膀下”；当小鸡追捕小蛾未成，便“跑回妈妈那里”，对幼小的生命充满了柔情；他喜欢它们“兄弟间的情谊”，他关切这些小生命：“几年以后，它们又会在哪里呢？”最后，当小鸡纷纷跑到他身上栖息时，他与小鸡融为一体。

他将自己的感情系之于小生命。他衣袋里的那只小舞鞋，是属于他“长眠的朋友”，即未在文章里出现的 Lyndall ——艾姆(Em)的 cousin。他把 Lyndall 生前穿过的小舞鞋放在自己的衣袋里，以示怀念。

沃尔多有美好的追求,他希望“看着黑暗消逝,看着那一天到来。那一天,试图亲近灵魂的灵魂不再遭排斥;那一天,人们因为心灵呼唤着爱和同情而不再被迫寻求孤寂。”他不但与自然和谐相处,他也追求人与人之间的“爱”和“同情”,追求人与人之间的和谐。

读者仔细阅读,还可以从这段文字里解读出更多内容。

这是一部写于一百三十多年前的小说,今天读起来仍觉其文字简单、易懂,轻松、自然,这是很难得的。翻译时,也需尽量保持原文风格。此外,关于文中 well 的译法需略做说明。

文章里“well”这个字连续出现好几次。如:

(1) Ah, to live on so, year after year, how **well**!

(2) **Well**, how **well**, to sit so on one side...

(3) ... **well** to live long...

(4) **Well** to live long...

(5) He could feel it when he folded his arms tight against his breast; and that was **well** also.

这几处的 well 可看作形容词,意为 in a satisfactory state,翻译时需要注意语气。

Goldsworthy Lowes Dickinson

戈兹沃西·洛斯·迪金森(1862—1932),英国作家,在第一次世界大战期间是一个和平主义者,后来在酝酿成立国际联盟过程中发挥了重要作用。政治著作有 *The International Anarchy, 1904—1914* (1926)。*The Greek View of Life* (1896)是他研究希腊社会的一部名著。后文选自他的 *Letters from John Chinaman*。

Literature in Cathay

Goldsworthy Lowes Dickinson

In China letters are respected not merely to a degree but in a sense which must seem, I think, to you unintelligible and overstrained. But there is a reason for it. Our poets and literary men have taught their successors, for long generations, to look for good not in wealth, not in power, not in miscellaneous activity, but in a trained, a choice, an exquisite appreciation of the most simple and universal relations of life. To feel, and in order to feel to express, or at least to understand the expression of all that is lovely in Nature, of all that is poignant and sensitive in man, is to us in itself a sufficient end. A rose in a moonlit garden, the shadow of trees on the turf, almond blossom, scent of pine, the wine-cup and the guitar; these and the pathos of life and death, the long embrace, the hand stretched out in vain, the moment that glides for ever away, with its freight of music and light, into the shadow and hush of the haunted past, all that we have, all that eludes us, a bird on the wing, a perfume escaped on the gale—to all these things we are trained to respond, and the response is what we call literature.

文学在中国

戈兹沃西·洛斯·迪金森

在中国，文学不只在一定程度上受尊重，而且我想，你们肯定以为在某种意义上，这种尊重是难以理解、过于强调了。可是，这里面是有道理的。长期以来，我们的诗人和文人教育他们的继承者不要在财富里、不要在权力里、也不要在繁琐的活动里去寻找美好的东西，而是用训练有素的、有选择的和敏锐的眼光在对最简单、最普遍的生活关系的鉴赏中去寻找。去感受（为了表达而去感受）或至少去理解大自然所有美好的表露，以及人类所有痛楚和敏感的表露，对我们来说，这本身就是目的，足够了。月光下花园里的一朵玫瑰花，草地上树木的影子，扁桃的花朵，松树的香味，酒杯和吉他；以上这些以及生与死的痛苦，长时间的拥抱，徒劳伸出的手臂，承载着自身的音乐和光明悄然而过、永远消逝在烦扰的往昔之阴影和寂静里的时光，我们所拥有的一切，从我们身边遁去的一切，正在飞行的鸟儿，随风飘逝的芳香——对于所有这些，我们已有训练能够做出反应，而这一反应就是我们所谓的文学。

译后语

关于行文节奏

语言的力量和美感是由多种因素形成的，节奏感是其中之一。

英语里常常有很长的句子，翻译时有时可以断句，即把一个长句断成几个符合逻辑的短句，这是常见的做法；有时可以采取划分意群的做法，即单词以上、小句以下的构成意义的单位。在翻译之前的阅读中需正确判断句子里的意群，并体悟其行文节奏。如：

Our poets and literary men/ have taught their successors,/ for long generations,/ to look for good/ not in wealth,/ not in power,/ not in miscellaneous activity,/ but in a trained, a choice, an exquisite appreciation/ of the most simple and universal relations of life./

清楚划分意群，不论是默读还是朗读，都可以感受到句子的节奏。翻译时如果处理得当，有时需略做变通，在照顾汉语表达习惯的前提下，可以使此节奏在译文里得到反映。如：

> 长期以来/我们的诗人和文人/教育他们的继承者/不要在财富里、/不要在权力里、/也不要在繁琐的活动里/去寻找美好的东西，/而是用训练有素的、有选择的和敏锐的眼光/在对最简单、最普遍的生活关系的鉴赏中去寻找。

这篇文章一共五句话，多数句子较长，但都有明显的节奏感，翻译时注意到节奏问题，不仅能把长句译清楚，还能使整篇文章有气势。

George Santayana

乔治·桑塔亚纳(1863—1952),西班牙人,哲学家、美学家、小说家,他的学术思想在欧美有广泛影响。桑塔亚纳1872年移居美国,入哈佛大学师从哲学家威廉·詹姆斯学哲学,毕业后留校任教。他一生大部分时间在美国和欧洲从事教学和研究。主要哲学著作有 *The Sense of Beauty* (1896)、*The Life of Reason* (1905—1906)、*Scepticism and Animal Faith* (1923)、*The Realms of Being* (1927—1940)。此外有三卷本自传 *Persons and Places* (1944—1953)和一部长篇小说 *The Last Puritan* (1935),这部小说曾荣登畅销书排行榜。后文选自他的 *Soliloquies in England*。

The Weather in His Soul

George Santayana

Let me come to the point boldly; what governs the Englishman is his inner atmosphere, the weather in his soul. It is nothing particularly spiritual or mysterious. When he has taken his exercise and is drinking his tea or his beer and lighting his pipe; when, in his garden or by his fire, he sprawls in an aggressively comfortable chair; when well-washed and well-brushed, he resolutely turns in church to the east and recites the Creed (with genuflexions, if he likes genuflexions) without in the least implying that he believes one word of it; when he hears or sings the most crudely sentimental and thinnest of popular songs, unmoved but not disgusted; when he makes up his mind who is his best friend or his favourite poet; when he adopts a party or a sweetheart; when he is hunting or shooting or boating, or striding through the fields; when he is choosing his clothes or his profession—never is it a precise reason, or purpose, or outer fact that determines him; it is always the atmosphere of his inner man.

To say that this atmosphere was simply a sense of physical

英国人灵魂里的气象

乔治·桑塔亚纳

让我直截了当地谈正题吧：是什么左右着英国人的言行举止呢？是他内在的情调，即他灵魂的气象。它不是某种宗教精神的，也不是神秘莫测的。设想一个英国人，在运动之余点着烟斗品茶或喝啤酒时；或者在花园里或壁炉旁懒洋洋地躺在舒适的安乐椅上时；或者在他精心梳洗之后，在教堂里毅然转向东方背诵（跪诵，假如他喜欢跪诵）信经，但丝毫也不意味着他相信其中的任何说法时；或者在他听着或哼着最粗俗、最伤感、最浅薄的流行歌曲，虽然无动于衷但也并不讨厌时；或者他在确定谁是他最好的朋友或最喜爱的诗人时；或者在他选择一个群体或一个恋人时；或者在他打猎、射击、划船或大踏步走过田野时；或者在他挑选服装或选择职业时——在他做这一切的时候，想必从来都不是因为某一确定的理由，或目的，或外界的事物在唆使他，而总是他内在的情调使然吧。

若说这一内在的情调仅仅是对于身体状况、

well-being, of coursing blood and a prosperous digestion, would be far too gross; for while psychic weather is all that, it is also a witness to some settled disposition, some ripening inclination for this or that, deeply rooted in the soul. It gives a sense of direction in life which is virtually a code of ethics, and a religion behind religion. On the other hand, to say it was the vision of any ideal or allegiance to any principle would be making it far too articulate and abstract. The inner atmosphere, when compelled to condense into words, may precipitate some curt maxim or over-simple theory as a sort of war-cry; but its puerile language does it injustice, because it broods at a much deeper level than language or even thought. It is a mass of dumb instincts and allegiances, the love of a certain quality of life, to be maintained manfully. It is pregnant with many a stubborn assertion and rejection. It fights under its trivial fluttering opinions like a smoking battleship under its flags and signals; you must consider, not what they are, but why they have been hoisted and will not be lowered. One is tempted at times to turn away in despair from the most delightful acquaintance—the picture of manliness, grace, simplicity, and honour, apparently rich in knowledge and humour—because of some enormous platitude he reverts to, some hopelessly stupid little dogma from which one knows that nothing can ever liberate him. The reformer must give him up; but why should one wish to reform a person so much better than oneself? He is like a thoroughbred horse, satisfying to the trained eye,

血液循环和消化功能的感觉，那未免过于粗浅；因为，尽管如此，灵魂的气象也是某种稳定的气质和日臻成熟的这种或那种的癖好的见证，都植根于灵魂深处。它给人以生活的方向感，实则是一种伦理准则，一种宗教背后的宗教。另一方面，若说它是对于任何理想的见识或对于任何原则的忠诚，那就把它说得过于直白也过于抽象了。这种“内在的情调”，在必须用凝练的语言表述时，可能生发出简短的格言或过于简单的理论，作为一种战斗口号；但那幼稚的语言并不能把它表述清楚，因为它孕育在比语言、甚至比思想还要深得多的层次上。它是许多无法言传的本能与忠诚的结合体，是对于一种生活品质的爱，只待勇敢地予以保持。它充满了执意的坚持和非摈弃不可的固执。它在各种微妙的、涌动于内心的见解之下进行战斗，就像一艘喷吐浓烟的战舰在各种旗帜和信号的指挥下进行战斗一样；你所要考虑的不是这些旗帜和信号是什么，而是它们既然已经升起就不再降落这是为什么。有时人在绝望中会回避他最乐于相处的知己——一幅具有大丈夫气概、儒雅、朴素和荣耀，而且显然是知识渊博和具有幽默感的形象——因为他这个相识有时会重新使用陈词滥调，陷入愚蠢的小小教条之中而不能自拔，又不听劝告。若想改变他就千万不要干涉他；可是，为什么偏要改变一个比自己好得多的人呢？何况他就像是一匹英国纯种马，在内行人看来

docile to the light touch, and coursing in most wonderful unison with you through the open world. What do you care what words he uses? Are you impatient with the lark because he sings rather than talks? and if he could talk, would you be irritated by his curious opinions? Of course, if any one positively asserts what is contrary to fact, there is an error, though the error may be harmless; and most divergencies between men should interest us rather than offend us, because they are effects of perspective, or of legitimate diversity in experience and interests. Trust the man who hesitates in his speech and is quick and steady in action, but beware of long arguments and long beards. Jupiter decided the most intricate questions with a nod, and a very few words and no gestures suffice for the Englishman to make his inner mind felt most unequivocally when occasion requires.

Instinctively the Englishman is no missionary, no conqueror. He prefers the country to the town, and home to foreign parts. He is rather glad and relieved if only natives will remain natives and strangers strangers, and at a comfortable distance from himself. Yet outwardly he is most hospitable and accepts almost anybody for the time being; he travels and conquers without a settled design, because he has the instinct of exploration. His adventures are all external; they change him so little that he is not afraid of them. He carries his English weather in his heart wherever he goes, and it becomes a cool spot in the desert, and a steady and sane oracle

无可挑剔，轻轻一拍就能领会你的意图，载着你穿越空旷的原野，和你完全融为一体。至于他说话时如何措辞，那有什么关系？你会因为云雀只会歌唱不会说话就对它失去耐心吗？假使它会说话，你会对它那些奇怪的念头感到厌烦吗？当然，假如有人武断地坚持与事实相反的意见，那肯定是错误的，虽然这错误未必有害；再说，人们之间有分歧应该使我们感到兴趣，而不是感到恼火，因为这些分歧是由于看问题的角度不同，或者由于经验和兴趣的多样性而引起的，而多样性总是合乎情理的。应当信任那种言语迟疑但行动迅速而坚定的人，但是要警惕无休止地争论和长着长胡子的人。即便面对最棘手的问题，朱庇特一点头就决定了，而当情况需要的时候，英国人只需三言两语而无需比比划划，就能使人准确无误地了解他的内心世界。

就本能而言，英国人不是传教士，不是征服者。他宁愿待在乡村，而不愿住在城市，宁愿待在家里，而不愿去陌生的地方。如果能做到本地人永远是本地人，陌生人永远是陌生人，而且和他保持一个他觉得舒适的距离，他会感觉很高兴，很轻松。而在外表上，他又非常好客，几乎任何人他都可以暂时地悦纳；他旅行，他征服，而没有一成不变的计划，因为探索是他的本能。他的冒险活动都是外在的，对他自己几乎没有什么影响，所以他不怕冒险。无论走到哪里，他在心里总是怀着他的"英国气象"——那是沙漠里一个清凉的处所，是人类的谵妄之中一个稳定而明智的圣堂。自从

amongst all the deliriums of mankind. Never since the heroic days of Greece has the world had such a sweet, just, boyish master. It will be a black day for the human race when scientific blackguards, conspirators, churls, and fanatics manage to supplant him.

希腊的英雄时代以来，走遍世界大约也很难碰到如此可爱、有正义感和孩子气的主人了。对于人类而言，倘若科学上的无赖、阴谋家、吝啬鬼和狂热之徒设法取代了他，那么这世界真的会变得暗无天日了。

译后语

此译文的译后语采用王宏印教授的点评：

乔治·桑塔亚纳是著名的哲学家、美学家。虽然多年在美国受教育并从事学术活动，但因为他的西班牙血统和他对美国社会的深刻认识，他对古希腊传统和欧洲文明有着衷心的喜爱。他的这篇写英国人性格的散文，思想异常深刻而比喻贴切新颖，观察洞悉入微而语言流畅自然，可谓英语文学中的名篇。这样一篇散文的翻译，自然要求一种特别的翻译方法和适当的翻译文体。这篇译文，可谓细微而达旨，委曲而流畅，细心阅读，总给人以美的享受。

首先一个问题是标题和开题几句的翻译。因为作者借助英国人对于天气的偏好，用 weather（天气）和 atmosphere（气候）与 soul（灵魂）和 inner（内在自我）构成基本的比喻性搭配，即 his inner atmosphere 和 the weather in his soul，同时指出它既不是宗教意义上的精神（spiritual），也没有神秘到莫测的地步（mysterious）。根据这种理解，再加上仔细的推敲，以兼有专业意思和文学意味的"情调"来译 atmosphere，用"气象"来译 weather，这样就产生了"内在的情调"和"灵魂的气象"两个基本词组，作为全篇的比喻基调。这样，标题只不过是一个扩充性说法而已——"英国人灵魂里的气象"。

比喻的贴切和精妙是桑塔亚纳散文的特点之一，译文采用尊重原作形象，适当发挥想象的译法，使抽象的思想明白可感，跃然纸上。下面引述的两个句子，首先一个是以战舰比喻英国人性格中的倾向，单一而复杂。只要想一下英国曾经有过的海上霸权地位，就知道这一比喻是何等地贴切而神妙。而译笔的流畅达意和发挥汉语优势的关系,以及译者的文学想象力恰到好处的使用,都是显而易见的。

It fights under its trivial fluttering opinions like a smoking battleship under its flags and signals; you must consider, not what they are, but why they have been hoisted and will not be lowered.

> 它在各种微妙的、涌动于内心的见解之下进行战斗,就像一艘喷吐浓烟的战舰在各种旗帜和信号的指挥下进行战斗一样;你所要考虑的不是这些旗帜和信号是什么,而是它们既然已经升起就不再降落这是为什么。

一想起英国人喜欢赛马,就知道第二个比喻把英国人比作纯种马,并从纯种马的角度来理解人与人的关系,是一种多么富有暗示性的哲理阐发。而译文在不中断叙述顺序的同时,也就顺乎自然地营造了一种天人合一的崇高意境了。

He is like a thoroughbred horse, satisfying to the trained eye, docile to the light touch, and coursing in most wonderful unison with you through the open world.

> 何况他就像是一匹英国纯种马,在内行人看来无可挑剔,轻轻一拍就能领会你的意图,载着你穿越空旷的原野,和你完全融为一体。

观察的仔细和致思的精密,反映在行文的流畅和思绪的激荡里,莫过于一连串现象的列举和逐渐推向一个普遍性结论的能力。这便是第一段的行文特点。在翻译上有限度地改变原文连续使用的"when..."结构,但同时保持原文分节停顿的分号";",可使全段文字产生统一中有变化的审美情趣。同时,长句开头处加一"设想"进行提示，列举结束时用一破折号“——”引出下面的译文，就起到了把多归结为一的收尾作用了：

> 在他做这一切的时候，想必从来都不是因为某一确定的理由，或目的，或外界的事物在唆使他，而总是他内在的情调使然吧。

到了全篇结束的时候，同样的写作手法又出现了。不过这里是结合了比喻在内的多种归一，与现代文明的贫瘠和苍白相比，作者的荒漠甘泉和俗地圣堂两个比喻，把思想的境界推到了一个至高无上的地位。译文把 become（变为）译为“是”字隐喻结构，加强了这两个比喻的收尾性效果，为全篇结束时把英国人的性格纳入希腊以来的文明史作为一种成就，起到了有力的铺垫作用。

He carries his English weather in his heart wherever he goes, and it becomes a cool spot in the desert, and a steady and sane oracle amongst all the deliriums of mankind.

> 无论走到哪里，他在心里总是怀着他的“英国气象”——那是沙漠里一个清凉的处所，是人类的谵妄之中一个稳定而明智的圣堂。

玄思与想象的结合是造就哲人式的文学家的一个必要的条件，也是构成桑塔亚纳这篇散文的个性化风格的一种成因。译者充分注意到这一点，可以说是译文成功的一个重要因素。词汇平面上一个明显的标志就是，原文采用专门术语的地方，就尽量译为专门术语，而原文采用文学语言的地方，就尽量译为文学语言。而在句法平面上，则较多地改英文比较直率的语气为汉语比较委婉的语气，比如假设、虚指、让步、设问、反问、重复、提示等手段，甚至包括少量文言虚词的使用，旨在有助于造成中文散文波澜起伏、一唱三叹的审美趣味。

以下列出一些典型例句,并附以必要的提示。

(1) Let me come to the point boldly; what governs the Englishman is his inner atmosphere, the weather in his soul.

让我直截了当地谈正题吧:是什么左右着英国人的言行举止呢?是他内在的情调,即他灵魂的气象。(设问、重复)

(2) To say that this atmosphere was simply a sense of physical well-being, of coursing blood and a prosperous digestion, would be far too gross...

若说这一内在的情调仅仅是对于身体状况、血液循环和消化功能的感觉,则未免过于粗浅……(文言虚词、假设语气、委婉讽喻)

(3) The reformer must give him up; but why should one wish to reform a person so much better than oneself?

若想改变他就千万不要干涉他;可是,为什么偏要改变一个比自己好得多的人呢?(假设语气、词类转换、生活用语)

一篇散文的成功写作,其因素是多方面的。同样,一篇散文的成功翻译,也要求译者多方面的功底和修养。译者和作者在语言能力、文学修养、气质习性上相一致的地方越多,则译文就越成功、越自然。

(王宏印点评)

Rudyard Kipling

拉迪亚德·吉卜林(1865—1936),英国作家,生于印度孟买,父亲约翰·洛克伍德·吉卜林(John Lockwood Kipling),写有 *Beast and Man in India* (1891)。拉迪亚德·吉卜林于 1871 年回英国上学。1882 年至 1889 年,作为记者在印度工作,创作了不少以印度为背景的作品。1907 年获诺贝尔文学奖。他的儿童文学作品 *The Jungle Book* (1894)获得好评。后来又写了 *The Second Jungle Book*。后文取自 *The Second Jungle Book*,是书中写得很好的一个片段,对月光和对动物的描写,都能看出作者塑造形象的语言技巧。

The Spring Running

Rudyard Kipling

It was a perfect white night, as they call it. All green things seemed to have made a month's growth since the morning. The branch that was yellow-leaved the day before dripped sap when Mowgli broke it. The mosses curled deep and warm over his feet, the young grass had no cutting edges, and all the voices of the Jungle boomed like one deep harp-string touched by the moon—the Moon of New Talk, who splashed her light full on rock and pool, slipped it between trunk and creeper, and sifted it through a million leaves. Forgetting his unhappiness, Mowgli sang aloud with pure delight as he settled into his stride. It was more like flying than anything else, for he had chosen the long downward slope that leads to the Northern Marshes through the heart of the main Jungle, where the springy ground deadened the fall of his feet. A man-taught man would have picked his way with many stumbles through the cheating moonlight, but Mowgli's muscles, trained by

春　跑

拉迪亚德·吉卜林

这正像人们所说的，是一个地道的白夜。自早晨，所有的绿色植物好像已经生长了一个月。昨天还有黄叶的树枝，莫格里折断一看，便有汁液滴出来。地上暖乎乎的苔藓没过他的双脚，小草还没有长出尖利的叶子，丛林里回荡着嗡嗡声，犹如竖琴的低音琴弦被月光拨动时发出的音响，月亮——“新交谈季”①的月亮——把它的光洒在石头上，洒在水洼里，穿过树干和藤萝之间的空隙，透过万千婆娑的树叶。当莫格里迈开步子跑起来，他便忘记了自己的不幸，怀着纯净的愉快的心情，高声唱了起来。那简直就是飞翔，因为他选择的是一条很长的下行山坡，穿过丛林的中心通向北泽，脚踩在松软而有弹性的地上听不见声音。即使是被别人提醒过的人，由于月光所造成的假象，在这样的地上跑步时也会经常被绊倒的，可是，莫格里的肌肉经

① 根据原著所述，丛林中各种动物在春季叫声特别，因此春季被称为“新交谈季”。

years of experience, bore him up as though he were a feather. When a rotten log or a hidden stone turned under his foot he saved himself, never checking his pace, without effort and without thought. When he tired of ground-going he threw up his hands monkey-fashion to the nearest creeper, and seemed to float rather than to climb up into the thin branches, whence he would follow a tree-road till his mood changed, and he shot downward in a long, leafy curve to the levels again. There were still, hot hollows surrounded by wet rocks where he could hardly breathe for the heavy scents of the night flowers and the bloom along the creeper buds; dark avenues where the moonlight lay in belts as regular as checkered marbles in a church aisle; thickets where the wet young growth stood breast-high about him and threw its arms round his waist; and hilltops crowned with broken rock, where he leaped from stone to stone above the lairs of the frightened little foxes. He would hear, very faint and far off, the chug-drug of a boar sharpening his tusks on a bole; and would come across the great gray brute all alone, scribing and rending the bark of a tall tree, his mouth dripping with foam, and his eyes blazing like fire. Or he would turn aside to the sound of clashing horns and hissing grunts, and dash past a couple of furious sambhur, staggering to and fro with lowered heads, striped with blood that showed black in the moonlight. Or at some rushing ford he would hear Jacala the Crocodile bellowing like a bull, or disturb a twined knot of the Poison People, but before they could strike he would be away and across the glistening shingle, and deep in the Jungle again.

过多年的锻炼，支撑着他就像支撑一片羽毛。当他踩到腐烂的树干和看不见的石头时，他从不放慢速度，也无所顾忌，仍能毫不费力地让自己平安无事。当他在地面上跑厌倦了，就像猴子似地把双手往上一伸，抓住最近的藤蔓，不是往上爬，而好像是漂进稀疏的树枝中间，然后他会沿着“树上的路”往前滑动，直到他的心情改变，便往下一跳，穿过空中的树叶划出一个长长的弧，又回到平地上。他经过静寂的很热的洼地，周围都是湿润的石头，夜里的花卉和藤蔓上的花蕾散发着浓郁的香味，几乎让他喘不过气来；黑暗的路上洒满带状的规则的月光，犹如教堂走道上的大理石；树丛里新生的小树长得齐胸高，树枝伸出来搂住他的身子；小山丘的顶上满是碎石块，他踩在上面往前跳着，石头下面就是狐狸窝，窝里的小狐狸吓得惊恐万状。他会听见远处传来野猪在树干上磨牙时发出的微弱的“喀嚓喀嚓”的声音；然后，便撞见一个巨大的灰色野兽，正在用它的獠牙把一棵大树的树皮划开撕成碎条，嘴里滴着白沫，眼睛冒出火光。或者，他躲开野猪之后又会听见动物犄角的碰撞声和嘴里发出的嘶嘶声，接着，就看见一对愤怒的黑鹿正低着头踉踉跄跄地相互顶撞，浑身流着在月光下呈黑色的一道道血迹，他便赶紧从它们身边跑过去。或者他来到水流湍急的浅滩时，会听见鳄鱼杰卡拉像公牛似地吼叫，或者惊扰了蜷曲成一团的毒蛇，但是，还没等它们来得及向他发起进攻，他已经跑开，越过闪闪发亮的卵石滩，跑进丛林的深处。

So he ran, sometimes shouting, sometimes singing to himself, the happiest thing in all the Jungle that night, till the smell of the flowers warned him that he was near the marshes, and those lay far beyond his farthest hunting-grounds.

就这样，他跑着，有时喊，有时唱。那天晚上丛林中数他最幸福，等闻到了花香，他才知道已经接近沼泽地，而那些沼泽比离他最远的猎场还要远得多。

译后语

此文里多有生动的描写,值得学习和借鉴。

1. 关于月光的描写

(1) **It** was a perfect **white night**, as they call it.

这里的 white night 很形象,引起联想,天上一轮明月,地上月光如洗。句子简洁,易懂,耐读。翻译这句话时,一考虑了句子的语序,若照原文语序翻译,也能懂,但不符合汉语习惯,因此,需对语序进行调整,故将从句 as they call it 往前提,提到符合汉语习惯的位置上;二考虑了句子的开头,原文的 It 作为主语代表天气夜色,译文也应有一个相应的主语,这里可以用"这"来表示,得如下译文:

这正像人们所说的,是一个地道的白夜。

这样译,文字通顺自然,符合汉语叙事习惯。

(2) —the Moon of New Talk, who **splashed** her light full on rock and pool, **slipped** it between trunk and creeper, and **sifted** it through a million leaves.

这句话描写月光洒满大地,无处不在。这里用了三个动词 splashed、slipped、sifted,描绘月光洒向林间、水石相映、树影斑驳的景象,如画一般。三个动词都产生了形象的修辞效果,译文用了"洒在""穿过"和"透过",与原文的效果相近。

月亮把它的光洒在石头上,洒在水洼里,穿过树干和藤萝之间的空隙,透过万千婆娑的树叶。

(3) ... and all the voices of the Jungle **boomed** like one deep

harp-string **touched by the moon**...

作家的想象很奇特，听见丛林里的嗡嗡声，联想到竖琴的低音琴弦被月光拨动时发出的音响，犹如仙乐，轻柔，美妙。这句话里有两个动词需处理好，boomed 是动词象声词，因此将其译成"回荡着嗡嗡声"；touched by the moon 译成汉语并不困难，但表述方式则需要考虑所描写环境的氛围。如下：

> 丛林里回荡着嗡嗡声，犹如竖琴的低音琴弦被月光拨动时发出的音响……

2. 关于动物的描写

(1) He would hear, very faint and far off, the chug-drug of **a boar sharpening his tusks** on a bole; and would come across the great gray brute all alone, **scribing and rending the bark of a tall tree, his mouth dripping with foam, and his eyes blazing like fire.**

这是描写林中的野猪在树干上磨牙时发出的声音，嘴里冒着白沫，眼睛射出火光，这一生动形象的塑造与现在分词的运用有关，如 a boar sharpening his tusks；与独立主格结构的运用有关，如"scribing and rending the bark, his mouth dripping with foam, and his eyes blazing like fire"。读者好像听见了野猪磨牙时发出的声音，看见了野猪磨牙时的样子。

(2) Or he would turn aside to the sound of clashing horns and hissing grunts, and dash past a couple of furious sambhur, staggering to and fro with lowered heads, striped with blood that showed black in the moonlight.

这句话和前面的句子类似，描写两只黑鹿用它们的犄角争斗时发出的声音和身体的姿态。

以上两句话都是描写林中野生动物的形象，有声音，有动作。翻译时妥善处理分词和独立主格结构对于再现原文的生动形象是重要的。

3. 关于具有动词意义的名词的使用

英语作家很会使用具有动词意义的名词，用好了不仅使文字简洁，还给人新奇之感。如：

(1) All green things seemed to have made a month's **growth** since the morning.

(2) ... where the springy ground deadened the **fall** of his feet.

(3) ... he threw up his hands **monkey-fashion** to the nearest creeper.

在第(1)、(2)句里，growth 和 fall 都是名词，译成汉语时倒不必追求词性上的对应，只是将句子的意思准确地表达出来就可以了。在第(3)句里，monkey-fashion 虽然也是由名词组成的词组，但在句子里却是作状语，因此，译成汉语时往往还是以状语形式出现。

4. 两点说明

(1) the Moon of New Talk 在书中有特定的含义，必须根据上下文去理解，因此，将 the Moon of New Talk 译成"新交谈季"的月亮。

(2) the Poison People，经查阅原著，指毒蛇。

Edward Verral Lucas

爱德华·维拉尔·卢卡斯(1868—1938),英国作家和评论家,当过英国杂志 *Punch* 的助理编辑,写过讽刺小品和游记,著有 *Old Lamps for New* (1911)、*Saunterers Rewards* (1933)和 *Only the Other Day* (1936)。他写的查尔斯·兰姆传记以及整理的查尔斯·兰姆和玛丽·兰姆通信集为读者称道。他的长篇小说 *Over Bemerton* (1908)被认为是他写得最好的小说。后文选自他的 *Old Lamps for New*。

The Windmill

Edward Verral Lucas

Chance recently made me for a while the tenant of a windmill. Not to live in, and unhappily not to grind corn in, but to visit as the mood arose, and see the ships in the harbour from the topmost window, and look down on the sheep and the green world all around. For this mill stands high and white—so white, indeed, that when there is a thunder cloud behind it, it seems a thing of polished aluminium.

From its windows you can see four other mills, all, like itself, idle, and one merely a ruin and one with only two sweeps left. But just over the next range of hills, out of sight, to the northeast, is a windmill that still merrily goes, and about five miles away to the northwest is another also active; so that things are not quite so bad hereabouts as in many parts of the country, where the good breezes blow altogether in vain ...

Thinking over the losses which England has had forced upon her by steam and the ingenuity of the engineer, one is disposed to count the decay of the windmill among the first. Perhaps in the

风车磨坊

爱德华·维拉尔·卢卡斯

最近，一次偶然的机会，我在一个风车磨坊里停留了一阵，不是在那里居住，很不幸，也不是磨麦子，而是一时兴致所至前去看看，从它最上面的窗户看看港湾里的船只，看看下面的羊群和周围绿色的世界。因为这个磨坊挺高，而且是白色的，确实很白，当它后面的天空出现雷雨云时，磨坊看上去就像一个擦得很亮的铝制建筑。

你从它的窗户可以看见四个别的磨坊，和这个一样，都是闲置的，有一个不过是一堆废墟而已，还有一个只剩下两扇翼板。可是，就在下一排小山的背面，在东北方向看不见的地方，有一个风车磨坊仍在欢快地运行，在西北方向大约五英里处还有一个也在运行；看来，这一带的情况还不坏，不像在这个国家很多地方那样，大好的风力白白浪费掉了……

若仔细想一想，由于蒸汽动力的发明和工程师的聪明才智给英格兰造成的诸多损失，你会把风车磨坊的衰落列为首当其冲的损失之一。也许，单就

matter of pure picturesqueness the most serious thing that ever happened to England was the discovery of galvanized iron roofing; but, after all, there was never anything but quiet and rich and comfortable beauty about red roofs, whereas the living windmill is not only beautiful but romantic too: a willing, man-serving creature, yoked to the elements, a whirling monster, often a thing of terror. No one can stand very near the crashing sweeps of a windmill in half a gale without a tightening of the heart—a feeling comparable to that which comes from watching the waves break over a wall in a storm. And to be within the mill at such a time is to know something of sound's very sources; it is the cave of noise itself. No doubt there are dens of hammering energy which are more shattering, but the noise of a windmill is largely natural, the product of wood striving with the good sou'-wester; it fills the ears rather than assaults them. The effect, moreover, is by no means lessened by the absence of the wind itself and the silent nonchalance of the miller and his man, who move about in the midst of this appalling racket with the quiet efficiency of vergers.

In my mill, of course, there is no such uproar; nothing but the occasional shaking of the cross-pieces of the idle sails. Everything is still; and the pity of it is that everything is in almost perfect order for the day's work. The mill one day—some score years ago—was full of life; the next, and ever after, mute and lifeless, like a stream frozen in a night or the palace in Tennyson's ballad of the "Sleeping Beauty". There is no decay—merely inanition. One or two of the

纯粹如画的风景而论，英格兰发生的最重要的事情莫过于发现了镀锌铁皮屋顶；可是，红屋顶毕竟给人一种安谧、丰富和舒适的美感，然而，仍在运行的风车磨坊不仅是美丽的，而且还有一种浪漫情调：一个受制于自然力并情愿为人类服务的工具，一个旋转的大怪物，常常让人感到惧怕的东西。任何人在四五级风里站在发出巨响的风车翼板附近都会心情紧张，可以与之相比的是在暴风雨里看着巨浪冲过防浪墙时的感觉。在这个时候身处磨坊之中，就知道声音的源头在何处；它本身就是发声的洞穴。毋庸置疑，还有其他很有冲击力的洞穴，声音更响，但风车的声音大多是自然的，是木制翼板在如意的西南风吹动下拼命旋转时发出的声音；它充盈于耳，但不对耳朵造成猛烈冲击。而且，这声音的影响，并不因为风的止息而减弱，也不因为磨坊主人和他的工人(他们在可怕的嘈杂声中像教堂司事那样静静地走来走去)默默不语和若无其事就减弱了。

当然，在我的磨坊里，没有这样的喧嚣，只有闲置的翼板横杆偶尔颤动的声音。一切都静止不动；但遗憾的是，一切都几乎是井然有序的，好像做好了一天工作的准备。大约二十年前的某一天，这个磨坊充满活力，随后，而且自那以后，就哑然无声，死气沉沉了，就像一夜之间结了冰的小溪，或像丁尼生的叙事诗《睡美人》中的宫殿。在我的磨坊里看不见衰落，只是空荡。有一两个

apple-wood cogs have been broken from the great wheel; a few floor planks have been rotted; but that is all. A week's overhauling would put everything right. But it will never come, and the cheerful winds that once were to drive a thousand English mills so happily now bustle over the Channel in vain.

苹果木做的轮齿从巨大的转轮上断了下来,地板上有几块木板已经腐烂,仅此而已。只要用一个星期的时间检修一下就会让一切恢复正常。但那样的事情不会再有了,曾经吹动上千家英国磨坊欢快运转的快乐的风,现在匆匆地掠过英吉利海峡,劳而无功。

译后语

关于行文语气和作者态度

作者写文章——叙事、议论或抒情——都流露一种情绪，都表明或暗示一种态度，这一情绪或态度在行文语气里体现出来。行文语气通过多种修辞手段得以显现，如用词、句式、重复、意象、象征以及一些押韵的运用。在“The Windmill”里，行文语气比较多地从用词和句式中看出来。比如，当作者来到一个停止运转的风车磨坊，并且发现附近的四个其他磨坊也闲着，他感到惋惜：

(1) Not to live in, and unhappily not to grind corn in, but to visit as the mood arose...

风车磨坊现在失去了它的功能，不能居住，也不能磨麦子，而只是供人闲时观景之用，作者（姑且将文章里的第一人称看作作者本人）颇觉不幸。

(2) From its windows you can see four other mills, all, like itself, idle, and one merely a ruin and one with only two sweeps left.

附近的四个风车磨坊不仅闲着，而且有一个变成了废墟，还有一个只剩下两扇翼板，在作者眼里，这是一片凋零的景象。

(3) Thinking over the losses which England has had forced upon her by steam and the ingenuity of the engineer, one is disposed to count the decay of the windmill among the first.

在作者看来，风车磨坊停转是英格兰的损失，是由蒸汽动力的发明和工程师的聪明才智造成的。不仅流露出作者的怀旧情绪,也暗示他对现代工业文明的保留态度。

(4) Everything is still;and the pity of it is that everything is in almost perfect order for the day's work.

作者的磨坊一切井然有序,好像已经做好工作的准备,但很遗憾,它现在已经停止运转了。但当作者看见有一个风车磨坊仍在运转时便情不自禁地流露出喜悦的心情:

(5) ... to the northeast,is a windmill that still merrily goes.

而且认为仍在运转的风车磨坊不仅美丽,还有一种浪漫情调:

(6) the living windmill is not only beautiful but romantic too.

文章里有几句采取对比写法,作者两种不同的心情交织在一起。

(7) ... so that things are not quite so bad hereabouts as in many parts of the country, where the good breezes blow altogether in vain...

(8) The mill one day-some score years ago was full of life; the next, and ever after, mute and lifeless...

二十年前,磨坊充满活力,后来便哑然无声,死气沉沉。

例(7)是时间的对比,例(8)是地点的对比。当作者看到英国很多地方的风力白白浪费掉,而这一带的情况还不坏的时候,他感到些许安慰。

文章的最后一句,"But it will never come, and the cheerful winds that once were to drive a thousand English mills so happily now bustle over the Channel in vain."概括了作者的惋惜和遗憾:风车的时代不会再来了,现在快乐的风白白掠过英吉利海峡,白白浪

费掉了。

翻译前仔细揣摩文章的用词和句式与行文语气的关系，进而体会作者的情绪和态度，翻译时尽量在这方面贴近原文，对把握译文的笔调有帮助。

Mark Rutherford

马克·拉瑟福德是威廉·黑尔·怀特(William Hale White,1831—1913)的笔名,英国维多利亚时期小说家,也作文学批评,同时为报纸写过大量文章。后文取自*Mark Rutherford's Deliverance*(1885)。

A Londoner's Holiday

Mark Rutherford

One Sunday we determined upon a holiday. It was a bold adventure for us, but we had made up our minds. There was an excursion train to Hastings, and accordingly Ellen, Marie, and myself were at London Bridge Station early in the morning. It was a lovely summer's day in mid-July. The journey down was uncomfortable enough in consequence of the heat and dust, but we heeded neither one nor the other in the hope of seeing the sea. We reached Hastings at about eleven o'clock, and strolled westwards towards Bexhill. Our pleasure was exquisite. Who can tell, save the imprisoned Londoner, the joy of walking on the clean sea sand! What a delight that was, to say nothing of the beauty of the scenery! To be free of the litter and filth of a London suburb, of its broken hedges, its brickbats, its torn advertisements, its worn and trampled grass in fields half given over to the speculative builder: in place of this, to tread the immaculate shore over which breathed a wind not charged with soot; to replace the dull, shrouding obscurity of the smoke by a distance so distinct that the masts of the ships whose hulls were buried below the horizon were visible — all this was perfect bliss.

一个伦敦人的假日

马克·拉瑟福德

一个星期日，我们决定去度假。这对我们来说是一次大胆的冒险，可是，我们已经下定了决心。城里有一列去黑斯廷斯的旅游火车，于是，我和埃伦、玛丽一清早就来到伦敦大桥火车站。那是7月中旬一个晴朗的夏日。因为天热，尘土也多，一路上很不舒服，可是，我们盼着看海，对这些都不在意。大约11点钟我们到了黑斯廷斯，然后，朝西向贝克斯希尔走去。我们高兴极了。除了被憋在城里的伦敦人，谁能说得出走在干净的海沙上那种愉快的心情呢！那是多么开心呀，更不用说那美丽的景色！摆脱伦敦郊区的垃圾和污秽，摆脱那里损坏的树篱、抛掷的砖头、破损的广告，以及多半已经给了投机开发商的田地上那被踩坏的青草：我们迎着不含煤烟的海风在干净的海岸上漫步；没有讨厌的弥漫的烟雾，一望无际，远处的船只虽然埋在天际线以下，船桅却清晰可见，这一切都让人欣喜至极。

It was not very poetic bliss, perhaps; but nevertheless it is a fact that the cleanness of the sea and the sea air was as attractive to us as any of the sea attributes. We had a wonderful time. Only in the country is it possible to note the change of morning into mid-day, of mid-day into afternoon, and of afternoon into evening; and it is only in the country, therefore, that a day seems stretched out into its proper length. We had brought all our food with us, and sat upon the shore in the shadow of a piece of the cliff. A row of heavy white clouds lay along the horizon almost unchangeable and immovable, with their summit lines and the part of the mass just below them steeped in sunlight. The level opaline water differed only from a floor by a scarcely perceptible heaving motion, which broke into the faintest of ripples at our feet. So still was the great ocean, so quietly did everything lie in it, that the wavelets which licked the beach were as pure and bright as if they were a part of the mid-ocean depths. About a mile from us, at one o'clock, a long row of porpoises appeared, showing themselves in graceful curves for half an hour or so, till they went out farther to sea off Fairlight. Some fishing boats were becalmed just in front of us. Their shadows slept, or almost slept, upon the water, a gentle quivering alone showing that it was not complete sleep, or if sleep, that it was sleep with dreams. The intensity of the sunlight sharpened the outlines of every little piece of rock, and of the pebbles, in a manner which seemed supernatural to us Londoners. In London we get the heat of the sun, but not the light,

也许，这不是特别富有诗意的喜悦；可是，大海的洁净、海上空气的清新，如同大海的任何别的特征一样，对我们极富吸引力，这却是事实。我们度过了一段十分美好的时光。只有在乡间才能注意到从早晨到中午、从中午到下午、从下午到晚上的变化；因而，只有在乡间，一天的时间看来才能延伸到它应有的长度。我们都带了食物，坐在海滩上一个峭壁的阴凉处。一排厚厚的白云浮在天际线之上，几乎没有变化，纹丝不动，白云高处的轮廓线及其下面的部分浸润在阳光里。平稳的蛋白石色水面看似地板，但它那难以察觉的涌动又使它不似地板，涌动的水面在我们脚下形成极其微弱的波纹。大海是那样的平静，海里的一切是那样的安静，拍打着海滩的涟漪，是那样的纯净，那样的清亮，好像它们是来自海洋中间深处的一部分。下午1点钟，距离我们大约一英里的地方，来了长长的一串鼠海豚，展示它们身体的优雅线条，大约过了半个小时，它们又朝费尔莱特村以外的远海游去了。几只渔船停在我们面前。小船的影子在海面上睡觉，或几乎在睡觉，偶尔一点微微的波动表示船影没有完全入睡，或者即便睡了，也是在睡梦之中。强烈的阳光把每一块小岩石和鹅卵石都照得轮廓鲜明，这在我们伦敦人看来很神奇。在伦敦，我们只有太阳的高温，而看不到太阳的光线；

and the separation of individual parts into such vivid isolation was so surprising that even Marie noticed it, and said it "all seemed as if she were looking through a glass". It was perfect—perfect in its beauty—and perfect because, from the sun in the heavens down to the fly with burnished wings on the hot rock, there was nothing out of harmony. Everything breathed one spirit. Marie played near us; Ellen and I sat still, doing nothing. We wanted nothing, we had nothing to achieve; there were no curiosities to be seen, there was no particular place to be reached, no "plan of operations," and London was forgotten for the time. It lay behind us in the northwest, and the cliff was at the back of us shutting out all thought of it. No reminiscences and no anticipations disturbed us; the present was sufficient, and occupied us totally.

在这里,阳光把每一个物体都变得如此清晰分明,真让人感到惊奇,连玛丽都注意到了,她说:“都像透过镜子看到的一样。”这太完美了,美到了极致。说它完美,因为,从天上的太阳到热石上翅膀闪亮的苍蝇,没有一样东西是不和谐的。一切都透露出一种同样的精神。玛丽在我们附近玩,我和埃伦静静地坐着,什么也没做。我们什么也不想要,也没有什么事情要去完成;周围看不见让人好奇的事情,也没有特别想去的地方,没有“活动计划”,暂时把伦敦抛在了脑后。伦敦在我们后面的西北方向,峭壁就耸立在我们身后,挡着我们不去想伦敦。不想过去,也不想未来;眼下就足够了,我们完全被眼下的情景占据了。

译后语

“A Londoner’s Holiday”是一篇关于伦敦人去海滨度假的游记，一篇如诗如画的散文。一家人离开污秽的伦敦郊区，来到海边，踩着洁净的海沙，呼吸着清新的空气，一览大海的景象，快乐的心情难以形容。

1. 关于细节描写

旅游者愉悦的心情来自对大自然、对天上海上各种景象的感受。抬眼望去，海天相接的地方浮着白云，形状不变，位置不移，白云高处的轮廓线及其下面的部分浸润在阳光里。轻巧、准确的文字描绘出阳光之下白云的形象：

A row of heavy white clouds lay along the horizon almost unchangeable and immovable, with their summit lines and the part of the mass just below them steeped in sunlight.

然后写海水，写海水的颜色，写平静的海面上涟漪微起拍打海滩的情景：

The level opaline water differed only from a floor by a scarcely perceptible heaving motion, which broke into the faintest of ripples at our feet. So still was the great ocean, so quietly did everything lie in it, that the wavelets which licked the beach were as pure and bright as if they were a part of the mid-ocean depths.

大海远处露出鼠海豚身体的曲线，泳姿优美，令人神往：

About a mile from us, at one o’clock, a long row of porpoises appeared, showing themselves in graceful curves for half an hour or so, till they went out farther to sea off Fairlight.

小船停在海面上,影子一动不动犹如睡眠,偶尔微微颤动如在梦中:

Some fishing boats were becalmed just in front of us. Their shadows slept, or almost slept, upon the water, a gentle quivering alone showing that it was not complete sleep, or if sleep, that it was sleep with dreams.

写阳光时没有直接写其明媚,而是写石头在阳光照耀之下的鲜明轮廓,给久居城里的伦敦人一种神奇之感:

The intensity of the sunlight sharpened the outlines of every little piece of rock, and of the pebbles, in a manner which seemed supernatural to us Londoners.

作者对这些细节如此细致、清楚、真实的描写,并巧妙地将这些细节交织在一起,绘制了一幅大海的立体的动态画面,把人带进另一个境界,使人陶醉。他描写海景时所选的词语和恰当的搭配,值得借鉴和模仿。

2. 关于译文的几点说明

(1) 简单句的翻译

文章叙述度假过程,描写自然景象,抒发内心感受,除少数几个较长的主从句以外,简短明了的句子比较多。其中一部分是简单句,如:

One Sunday we determined upon a holiday.

It was a lovely summer's day in mid-July.

Our pleasure was exquisite.

还有较长的并列句,可视为简单句的组合,如:

We wanted nothing, we had nothing to achieve; there were no

curiosities to be seen, there was no particular place to be reached, no "plan of operations" and London was forgotten for the time.

翻译这样的句子，就本文而言，多数情况下，可依照原文的语序，无需重组句子结构，但需斟酌，尽量译出原文的行文语气。

(2) 关于 to give sth over to 的意思和翻译

这个动词搭配出自文中的"its worn and trampled grass in fields half given over to the speculative builder"。《牛津高阶英汉双语词典》说，to give sth over to 是 to use sth for one particular purpose，即"把……留作特定用途"。故将这句话译作"以及多半已经给了投机开发商的土地上那被踩坏的青草……"。

(3) 关于 a distance 和 distinct 意思的确定

这两个词出自文中的"... to replace the dull, shrouding obscurity of the smoke by a distance so distinct that the masts of the ships whose hulls were buried below the horizon were visible...", 其中 a distance 既可作"距离"解，也可作"远"或"远处"解，也就是距离伦敦很远的海滨，本文译者倾向后者，后面的 distinct 可解释为"清晰"，这样能使上下文的意思一致。故将这句话译为：

> 没有讨厌的弥漫的烟雾，一望无际，远处的船只虽然埋在天际线以下，船桅却清晰可见……

Robert Bridges

罗伯特·布里吉斯(1844—1930),英国诗人,1913 年至 1930 年的桂冠诗人。*The Testament of Beauty* (1929)被认为是他最伟大的作品。后文取自 *Memoir Prefixed to Poems of Digby Mackworth Dolben*。

A School Portrait

Robert Bridges

I had not visited Eton for many years, when one day passing from the Fellows' Library into the Gallery I caught sight of the portrait of my school-friend Digby Dolben hanging just without the door among our most distinguished contemporaries. I was wholly arrested, and as I stood gazing on it, my companion asked me if I knew who it was. I was thinking that, beyond a few whom I could name, I must be almost the only person who would know. Far memories of my boyhood were crowding freshly upon me: he was standing again beside me in the eager promise of his youth; I could hear his voice; nothing of him was changed; while I, wrapt from him in a confused mist of time, was wondering what he would think, could he know that at this actual moment he would have been dead thirty years, and that his memory would be thus preserved and honoured in the beloved school, where his delicate spirit had been so strangely troubled.

This portrait-gallery of old Etonians is very select: preeminent distinction of birth or merit may win you a place there, or again

一幅校内肖像

罗伯特·布里吉斯

我很多年没回伊顿公学了。一天，在从研究员图书馆去画廊的路上，我看见学生时代的朋友迪格比·多尔宾的画像和当代杰出名人们的肖像一起挂在门外。我完全被吸引了，我停下来盯着画像出神的时候，我的同伴问我是否知道那是谁。我想，除了几个我可以叫出名字的人以外，我差不多是唯一认识他的人了。遥远童年时代的记忆争先恐后涌进我的脑海：他又重新站在我的身边，焕发着青春年华；我可以听见他说话的声音；他没有一点变化；因为我们之间相隔一段宛若迷雾的年月，我在想，假如他知道这会儿他已经死去三十年了，他上学时，那脆弱的心灵曾经莫名其妙地烦恼过，而现在，他可爱的母校以这样的方式纪念他，给他这样高的荣誉，他会怎么想呢？

这个为老伊顿校友建立的肖像画廊在决定人选时是很慎重的：出身显赫或表现突出有可能得到一个位置，或者与校方有正式的联系，而校方也乐

official connection with the school, which rightly loves to keep up an unbroken panorama of its teachers, and to vivify its annals with the faces and figures of the personalities who carried on its traditions. But how came Dolben there? It was because he was a poet, —that I knew;—and yet his poems were not known; they were jealously guarded by his family and a few friends: indeed such of his poems as could have come to the eyes of the authorities who sanctioned this memorial would not justify it. There was another reason; and the portrait bears its own credentials; for though you might not perhaps divine the poet in it, you can see the saint, the soul rapt in contemplation, the habit of stainless life, of devotion, of enthusiasm for high ideals. Such a being must have stood out conspicuously among his fellows; the facts of his life would have been the ground of the faith in his genius; and when his early death endeared and sanctified his memory, loving grief would generously grant him the laurels which he had never worn.

于完整地再现教师队伍的全貌,用那些保持学校传统的名人的形象丰富学校的年鉴,学校这样做是完全正确的。但是,多尔宾的肖像怎么会来到这里呢?因为他是一个诗人,这我很清楚;然而他的诗并不为人们所知;他的诗是由他的家人和几个朋友精心保管着;要说学校当局只凭见到的几首诗就同意以这种方式纪念他,理由不太充足。还有另外一个理由:他的肖像本身就可以解释这个问题;虽然你也许不能从肖像里看出他是诗人,但你可以看出他是一个圣人,一个沉思的人,和他无瑕、执着、热烈追求崇高理想的一生。这样的人在他的同事当中一定是出类拔萃的;他生活的事实与经历足以使我们相信他的天赋;他的英年早逝使得我们对他的怀念变得亲切而神圣;出于对他的爱而产生的悲哀慷慨地赋予了他生前未曾享受过的荣誉。

译后语

文贵简

“A School Portrait”是一篇回忆往昔朋友的文章，讲作者回母校伊顿公学访问，在校园里看见已故三十年的老同学的肖像和当今名人的肖像挂在一起时，瞬间的感慨。

文章分两段，很像中国词的上、下两阕，上阕写景(这里是人文景观)，描写作者在校园里看见多尔宾的画像之后引起回忆；下阕抒情，分析他的朋友能与当今名人并论，是因为他有圣人的品格。

由于内在的逻辑性强，文章不求形式联系。第一段四句，第二段五句。句与句之间不用连接词，段与段之间也没有字面上的转承。

分析一下文章的内容便可以看出这一内在联系。在第一段里，“我”多年之后回到伊顿，发现朋友的肖像挂在门口，被吸引了。和“我”同行的伙伴问“我”是否知道他是谁，岂止是知道，“我”几乎是唯一知道他的人。然后，童年的往事争先恐后地浮现在脑海里。“我”想，假如多尔宾知道他死去三十年后竟然享受此等殊荣，他会作何感想呢？这一问抒发了作者的无限感慨，也引发了读者的神思。

第二段一开始，作者说，既然入围肖像馆的选择是非常严格的，那么多尔宾是怎么被选进来的呢？作者、读者自然会想到这个。回答这个问题，作者先抑后扬，先说多尔宾是诗人，但这不是他入选的原因,就决策人所能见到的他的诗来说,也不足以使他入选。然后作者说,真正的原因是,多尔宾具有圣人的品德、完人的习惯、执着的追求以及为实现崇高理想而表现的热情。最后说,这样的人在他的同辈当中一定是出类拔萃的;他的生活事实使得人们相信他的天赋;他的早逝使人对他倍加怀念,他在世时虽未享受过如此荣誉,但人们因爱他而产生的悲痛补足了这个遗憾。最后两句是文章的精髓。读罢此文,读者会感觉到作者对朋友认识的深邃、感情的真诚、文章内容的充实、行文节奏的有致。

这里不妨借用毛泽东关于写文章的论述,他说,看一篇文章好不好,不一定看文章各段落之间的文字上的联系如何,主要是看文章的内在联系如何。如果内在联系得紧,那么倒不一定追求形式上的联系。(《今晚报》,1999/7/1)像这篇内在逻辑紧密、发展脉络清晰自然的文章,倘若在句与句或段与段之间加上连接词,反而会感到多余。

文章的又一个特点,不修饰,不用典,文笔简。

清代桐城派散文家刘大櫆《论文偶记》说:"文贵简。凡文笔老则简,意真则简,辞切则简,理当则简,味淡则简,气蕴则简,品贵则简,神远而含藏不尽则简。故简为文章尽境。"

"文笔老"是说文笔老练,用词、造句不拘一格,不刻意追求形式和修辞,说理抒情,"从心所欲","意则期多,字则期少",寥寥几笔,能把情理说透;"意真"是说态度诚恳,感情真挚,这是文章的命脉;"辞切"是说言辞贴切,行文自然;"理当"是说言之有理,令人信服;"味淡"是指言辞不着粉饰,明辨深藏简发;"品贵"是说论品贵,格调高,气质好;"气蕴"和"神远而含蓄不尽"是属文章风格范畴的事。反复品鉴,这篇文字有"简"的品格。

“简”是一种美，这种美（其他美的品格亦然）不仅表现在字词、造句、修辞上，或句与句、段与段之间的组织上，更在文章整体上所表现的艺术境界。这或许就是英国散文家 Arthur Clutton-Brock 在“The Cardinal Virtue of Prose”中所说：“Unhasting, unresting, he pursues it... making his own beauty out of the very accomplishment of it, out of the whole work and its proportions, so that you must read to the end before you know that it is beautiful.”

欣赏一篇文章和欣赏一幅国画或一首乐曲一样。观赏一幅国画，我们所注意的不仅是它的一笔一画或某一线条、某一着色，更重要的是其画面的整体艺术氛围对观者所产生的审美效果；听一首乐曲亦然，我们所注意的不仅是一个个的音符或乐句，更是全曲的艺术境界对听者所产生的感染力。作家冯骥才写过一篇文章《阐释五大道》，写关于在天津市区五条街道上遗留下来的殖民地时期的建筑。他说：“历史留给我们的绝不是一幢幢房子，还有它迷人的氛围。而这又不只是一种建筑氛围，更是一种历史人文的气息。”（《今晚报》，1999/8/18）他说的这种“氛围”“气息”普遍存在于艺术之中，好的文章里有这种“氛围”和“气息”，有的人能感觉到，有的人感觉不到。

文章（或绘画或音乐）的整体艺术效果来自三个方面：作者、题材和表现手段。所谓作者，就是指他的思想情感、个性气质和审美情趣，这些都自觉或不自觉地渗透到作品的字里行间；题材是指作者赖以发现美的客观素材，也就是文章所着力挖掘的内容；表现手段是指作者运筹文字的谋略。这三者相互联系。作者是主观因素，题材是客观因素，主、客观因素的结合是产生审美的源泉；文字是媒介，是表现美的手段。文章的审美价值主要表现在文字上，但要体会由文字所创造出来的艺术境界，更全面、更深刻地把握文章的审美内涵，需要把作者和题材考虑进来，艺术境界是作者的精神气质和所描写的素材在文字内外散发出来的美的光芒。

多尔宾的人品和作者对其人品用简朴的文字所作的深刻的分析和诚挚的评价，构成了这篇散文的艺术境界。在这篇文章里，作者所表达的全部思想和情感，归结到最后两句话。以 There was another reason 为开始的一句，是对多尔宾的正面评价，在他的肖像里，"you can see the saint, the soul rapt in contemplation, the habit of stainless life, of devotion, of enthusiasm for high ideals."最后一句，从三个与多尔宾相联系的客观方面出发，赞美多尔宾：

(1) Such a being must have stood out conspicuously among his fellows;

(2) ... the facts of his life would have been the ground of the faith in his genius;

(3) ... and when his early death endeared and sanctified his memory, loving grief would generously grant him the laurels which he had never worn.

字词的选择和文章整体的风格是和谐的，简单、准确、形象，下面各句中黑体的词或词组都是好例子：

(1) **I caught sight of** the portrait of my school-friend Digby Dolben...

(2) I was wholly **arrested**...

(3) Far memories of my boyhood **were crowding** freshly upon me...

(4) This portrait-gallery of old Etonians is very **select**...

(5) they were **jealously** guarded by his family and a few friends...

句子的结构也是一样，有的句式虽长而复杂，但因和作者情感发展的脉络相一致，读起来并不觉得繁复、冗长，反而觉得清新、自然，如：

... while I, wrapt from him in a confused mist of time, was wondering what he would think, could he know that at this actual moment he would have been dead thirty years, and that his memory would be thus preserved and honoured in the beloved school...

Max Beerbohm

马克斯·比尔博姆(1872—1956),英国散文家,因其优雅的风格,被誉为散文大师。主要作品有小说集 *Seven Men* (1919),散文集 *And Even Now* (1920)、*Mainly on the Air* (1947);*Yet Again* 是他从发表在诸多刊物上的散文中选出来的一个结集。后文即出自该集。

The Morris Dancers

Max Beerbohm

It was in the wide street of a tiny village near Oxford that I saw them. Fantastic—high-fantastical—figures they did cut in their finery. But in demeanour they were quite simple, quite serious, these eight English peasants. They had trudged hither from the neighbouring village that was their home. And they danced quite simply, quite seriously. One of them, I learned, was a cobbler, another a baker, and the rest were farm-labourers. And their fathers and their fathers' fathers had danced here before them, even so, every May-day morning. They were as deeply rooted in antiquity as the elm outside the inn. They were here always in their season as surely as the elm put forth its buds. And the elm, knowing them, approving them, let its green-flecked branches dance in unison with them.

The first dance was in full swing when I approached. Only six of the men were dancers. Of the others, one was the "minstrel", the other the "dysard". The minstrel was playing a flute; and the dysard I knew by the wand and leathern bladder which he brandished

跳莫里斯舞的人们

马克斯·比尔博姆

我是在牛津附近一个小村子的一条大街上看见他们的。他们穿着华丽的服饰扮演着奇特的——非常奇特的——形象。但是，这八个英国农民看上去都很朴素，都很认真。他们从临近的村庄，他们的家乡，一路走到这里。他们的舞蹈动作挺简单，跳得也挺认真。我听说其中一个人是鞋匠，另一个是面包师，其余的都是农民。他们的父亲，他们父亲的父亲，在他们之前都曾来这里跳过舞，甚至每年5月1日的五朔节也来跳。他们深深地植根于古代的习俗之中，就像小旅店外面的榆树植根于土壤之中。他们到时候准来，就像那棵榆树准时发芽一样。那棵榆树熟悉他们，赞许他们，让它那布满绿色斑点的树枝和他们一起跳舞。

我来的时候，第一个舞蹈正跳得起劲。只有六个男人是跳舞的，其他两人，一个是"游吟歌手"，另一个是小丑。歌手正在吹笛子；小丑——我是从他边走边挥舞的魔杖和皮球认出他的——他蹦蹦

as he walked around, keeping a space for the dancers, and chasing and buffeting merrily any man or child who ventured too near. He, like the others, wore a white smock decked with sundry ribands, and a top-hat that must have belonged to his grandfather. Its antiquity of form and texture contrasted strangely with the freshness of the garland of paper roses that wreathed it. I was told that the wife or sweetheart of every Morris-dancer takes special pains to deck her man out more gaily than his fellows. But this pious endeavour had defeated its own end. So bewildering was the amount of brand-new bunting attached to all these eight men that no matron or maiden could for the life of her have determined which was the most splendid of them all. Besides his adventitious finery, every dancer, of course, had in his hands the scarves which are as necessary to his performance of the Morris as are the bells strapped about the calves of his legs. Waving these scarves and jangling these bells with a stolid rhythm, the six peasants danced facing one another, three on either side, while the minstrel fluted and the dysard strutted around. That minstrel's tune runs in my head even now—a queer little stolid tune that recalls vividly to me the aspect of the dance. It is the sort of tune Bottom the Weaver must often have danced to in his youth. ... After they had drunk some ale, they formed up for the second dance—a circular dance. And anon, about the notes of the flute and the jangling of the bells and the stamping of the boots, I seemed to hear the knell actually toll. *Hoot! Hoot! Hoot!*

跳跳地把那些靠得太近的大人或小孩儿推开、赶走,给跳舞的人打场子。他和其他人一样,穿一件宽松的白色衬衫,用各色各样的彩条装饰着,戴着一个高顶礼帽,一定是他祖父戴过的。帽子古里古怪的形状和质地,与它上面一圈新颖的纸制玫瑰花冠形成奇特的对照。有人告诉我,每一个莫里斯舞者的妻子或恋人都煞费苦心把自己的男人打扮得比同伴更华丽。可是,她们这一番虔诚的努力并没有达到她们的初衷。这八个人身上都缀着这么多崭新的彩带,把人们弄得眼花缭乱,已婚的或者未婚的女人们怎么也看不出他们当中哪一个人的服饰最风光。除了穿奇装异服,每一个舞者当然都手拿几条彩巾,这是他们表演所必需的,就跟绑在他们腿上的小铃铛同样必要。这六个舞者站在两边,每边三个,面对面地跳着,以稳健的节奏,手挥舞着彩巾,腿震荡着铃铛;与此同时,歌手吹着笛子,小丑围着场子昂首阔步地走动着。那个歌手吹的调子甚至到现在仍在我的脑海里回响,那是一个挺怪的平淡的小调,一听就让我清晰地想起舞蹈的情景。这个调子,织布工博顿在他的青年时期听了一定是常常要翩翩起舞的。……他们喝了点麦芽啤酒就又站好队开始跳第二支舞蹈,是一个转着圈跳的舞蹈。很快,一个声音盖过了笛子的音符、腿铃的叮铃声和靴子跺地的声音,我好像听见了破坏舞蹈的丧钟已经敲响。呜!呜!呜!

A motor-car came fussing and fuming in its cloud of dust. *Hoot! Hoot!* The dysard ran to meet it, brandishing his wand of office. He had to stand aside. *Hoot!* The dancers had just time to get out of the way. The scowling motorists vanished. Dancers and dysard, presently visible through the subsiding dust, looked rather foolish and crestfallen. And all the branches of the Tory old elm above them seemed to be quivering with indignation.

一辆汽车卷着一阵灰尘,突突冒着黑烟,急匆匆开过来。呜!呜!小丑跑上前去挥动手中的魔杖想拦住它。但是他不得不站开。呜!跳舞的人们及时躲开了汽车。满脸怒色的车手们消逝了。灰尘落下之后,跳舞的人们和小丑很快又出现了,似乎有点不知所措,垂头丧气。他们头顶上那棵守旧的老榆树上所有的树枝好像都气愤得浑身发抖。

译后语

本文描写英国乡间的舞蹈者们在临近的村庄跳莫里斯舞的情景，这是古朴的民间文化活动。跳舞的人高兴，妇女们高兴，看热闹的人也高兴，这是乡村的节日。但突然到来的一辆汽车，把跳舞的人们冲散，把跳舞的场地弄得乌烟瘴气，舞蹈者们生气，连老榆树也气得浑身发抖。从这一情节看，文章带有生态文学的意味，谴责现代工业文明的无礼，它破坏了人文生态，也破坏了自然生态。

这篇文章的风格和它所描写的英国民风一样，是古朴的，都是普通的字词，普通的句子，结构简单，长度适中。翻译时注意体现这一特征。

几点说明：

1. 关于标题“The Morris Dancers”，如何翻译是好，需要斟酌。这些 Morris Dancers 当中，有的是鞋匠，有的是面包师，其余都是农民。根据这个情况，这里没有将其翻译成“莫里斯舞蹈家”，或“莫里斯舞蹈演员”，因为“家”或“演员”都带有专业性质；而将其翻译成“跳莫里斯舞的人们”，这暗示他们都是业余的。

2. 下面的两句话里有两组意思相同的词：simple（形容词），simply（副词）；serious（形容词），seriously（副词）。

(1) But in demeanour they were quite **simple**, quite **serious**, these eight English peasants.

(2) And they danced quite **simply**, quite **seriously**.

第一句指的是他们的举止（in demeanour），故将 simple 翻译成

"朴素",将 serious 翻译成"认真"。第二句指的是他们的舞蹈动作(they danced),故将 simply 翻译成"简单",将 seriously 翻译成"认真"。这样处理比较妥当。

3. They were as deeply rooted in antiquity as the elm outside the inn.

这句话是说他们离不开传统习俗,就像那棵榆树离不开土壤一样。所以我们将前半句翻译成"他们深深地植根于古代的习俗之中"(翻译成"古代的习俗深深地扎根于他们的心中"也未尝不可),是为了和后半句"就像小旅店外面的榆树植根于土壤之中"形成对应。

4. They were here always in their season as surely as the elm put forth its buds.

我们用口语化的说法翻译前半句,即"他们到时候准来",这样就把 in their season 和 surely 的意思都包括进来了,比较简洁。

5. But this pious endeavour had defeated its own end.

这里是说,根本无法挑选谁的打扮是最好的,译文尽量与原文贴切些,故将其翻译成"并没有达到她们的初衷"。

6. Dancers and **dysard**... looked rather **foolish** and **crestfallen.**

这里的 foolish 意思和汉语里的"傻了"或"傻眼了"很相似,但英语的 foolish 和 crestfallen 是平行的,形式上和声音上有均衡感,故将其翻译成"不知所措,垂头丧气",以取得和原文类似的效果。

dysard 是个生僻词。根据原文的上下文,意为"小丑"。

John Masefield

约翰·梅斯菲尔德(1878—1967),英国诗人、作家。1930年获英国“桂冠诗人”称号,直到1967年逝世。创作了数量可观的诗歌和小说,著名的有叙事诗“Salt-Water Ballads”(1902)、“The Everlasting Mercy”(1911)、“Dauber”(1912);著名的小说有*The Midnight Folk*(1927)、*The Box of Delights*(1935)等;此外还有多部自传体裁的作品,如*Sea Life in Nelson's Time*(1905)等。后文选自*A Tarpaulin Muster: A Memory*(1907)。

The Clipper

John Masefield

When I saw her first there was a smoke of mist about her as high as her foreyard. Her topsails and flying kites had a faint glow upon them where the dawn caught them. Then the mist rolled away from her, so that we could see her hull and the glimmer of the red sidelight as it was hoisted inboard. She was rolling slightly, tracing an arc against the heaven, and as I watched her the glow upon her deepened, till every sail she wore burned rosily like an opal turned to the sun, like a fiery jewel. She was radiant, she was of an immortal beauty, that swaying, delicate clipper. Coming as she came, out of the mist into the dawn, she was like a spirit, like an intellectual presence. Her hull glowed, her rails glowed; there was colour upon the boats and tackling. She was a lofty ship (with skysails and royal staysails), and it was wonderful to watch her, blushing in the sun, swaying and curveting. She was alive with a more than mortal life. One thought that she would speak in some strange language or break out into a music which would express the sea and that great flower in the sky.

快帆船

约翰·梅斯菲尔德

我刚一看见她时，前帆下桁以下的船身全被浓雾裹着。上桅帆和迎风飘动的轻帆映着晨曦的微光。然后大雾滚动着离开了她，我们这才看见船身和刚刚挂起的舱内红色舷灯发出的微弱的闪光。她时起时伏地前进，朝着天空画着一个个的弧。在我眼睛盯着她时，船身上晨光逐渐加深，最后，船上的每一条风帆都被映红，透着玫瑰色，好像阳光穿过蛋白石一样，又像火红的宝石。她此时光辉灿烂，她是不朽的美人，那只微微摆动的、体态轻盈的快帆船！她一路随波起伏，驶出迷雾，进入破晓的熹微，她活像一个魂灵，又像一个理智的存在。她的船身泛着光，栏杆泛着光；小船及其索具都染上了颜色。这是一只崇高的快帆船（张着天帆和豪华的索帆），看着她在阳光里泛着红光，左右摆动着，上下颠簸着，令人心旷神怡。她比现世凡人的生命更有生命力。人们会以为她就要用一种陌生的语言开口说话，或演奏一首乐曲来抒发大海的豪情和太阳的辉煌。

She came trembling down to us, rising up high and plunging; showing the red lead below her water-line; then diving down till the smother bubbled over her hawseholes. She bowed and curveted; the light caught the skylights on the poop; she gleamed and sparkled; she shook the sea from her as she rose. There was no man aboard of us but was filled with the beauty of that ship. I think they would have cheered her had she been a little nearer to us; but, as it was, we ran up our flags in answer to her, adding our position and comparing our chronometers, then dipping our ensigns and standing away. For some minutes I watched her, as I made up the flags before putting them back in their cupboard. The old mate limped up to me, and spat, and swore. "That's one of the beautiful sights of the world," he said. "That, and a cornfield, and a woman with her child. It's beauty and strength. How would you like to have one of them skysails round your neck?" I gave him some answer, and continued to watch her, till the beautiful, precise hull, with all its lovely detail, had become blurred to leeward, where the sun was now marching in triumph, the helm of a golden warrior plumed in cirrus.

她时起时伏朝我们驶来，忽而高高纵起，忽而往下坠落，一会儿露出吃水线下面的测深铅锤，然后猛扎下去，水雾飞花淹没了锚链孔。船头向前倾垂，然后船身向上穿越，阳光正好照进船楼的天窗；光线在船身上明灭闪烁；当她涌起的时候，便抖掉全身的海水。我们站在船上的人没有一个不为快帆船的美所打动。我想，如果快帆船离我们再近一点，他们准会欢呼起来；可是，事实上，我们升起船旗对她做出回应，确定了我们的位置，核准了经纬仪，降下了各色彩旗，然后站开。在我整理降下的旗子，准备把它们放回旗柜时，我一直盯着她，足有好几分钟。这时老水手一瘸一拐地朝我走来，吐了一口唾沫，斩钉截铁地说："这是世界一大美景——这，还有麦田，还有抱着孩子的女人。它是美和力的化身。你愿意摘下一片天帆戴在你的脖子上吗?"我随便答应了他一句，继续看着快帆船，直至她漂亮的、棱角精确的船身，连同她精美的各个细部变得模糊时，太阳正照着她的下风面并凯旋高升，身披金色盔甲的勇士的舵轮拨打起羽毛状的水云。

译后语

一幅壮丽的画

一个富于想象和敏于审美的读者，读了这篇文章，脑海里会浮现出一幅壮丽的动态画面：黎明之际，在大雾弥漫的海上，驶来一只帆船，风帆映着晨曦，随着海浪的起伏，画着一个个弧向前进；太阳升起，阳光照在船帆上，泛着玫瑰红色，像一块块燃烧的宝石。帆船继续前进，"我"和船员们被这壮丽的景色所感动，所陶醉，直到激动不已的老水手说"这是世界一大美景"时，作者对帆船的描写达到高潮。

读罢此文，我们也像文中的"我"一样，被这壮丽的景色所感动，所陶醉，也像文中的老水手一样，为这壮丽的景观而激动不已。

一个具有审美经验的人读了这样的文章，他所获得的审美愉悦会使他暂时进入"物我两忘"的境界，就像一首好的乐曲能把人带进另一个世界，但之后他会思索一个问题："为什么一篇小文章能在读者心中引起偌大反响？"这恐怕一方面由于作者所描写的内容和所抒发的情感真实感人。作者约翰·梅斯菲尔德是英国诗人，小说家，早年有过海上冒险经历，他对海景的描绘，从细节到宏观，不仅真实，而且具有典型性；另一方面他运用散文的形式和语言，成功描绘了大海的壮丽场景，成功抒发了内心的审美感慨。

朱光潜在谈艺术与自然的关系时说："艺术根据自然，加以熔铸雕琢，选择安排，结果乃是一种超自然的世界。换句话说，自然须通过作者的心灵,在里面经过一番意匠经营,才变成艺术……我们要了解情与辞的道理,必先了解这一点艺术与自然的道理。情是自然,融情于思,达之于辞,才是文学的艺术。在文学的艺术中,情感需经过意象化和文辞化,才算得到表现。"他还说:"英国诗人华兹华斯有一句名言:'诗起于在沉静中回味过来的情绪。'在沉静中加过一番回味,情感才由主观的感触变成客观的观照对象,才能受思想的洗炼与润色,思想才能为依稀隐约不易捉摸的情感造出一个完整的可捉摸的形式和生命。这个诗的原理可以应用于一切文学作品。"(《谈文学》,第112页)

他的意思是,只有情感是不够的,情感的自然流露还不足以产生文学作品。情感必须经过"回味",受过思想的"熔铸",然后通过具体的"意象"和适合的语言才得以表现。

如果对"The Clipper"做一分析,我们对朱光潜所说的"情感""意象"和"文辞"三者的关系会有一个清晰的印象。

本文从第一人称"我"的视角出发,"我"之所观,"我"之所感,构成了文章的焦点和脉络,从而引导读者观"我"之所观,感"我"之所感。一开始,作者描写"我"最初看见帆船时(When I saw her first)的情景;在第4句至第7句,又以 and as I watched her 起始,进一步描写帆船行进的情景及其色彩的变幻,此间使用了明喻(simile),将帆船比作有生命、有思想的生灵(like a spirit, like an intellectual presence);在第8句至第14句,从描写帆船的状貌进而描写它的内蕴 She was a lofty ship,也是以 and it was wonderful to watch her 起始来对帆船做深化的描绘;第15句至第20句以 For some minutes I watched her 开始,正当"我"凝神注视帆船时,老水手一瘸一拐地走过来,吐了一口唾沫之后大发感慨。这一部分最生动、最精彩。当老水手问"我"是否愿意摘下一面天帆做围巾时,"我"好歹答应了一声,又继续注视着帆船"I gave him some answer, and continued to watch her...",直到远去的帆船又模糊起来,只有舵轮在阳光照耀下激起一片烟雾。

这里作者"见景生情",但作者对其情感有条理的、步步深入的描写和精湛的比喻显然是经过回味、思考和精心铺排的。I saw her、I watched her、to watch her 等类似句式的重复使用,不仅预示作者情感的步步深化,也对语段和语篇产生了衔接和连贯的效果。

关于本篇的语言,有三个方面应当提及,即色彩词、动作词和比喻的运用。

色彩词汇的运用是这篇文章的一个特色。帆船在阳光的照耀下,形成一幅斑斓的画图。作者使用一系列鲜明的色彩词,使读者几乎可以凭视觉看见船体折射出来的不断变换的色彩和光亮,如 a faint glow、the glimmer of the red sidelight、burned rosily like an opal turned to the sun、radiant、the red lead、gleamed and sparkled 等。如果读者把这些绚丽的色彩放在雾霭蒙蒙的海面和冉冉升起的太阳的背景之下去想象,那将是一幅多么壮丽的景观。

动作词汇的运用也是这篇文章的一个特色。作者观察细致,对行进的帆船作了生动的描绘,一句话是一个画面。富于想象的读者不仅可以看见正在行进的帆船的丰姿,甚至可以听见帆船行进时激打海水的声音。如果读者进而想象自己身临其境,面对这样的景色,是不会无动于衷的。请看:"She was rolling slightly, tracing an arc against the heaven..." "Coming... out of the mist into the dawn...""swaying and curveting""She came trembling down to us rising up high and plunging...""then diving down""She bowed and curveted...""she shook the sea from her as she rose"。

暗喻(metaphor)和拟人法(personification)的运用赋予了帆船以生命,以灵感,如"She was alive with a more than mortal life." "One thought she would speak in some strange language or break out into a music..."老水手具有很高的审美素质,他的想象很奇特,"How would you like to have one of them skysails round your neck?"他发现了帆船的"beauty and strength",他看出了"That's one of the beautiful sights of the world."

作者约翰·梅斯菲尔德用文字所编织的这一色彩斑斓、无比壮观的图画,感染了读者,使我们对帆船产生无比崇敬的心情,也使我们不禁相信,它好像肩负着一个神圣的使命。